Tearful
TRIUMPH

Inspired by True Events

ROBERT M. BOOTH

DEDICATED TO NAJED & GAIL AZZAM

Living Hope Publishing

Cover Design by Kristen Ingebretson
https://www.kristening.com/

LCCN: 2024910300
ISBN: 979-8-9886113-0-1
eISBN: 979-8-9886113-1-8

What people are saying about
Tearful Triumph

"*Tearful Triumph* is a wonderful story describing the power of the gospel of Christ to bring tremendous peace within even the most confused and conflicted circumstances. . . . I know this book will touch the lives of many, and I pray you will find the triumph that is given to all who will turn to Christ for comfort and salvation.

GARY COOK, PhD, Chancellor, Dallas Baptist University

"This novel helps the readers feel the pain and challenges of the daily lives and losses of those living in the Holy Land as it calls believers in Christ to live out the reconciliation of the gospel, even in the middle of a war zone. It demonstrates the power of forgiveness through Jesus to transform not only an individual, but also families and estranged communities. . . . This book casts a hopeful vision for the future, reminding us of what is possible and of how Jesus calls us to live."

ALICIA JACKSON, PhD, Associate Professor of Old Testament, Vanguard University

"This story is beautifully told sharing the love that resides inside the lives of our dear Arab Christian brothers and sisters. It has the potential to heal the wounds between the various ethnic groups. My prayer is that it will become a life-altering story for all the people of the world!"

DONNA CHISAM, Retired Director of Friends of Nazareth

This story is dedicated to Najed and Gail Azzam whose lives in the land of Israel are a testimony of the saving grace and wondrous love of Jesus Christ, the Son of the living God, Who gave His life upon the cross for the salvation of all mankind.

Contents

Therefore, if anyone is in Christ, he is a new creation; old things have passed away; behold, all things have become new. Now all things are of God, who has reconciled us to Himself through Jesus Christ, and has given us the ministry of reconciliation, that is, that God was in Christ reconciling the world to Himself, not imputing their trespasses to them, and has committed to us the word of reconciliation.
(2 CORINTHIANS 5:17-19 NKJV)

Chapter 1

Trying to Reach Amal

ashira's world crumbled around her. The bombing at the Park Hotel threatened to shut down the West Bank again. The Israelis were sure to retaliate. Yet she believed in her heart that she and her father would make it back in time. The looming possibility of a forced curfew only added to the pressure to speed ahead.

They had made it out of Bethlehem; the checkpoint faded from sight in the rearview mirror. Bashira now looked to the horizon, scanning it with her deep brown eyes while praying silently in her heart. The afternoon sun made her task more difficult; its heat produced waves in the air, roughly parallel to the horizon, obscuring her vision, causing her to blink her eyes periodically to erase any false images of her uncle's car. She yearned to see his car approaching.

Thoughts raced through her mind faster than her father's old car could carry her. *We must make it in time to reach Amal*, she thought. Her little niece, who had been visiting with her extended family in Nazareth, wasn't due to return for another week. It grieved Bashira to have to interrupt her niece's time with her great uncle and aunt. But the decision had to be made; all their plans, and everything else they could call routine, had changed.

The only topic anyone from Bethlehem cared about now was the storm beginning to gather over the West Bank, heralded two years earlier by the cry for *intifada*. Fear tried to paralyze her as memories of the day she had lost her sister and brother-in-law flooded back into her thoughts. It had been nearly a year and a half since Amal had come to live with them after the death of her sister. The life of her family had been scorched by the flames of hatred, fanned by the endless conflict in the land. Violent acts followed by retribution produced a never-ending cycle of suffering that ripped apart the lives of those who lived here and prolonged their sorrows. *How many more must die?* she thought.

The constant rattle of the ailing engine in her father's beat-up 1978 Fiat as it raced down the road blocked out all other distractions, giving Bashira time to remember how much she missed her sister. Their long talks had painted in their imaginations the childhood dreams they shared with one another. The memories of her sister's beautiful wedding day came to mind, quickly followed by memories of the birth of Amal.

Her parched mouth framed a thin smile as she recalled her sister holding Amal in her arms, sharing her tender mother's love with her newborn daughter. Bashira's smile tightened. She pursed her lips together, trying to hold back the grief over her sister's death which seemed to ebb and flow through the floodgates of pain hidden beneath her tender countenance. *That day stole such beauty and life from our family.* In a twinkling of an eye, the bomb blast had ripped through the pizza restaurant in Jerusalem, destroying the lives of her sister and brother-in-law. Their decision to break away from the conference they were attending to enjoy a private moment together put them at the confluence of everyday affection and a random act of terror. Bashira wondered still, *If only . . .* Instead, her family remained forever changed.

Her sister and brother-in-law were gone. Amal was now in the care of her family, and she had become much more than Bashira's niece. More than a special link to the memory of her sister, Amal had become the center of her extended family's life. With all her laughter and energy, she had become a treasure that had to be kept safe at all costs, not only for her own sake but also for the sake of her whole family.

"*Baba,* can't you go faster? We've got to hurry," Bashira said.

Hunched over the steering wheel of his dilapidated car, Samir pressed the accelerator to the floor and began to bounce his torso up and down in what seemed to be his effort to add to the speed of the car. Bashira noticed him tap on the temperature gauge. She took note of his signal and added this situation to her prayers.

"*Habibti*, we can't go any faster," her father said. "Just keep on looking for Rashad's car and let me know when you see it."

Her thoughts did not cease to assail her as she refocused her eyes on the road up ahead. Once again, this time in Netanya, a bomber had placed his own cry for revenge or perhaps his misguided desire for eternal glory above the value of so many innocent lives, including her sister and brother-in-law. Now, with the military stepping in to set up the inevitable curfew, it would be impossible to get Amal back until the siege was over.

Bashira shuddered. They had to reach Amal in time.

She blinked her eyes to clear her vision and shouted, "I see them *Baba!* Look! We should reach them at the bottom of the hill. See? There!"

As they completed the curve, Samir said, "I see them now." Bashira heard the high whine of the engine relax as her father eased his foot off the gas pedal. She let out an audible sigh of relief of her own.

"There they are!" said Bashira.

Samir crossed the road to park his car on the southbound shoulder, facing his brother's car. Before Samir could bring his car to a full stop, Bashira jumped out and ran toward her uncle's car. Rashad stepped out as a chauffeur to open the back door for the child. Bashira swooped up her niece in her arms. She held her tightly while swinging her shoulders back and forth as if to emphasize her desire to be even closer to her. Knowing

Amal had now returned safely, Bashira turned to give her uncle a hug with Amal still on one arm.

"Thank you, *Amo*," she said. "I was so concerned we wouldn't make it in time."

Samir came up behind Bashira. He greeted his brother with a hug and three kisses alternating on his brother's cheeks. Samir reminded them all that they had no time to linger. The border could close at any time, so they had to hurry back. In response, Bashira carried Amal back to Samir's car.

"I love you, *Amo*," Bashira shouted, closing the door to the back seat of her father's car. Holding her little niece in her lap, she waved to her uncle through the window with tears in her eyes. Her father turned the car around and headed toward home. Her uncle stood on the shoulder of the road and waved goodbye until they drove out of sight.

∞∞∞∞∞∞∞∞∞∞∞∞

Above them, out of Bashira's view and beyond her concerns, a formation of three Israeli Sikorsky UH-60L Black Hawk helicopters heading toward Bethlehem had taken notice of this innocent roadside meeting. The point chopper's door gunner held his attention focused on what he now saw as two vehicles pulled over on the side of the road, one showing yellow Israeli plates and the other white West Bank tags.

The helicopter pilot called over the radio. "Sir, should we engage?" He moved the helicopter in closer behind the south-bound car. The door gunner trained his 7.62mm M60 door-mounted machine gun on the vehicle.

He heard nothing in response. Colonel Yakov had seen the two cars. He had watched them come to a halt, had seen a young woman come out of the smaller car and run towards the larger one to pick up a child in her arms and jump back into the car she had arrived in. He saw the driver turn the car around and drive back towards Bethlehem.

Yet the commander of the IDF strike team sat stiff in his jump seat. Colonel Yakov recalled how over the last many months he had surveyed the scenes of bombings and the riots that ensued, wondering how this would all end. It seemed to him like yesterday that his attack ship flew its sweeping arc over the scene of torn bodies and twisted metal strewn across the street beyond a bus stop. Those images were forever riveted to his mind.

He could summon an instant replay of the scene at any time, graphically recalling the sound of ambulance sirens and rescue workers racing to care for each person they could reach. Police rushed to cordon off the area. Stunned civilians walked about holding each other, lifting up silent cries of grief that could not be heard from the streets below. On that day, the colonel had also sat in stony silence surveying the bodies of innocent men, women, and children caught in the deadly blast. This mission was to be the beginning of the end of those actions. They had to be stopped. *But at what cost?* he thought.

"Press on," came the command over the radio from the colonel. "We have bigger issues waiting ahead."

The roar of the wind circling through the cabin ceased as they closed the gunner's door. The colonel sat with his eyes focused on the craggy, mountainous terrain below. Eighteen months later, he still asked why? The thought haunted Colonel Yakov. *Just a dumb political speech,* he thought. *Could have been given anywhere, but Sharon had to make a statement from the Temple Mount for the sake of what—more headlines—for an election?*

"We've got headlines now all right," Colonel Yakov muttered to himself. "Global ones, with the whole world watching on TV, anxiously waiting for an outcome that only time can determine."

Operation Defensive Shield was now in full swing. It had become the largest military campaign in Israel since the Six Day War in 1967.

◇◇◇◇◇◇◇◇◇◇◇◇◇

Bashira, hearing the helicopter as it pulled out of its preemptive attack dive, gasped at the sound of the fly over.

"*Baba*, are they after us?" she asked.

Samir glanced out the window to see the helicopter squadron pass over them.

"No, *habibti*, they are headed for the city." Bashira pulled her little niece in toward her even closer.

Amal looked up at Bashira with big dark brown eyes of her own. Bashira had trimmed Amal's bangs before her trip to Nazareth. Now they fell over her forehead, concealing the uncertainty expressed on her brow. Bashira brushed them back to tenderly kiss the soft, smooth skin of Amal's forehead.

"Everything is going to be fine, *Amulti*," she said. Her niece smiled back with candy-stained lips, wet from drinking the small bottle of water Bashira had given her. "I see *amo* has been giving you treats," Bashira said, shaking her pointed finger at Amal in a mock scolding. Although Bashira's parents were legally responsible for Amal, Bashira cared for her as if she was her mother. A bond had developed between them that both Bashira and Amal dearly cherished.

Bashira looked out of the window again. The sun shone behind them now. She had no trouble seeing the road ahead, at least until they reached Bethlehem and home. From that point on, the future seemed uncertain. Amal had settled in quietly onto Bashira's lap. Bashira wrapped her left arm around her, giving her a reassuring hug. With her right hand, she felt for the necklace that she wore every day; it was her constant companion. Her grandfather had given it to her not long after her sister had died. The chain of the necklace was made of black onyx beads strung on a gold wire.

The pendant, a fish-shaped ichthys made of gold and green Roman glass, hung from the chain. It remained the most precious gift she had ever received.

Her thoughts settled as the speed of the car had decreased to run a steady rhythm across the bumpy road. They were approaching the checkpoint from the Israeli side now. Having returned in time, they re-entered Bethlehem without incident. Bashira knew that if the family was together, they would find the strength to overcome the hardships ahead of them. The refugee camps had been locked down before they left. *Soon the whole city will be placed on curfew*, she thought. *But we will be okay*, she told herself. Clouds of smoke now marked the horizon, rising above her beloved Bethlehem. She looked at her father. Thanksgiving welled up in her eyes. She knew that she was loved. And she also knew that together they had the strength to face the future.

Samir caught her glance, turned toward her, and said, "We're going to make it, *habibti*. Don't worry."

Bashira smiled back. She continued to tell herself that she could handle whatever these unsettled days brought to her family; they would all be together soon. She pushed back against the fear of losing them.

Chapter 2

BETHLEHEM

As a seasoned international TV journalist with World Broadcasting Network (WBN), Mike Olson had covered the region for almost a decade. Even so, he found it difficult to adjust to the monotonous dry heat that surrounded him. He grew up in the rolling hills of southwestern Iowa, a land distinguished by the variety of the seasons and evidence of humidity—fireflies, thunderstorms, and bitter cold winters. The heat here seemed relentless; it pushed back against him as a constant reminder that he was stretching his limits. As the youngest reporter for a major cable network in the Middle East, Mike held an esteemed position that stretched him in other ways. His career had skyrocketed, driven by his passion to present the whole story—to dig deeper for an angle that lay beneath the obvious politically correct perspective of the events he witnessed. His work ethic inspired both envy and scorn from his colleagues, generating a different, but also oppressive form of heat—no less dry and monotonous than the air around him.

Dust had also become a constant and tiring companion. The Land Rover he drove stirred up great quantities of it as he raced towards Bethlehem; although, what distracted him most on these rides was the constant banter of his long-time friend and cameraman, Jack Winslow.

Jack had been with Mike on many news reports, getting his own share of Emmy nominations for footage he had captured during the conflicts they covered together in Southern Lebanon. Mike and Jack had been partners for most of Mike's five years as a journalist in the Middle East. They knew each other well, sometimes getting on each other's nerves as family members can when they are confined to close quarters for a long time. The Land Rover they now occupied could be considered close quarters, yet it was not a setting unfamiliar to either of them.

They had proven their grit as combat reporters. The combination of Jack's steady hand on the camera while under pressure and Mike's integrity in reporting the facts without political spin had given them special access to the top command of the Israeli Defense Force (IDF). This favor gave them privileged views of the IDF's maneuvers in the field. Bethlehem held their next assignment.

With his gaze focused beyond the dust-stained windshield of the Land Rover, Mike interrupted Jack's ongoing monologue, "Remember when we had such a difficult time getting into Gaza?"

Jack didn't seem to mind the interruption. "Yeah, we had to switch from an Israeli taxi to an Arab one before they would let us in. Man, that was crazy."

"How about when Pope John Paul visited and all that Y2K stuff was on everybody's mind?"

Jack replied with a slight chuckle. "Oh yeah. I remember the checkpoint in Jericho when we rode with that crazy Israeli driver. What was his name? I'll never forget him hollering, 'Look! Palestinian police and Israeli soldiers sitting together having lunch!'"

Mike perked up, smiling. "How did he put it? 'The Messiah must be due any day now.'"

They both laughed.

Mike continued to stare at the road ahead and spoke as though Jack was not beside him.

"It felt then like some semblance of peace was coming to this land—businesses opening up, folks traveling back and forth freely between the West Bank and—and now this nightmare."

∞∞∞∞∞∞∞∞∞

Driving up out of the valley, they saw smoke hanging over Bethlehem. As they approached the city, they could hear the crackle of rifle fire intermixed with the dull thud of muted explosions. Mike brought the Land Rover to a slow stop at the roadblock in front of them.

The IDF soldiers, with their weapons ready, had signaled them to stop and provide identification. Mike expected this level of security. He had become familiar with the protocols of the IDF, many of which were the brainchild of the man who had arranged for Jack and him to get past the roadblock. The soldier motioned to Mike to pull his vehicle over and park by the side of the road. He told Jack to stay inside the Land Rover. Mike got out. IDF soldiers escorted him over to a small building next to the road that had been converted into a temporary command center.

Once inside, Mike could see that the small space had been cordoned off with office dividers one and a half meters tall. Computer networking cords hung in bundles from the ceiling. Fans had been set up in each corner of the room. The atmosphere hummed with the unintelligible sound of voices all speaking at the same time. Colonel Yakov, involved in one of these conversations, looked up when he saw Mike enter.

"Isaac. Shalom, my friend," Mike said, waving to the colonel.

The colonel walked over to Mike and with a slight smile said, "I wondered when you would get here."

Colonel Isaac Yakov saved his smiles for the rarest of occasions. He had to. He couldn't afford allowing others to know what he was thinking. Commanding Israel's select strike forces, including the Reserve Infantry Brigade from Jerusalem and the special forces Shaldag Unit, required him to make decisions that he knew would put his men in harm's way. He carried this burden alone, prioritizing the mission he was charged with to achieve. Regardless of how he cared for his men, his decisions bore the weight of life and death. He kept his emotion on a tight rein within him.

Mike began his special relationship with Colonel Yakov while covering various engagements during his time in Lebanon. As a civilian, Mike had earned a certain amount of respect from Isaac because he had proven himself able to deliver a trustworthy commentary on the fighting during the campaign there. Over time, Isaac found he could discuss certain military decisions with Mike and remain confident of receiving honest, straight-forward news coverage. He knew this was a rare find. In short, Colonel Yakov, a man who had seen his share of combat, could remain cautiously "at ease" with Mike, even though Mike wasn't a military man. As the military operations had unfolded there, Mike had grown more comfortable in their relationship and had started calling Colonel Yakov by his first name. The colonel appreciated Mike's friendly demeanor and allowed this particular lapse of protocol to continue.

"I got here as soon as I could," Mike replied, with a smile of his own.

"Well, it's a mess up ahead, Mike. A group of priests and nuns are being held hostage in the church. There are snipers all over the area."

"What about your guys?"

"They're hunkered down. We don't want to fire into the church. We're trying to minimize casualties among the hostages."

Mike knew that Colonel Yakov had been instrumental in developing the IDF's techniques for urban warfare and respected him for his ability to think strategically to get results. He also knew this uprising had become more violent than any Israel had previously encountered, requiring new rules of engagement. No longer were the Palestinians armed only with rocks and Molotov cocktails; the insurgents were now using automatic weapons. The enemy's tactics had also changed. The resistance forces had embedded themselves in public spaces. This tactic often resulted in collateral civilian casualties when the IDF returned fire.

Colonel Yakov continued to brief Mike. "We're up against a bizarre situation where the combatants are young and old alike. The radical Palestinians will make deliberate use of civilians, regardless of increasing the number of casualties. Anyone can be a threat—and a casualty."

"That's not what we're hearing," said Mike. "You know the story: 'They've got slingshots and you're using Merkava Mark III state-of-the-art tanks against them.' To the outside world Isaac, it doesn't quite sound like a fair fight."

"Yeah, well that's why you're here, to get out the real story. Every time we respond to their assaults, the media blames us for using excessive force. The truth is, we need to expose the insurgents' tactics so that the world can understand what is really going on here."

"I'll do what I can. You've got a real mess on your hands. I've heard the Vatican is trying to intervene to get the hostages released."

Isaac frowned. "The Cardinal met with the Prime Minister and is asking for us to stand down."

"Sounds right. This cease fire might be the break from world attention that you're looking for."

"Yeah, but it won't last. No matter what we do, this is going to be ugly."

Mike looked out the window, past Isaac into the narrow streets ahead. "Southern Lebanon was bad enough," he said, talking into the air, "and yet we got the truth out then." Turning to Isaac, he continued, "Jack and I will do our best. Just get us into the right place at the right time and we'll tell the story as we see the facts unfold."

Isaac placed his hand on Mike's shoulder. "I know you will. Tell it like it is, my friend."

"Okay, ugly or not, Jack and I have to get in close to cover this thing."

"I hear you, but it's your neck."

"We'll be fine."

"I'll notify Lt. Reubens, my best platoon leader, to keep an eye out for you," Isaac said. This time he didn't smile.

Colonel Yakov had made it clear to Mike that this situation could still go any number of ways, many of which would cause the casualty count to rise. Mike shook Isaac's hand and turned to leave. This was his job, but it never got easier.

∞∞∞∞∞∞∞

Returning to the roadblock, Mike briefed Jack on his conversation with Isaac. He then started the Land Rover and drove them off toward the center of town. They made their way through the ancient, winding streets. The sounds of automatic weapon bursts became louder as they neared the ancient Church of the Nativity, the oldest basilica in the Holy Land, built by the Roman Emperor Justinian in 525 AD. Mike pulled the Land Rover over on the far edge of the square adjacent to the church, safely behind the lines of defense set up by the IDF. Shattered glass and fractured concrete littered the street.

"Get the gear, Jack," he said.

Mike saw a young Israeli officer approaching, hurrying to meet them while calling out to get his attention.

"Sir, I'm Lieutenant Calev Reubens. Colonel Yakov told me to be on the lookout for you and your cameraman. I understand you are trying to get in close for some filming?"

"That's right," Mike said.

"Okay with me sir, but it's pretty hot right now. The courtyard is a shooting gallery—I don't know how you'll get close enough to film, but it's up to you, sir."

Mike looked at Calev and smiled. "First things first, Lieutenant. Stop calling me 'sir.' I'm just a civilian trying to tell the story."

"Glad to hear it, sir," Lieutenant Reubens replied.

Mike rolled his eyes. Jack joined them with his camera and equipment. "Ready to go," he told Mike.

The rapid fire of automatic weapons echoed throughout the narrow streets all around them. Mike took a deep breath. Calev took off, crouching in between vehicles, signaling Mike and Jack to follow. They drew close to the perimeter set up in the square. They could now hear shouts coming out from the church. "There are wounded and dying in here. I beg you, stop shooting!"

In response, shots rang out from the apartment buildings surrounding the area, and a rocket-propelled grenade exploded in the plaza to their left. Mike and Jack ducked for cover, then carefully moved forward amid the intense shooting.

Mike looked back through the corner of a damaged building to check and see if Jack was filming. The red light on Jack's camera showed he was up and running, catching all the action on video. Hostile fire hit some Israeli soldiers. Medics raced through the fire fight to care for them. Other IDF soldiers fired back, wounding some fighters firing from the doorway of the church.

Mike overheard Calev on the radio talking to Colonel Yakov.

"Colonel, snipers are moving throughout the buildings along the southern end of the square."

Safe for the moment behind armored vehicles, Mike and Jack waited for a lull in the firing to see where they might be better able to position themselves.

More Palestinian gunmen ran toward the entrance of the Basilica. The IDF let loose a barrage of automatic weapons fire, wounding the gunmen before they could enter the church. Their comrades began dragging those that couldn't walk through the doorway. Some priests were also hit by the shooting, along with an older nun who had ventured out to help those who had been wounded.

Mike now heard the rumbling of tanks, accompanied by several armored vehicles, as they entered the courtyard. The shooting stopped as the turrets turned toward the upstairs windows of the adjacent buildings, determined by the IDF to be the source of the previous weapons fire. IDF troops moved in to surround the Basilica.

An IDF spokesman, using a bullhorn, ordered the gunmen to surrender. Time seemed to stand still. No one knew what would happen next. Finally, stooping through the ancient doorway of the church, an elderly orthodox priest in black robes and skull cap stepped forward with his arms raised. Mike watched, now from his cover behind the armored vehicles, as Calev and his team of elite Shaldag commandos quickly surrounded the priest. The soldiers escorted him behind one of the other armored vehicles and out of harm's way. Mike could see them talking. After a few minutes, the priest returned to the church.

The intensity of the setting began to subside. Emergency medical vehicles now entered the courtyard. More priests came out of the church to help several nuns escort some of the wounded Basilica staff to the ambulances. All the while, the soldiers maintained their aim on the church and the surrounding buildings.

As the emergency vehicles left, Mike connected with Calev. He explained that the gunmen had agreed to let some of the wounded leave but would continue to hold the rest as hostages. "It looks like we have a cease fire for a while. The negotiators are coming to see if they can calm the situation further and secure the release of the rest of the hostages. We'll see. Let me know if you need anything. I have to get back to my squad."

Mike turned to Jack. "We might as well shoot the report from right here. Let me know when you are ready."

"I'll be ready in a minute," Jack said. "Just let me check the angle and sound."

Mike continued to stare at the scene in a moment of reflection. *Here we are in the place of Christ's birth. If the Prince of Peace is watching, he must be weeping over what is happening today.* Although raised as a Methodist, Mike wasn't a religious person, but the irony of this scene would have struck anyone with the slightest knowledge of the story of Christmas.

Jack called out to Mike. "I'm ready when you are."

Mike turned towards him. "Let's do this."

Jack gave him the countdown using his fingers— three, two, one. He pointed to Mike and the red light on his camera came on.

"Fighting has erupted today around the Church of the Nativity in Bethlehem, built to honor the birth of the Savior. This ancient Catholic site has become the scene of an intense firefight. Palestinian gunmen have now taken control of the Basilica, holding an undisclosed number of priests and sisters of the church inside as hostages. While the shooting ricocheted around the square, Israeli troops used every effort to contain their fire and prevent damage to the site that Christendom heralds as the birthplace of Jesus Christ.

"This restraint may not last for long. The IDF will not continue to take casualties without initiating more drastic measures, nor will they allow any sacred site, priests, or nuns to become an obstacle for putting an end to this operation. This standoff has now become the focal point of Operation Defensive Shield. Ongoing political talks hold out hope for progress in bringing this siege to an end, yet negotiators do not anticipate that calm will return to this sacred site any time soon.

"This is Mike Olson, reporting live from the uprising here in Manger Square at the Church of the Nativity in Bethlehem."

Mike ended his report. The cease fire had held. He looked around to see black American State Department Suburbans and Palestinian Authority Land Rovers entering the area. Jack began to film the teams of staff and guards getting out of the vehicles. IDF team members shouted for everyone to hold their positions. Mike then saw Colonel Yakov waving his team to the side.

"Looks like the diplomats will take it from here," Jack said, putting his camera and gear away. Now men in civilian clothes, along with medical teams, entered the Basilica. Colonel Yakov saw Mike and came over to him. Mike relaxed a bit at the sight of a familiar face. The colonel gave Mike a nod, glancing over at Jack. He stood beside Mike, looking at the group of civilian vehicles surrounded by the diplomatic core.

"Here comes the political cavalry," Colonel Yakov said. "The gunmen will have their say now, but believe me, it won't do them any good. Headquarters is determined that this will not end in some kind of stalemate."

Mike looked at Isaac and back at the folks heading into the Basilica.

"You know, Isaac, the more I cover these conflicts, the more they seem to be like some ridiculous high-stakes political card game played out using real lives as poker chips. Politicians raise the ante, talking like things will get better; all the while people are getting killed."

Isaac looked at Jack, acknowledging his presence, and turned back to Mike.

"Don't get too philosophical on me, Mike. You're right about one thing, though. A lot more blood is going to be spilled on both sides before this is over."

Isaac turned and walked away.

"Let's get this off to the network," Mike said to Jack. He sent him back to the Land Rover to make the preparations. Mike then walked toward the Basilica. He made his way through the growing crowd of government officials. Nearing a group of soldiers huddled behind an armored vehicle, he saw their commander pointing to a map and overheard him say, "They're well entrenched. The random fire coming from here is also problematic." With his finger tracing the outline of a perimeter, he barked out, "Lt. Reubens, scout out which areas in these buildings we need to take down. We'll work out the timing and put together the right squads."

Mike made his way over to Calev, who seemed surprised to see him so close to the action.

With a quizzical look on his face, Calev said, "Sir, if you don't mind me asking, how'd you get this clearance?"

"Your colonel gave me this access," Mike said, looking down at the maps. "I covered the operations in Southern Lebanon when he was there and the Temple Mount a year and a half ago when all this hell broke loose. He seems to believe I do a pretty fair job of reporting the events as they happen."

"You know sir," Calev said, "it's still not clear to me what happened on the Temple Mount that day or who started firing first. All I remember is that it just went crazy. And now, we've got to deal with trying not to damage this church or injure the folks inside. It's a mess. For now, though, the politicians and the gunmen will have their time to discuss how to work something out. I gotta run, sir."

"Okay Calev. We'll catch up later."

Mike made his way back to the Land Rover.

"Jack, let's get out of here and see if we can shoot some footage outside of this area."

Jack muttered under his breath. "We'll shoot something all right. I'm just hoping we don't get shot."

Mike smiled at him and patted him on the shoulder, knowing they had retreated out of the range of danger. Jack continued to pack the film equipment back in the Land Rover.

Mike watched Jack arrange the gear for a while. He then threw the rest of his stuff in the back seat of the Land Rover and jumped in the front passenger's seat. Jack got in behind the wheel and cranked up the engine. He started weaving the vehicle through the soldiers stationed at the perimeter of the area and they made their way past the barbed wire barriers now set to mark the boundary of the hot zone.

"Where to bud?" Jack said. "You're the one determined to get us killed."

Chapter 3

THE WEST BANK

After crossing the barbed wire barriers, Mike and Jack traveled slowly through the winding streets of Bethlehem. Many people in the crowds that surrounded them made their way to the *souq*, an open-air market, where they pressed in to haggle with the stall owners over whatever meager supplies were available. The Israelis had responded to the violence at the Basilica by imposing a curfew and blockading the city, so the people of Bethlehem scrambled to gather whatever supplies remained.

Mike looked out the window of the Land Rover. Throngs of people swirled about him. He could hear them talking with one another in loud, shrill voices animated by emphatic hand motions and facial gestures. Soldiers dressed in green fatigues stood stationed at checkpoints. They held their TAR-21 Tavor automatic assault weapons, specially designed for urban warfare, at the ready. Other soldiers stood at ease in front of armored vehicles, mostly silent but alert, watching the movement of the crowd. Mike had seen civilians closely guarded by armed soldiers before; it seemed to be the norm in this part of the world whenever violence erupted.

Jack slowed the Land Rover to a crawl as a crowd of women, young and old, pushed by them carrying empty plastic water jugs. Children played at their sides oblivious to the stark conditions that surrounded them. Mike and Jack then began to feel the stares of a group of idle young men gathered on the street. Their looks seemed to display malice and hatred, possibly fueled by a sense of injustice being inflicted upon them and compounded by their inability to change the situation. What looked like anger contorted their faces, highlighting the fire in their eyes. Mike began to fidget, bouncing his right knee on the ball of his foot without his conscious control. He soon recognized this motion and came to grips with his own feelings of uneasiness.

"Stop this thing," said Mike. "Let's get out and walk around a bit. We can't talk to anyone or film anything from inside this vehicle."

Jack's look let Mike know he thought he was crazy. He mumbled to himself. "Yeah. Let's get out here and see who gets shot first."

"Quit your whining," said Mike.

Jack continued to grumble as he found a small parking place. They got out of the car. A warm, dry breeze hit them in the face. The morning shadows had fled. Mike knew it would be hot for the rest of the afternoon.

Jack grabbed his high-definition mini-camera out of the back of the Land Rover and had to catch up with Mike who had not paused to wait for him. Together they walked through the narrow streets, taking some footage here and there and sharing observations with each other. Mike had become a keen observer of people. He applied his skills to strengthen his reporting. His passion was to get the story right using every angle available. To do this he knew he needed to spend time with the people.

From the corner of his eye, Mike caught sight of a young woman squatting down to try and console a little girl in tears. He turned his head toward her, drawn by what he thought was curiosity, but soon became a more compelling reason: he simply could not take his eyes off her. Mike froze, speechless. Of course, he had seen his share of lovely women in his line of work, but before him now knelt the most strikingly beautiful young woman he'd ever seen. Her brown eyes sparkled with a bright intensity. Her long, thick, dark hair hung loosely around her shoulders in perfect swirls accentuating the high line of her cheeks. She held a gentle smile on her face as she comforted the little girl. Mike saw a glimmer in her smile of the kindness he imagined she must carry in her heart. She seemed to him to be out of place in this city caught up in crisis. His gaze had caught her for only a moment, yet it seemed to him to have stopped the movement of time.

Mike shook himself back to reality. He watched the young woman try to pick up the little girl, spilling the contents of her bag into the street. Propelled without thinking, Mike rushed up beside her and stooped down to pick up the groceries.

"Here, let me help you," he said.

The little girl, carrying a worn-out doll whose demeanor—unlike the girl's—was vague and painted on its face, stopped her sobbing for a moment, surprised at the attention of the American. The young woman continued to comfort her, speaking in Arabic, as she bent down to pick up the contents of the spilled bag.

"It's okay. I can get it," she said to Mike in perfect English.

Mike continued to help her collect everything as if he hadn't heard her. While kneeling, he reached into his backpack. The little girl moved closer to the woman to find security by hugging her leg.

"Here sweetie, would you like some water?" Mike said.

He reached out to hand the bottle of water to the little girl. The young woman motioned for her to refuse. Missing the signal, the little girl reached up and took the bottle, bringing a frown to the young woman's face.

"What do you say?" the young woman said in English. The little girl spoke in Arabic as she tried to open the water. "—in English," said the young woman, encouraging her.

The little girl stopped trying to turn the cap and looked sheepishly up at Mike.

"Thank you," she repeated, this time using her best English.

"You're welcome, sweetheart. Can I help you take off that cap?"

She lifted the bottle with both hands to give it to Mike. He took the bottle from her while reaching into his pocket with his other hand to pull out and present a chocolate bar. The little girl, all smiles now, grabbed it with glee.

"Where are your manners?" the young woman said. Mike saw the displeasure in her eyes towards his gift for the little girl. He noted it but continued to interact with her. He was glad to share what he could to bring a smile to the face of this lovely little girl. Mike opened the bottle of water and gave it back to her.

Then he looked at the young woman. "Here then, let me help. You've got your hands full."

"We're fine. Thank you anyway."

Mike finished picking up the groceries. He had no intention of letting the young woman refuse his help. He then stood, holding the bag of groceries so that she was able to pick up the little girl.

"Thank you," she said.

"My name is Mike. Is this your little girl?"

The young woman gave Amal a squeeze and said with a smile, "No. She is my niece."

"And her name is Amal? That's what I thought I heard you call her."

"Yes."

Amal, hearing her name but not sure why, looked back and forth between her aunt and the man who had just given her the chocolate.

"Do you mind if I ask your name?" Mike held his breath wondering if he had crossed a cultural boundary that would cause her some embarrassment. His intention was simply to continue the conversation. He hoped that he hadn't made a stupid mistake.

To his delight, a sweet little voice said softly, "Bashira—her name is Bashira."

Mike smiled at Amal and said, "Thank you." And then looking at Bashira said, "What a wonderful name. Do you live nearby?"

"Yes, just over there." She pointed to the apartments at the far end of the street. "We were trying to get to my grandfather's apartment near the square, but the soldiers won't let us pass."

Mike noticed the matter-of-fact way in which she mentioned the soldiers' orders. He noted an absence of anger or malice in her voice. Instead, he heard a calm demeanor that seemed out of place and in stark contrast with what he had recently experienced in the intense stares of the young men. *Interesting*, he thought.

The young woman led the way across the street toward her home. Mike walked beside her while Jack, dumbfounded by the interaction he had just witnessed, brought up the rear carrying his camera and backpack. People along the streets stopped to stare at the two Americans walking with the Palestinian woman and the little girl.

Mike regained his bearings, remembering again why he was on the streets, and asked, "You mentioned the soldiers. Has the fighting come close to you and your family?"

"At times."

She looked down the street for a moment to her left, in the direction of where she had mentioned her grandfather lived, and then behind them toward an apartment building they had just passed. Mike could see bullet holes, like pockmarked scars, around the doors and windows of various buildings.

He kept the conversation moving. "Looks like the fighting has come very close."

"Those are old scars from another time. The recent fighting has not come this close. We hope that it doesn't."

"I hope so too. It seems that there's a stalemate at the Basilica right now. The politicians are trying to work out a solution—"

Choking immediately on his words, he felt a sense of awkwardness release an unexpected twinge in his gut. He had to consciously remind himself that a potential solution in his mind might mean something completely different to this young woman in front of him, or she might care less for politicians and their multitude of failed plans. Her presence had caught him off guard; after all, he was tracking down a news story. But now, this beautiful young Arab woman had taken him off his game. His thoughts were broken by her words.

"Are you one of them?"

"A politician!! God forbid! I'm a reporter with WBN, World Broadcasting Network.

Bashira stopped in her tracks, still clutching Amal, and turned to face Mike, who stumbled as Jack tried to avoid crashing into all three of them from behind.

"Now I know why you look familiar! I've seen you many times on TV. What are you doing here today?"

"There's a break in the fighting as the negotiators meet. We thought this might be a good opportunity to try and see what's happening beyond the Basilica." Mike paused for a moment to emphasize what he was about to say. He considered this to be his trademark as a reporter. "There's always more to a news event than what the eye can see."

Now that his attention was back on the trail of reporting the news, he began to feel more at ease, coming to his senses as if he had just splashed cold water on his face. "We need to get out and try to gain some insight on what's happening on both sides of this conflict. By the looks of things, it's pretty rough here."

Bashira remained silent as she resumed walking, carrying Amal. They approached the apartment building that was her home. Mike saw the same tell-tale pockmarks of bullet holes covering the outside walls of some of her neighbors' homes, an ornamentation no one desired nor welcomed, commemorating what they all would like to forget. He slowed his pace, taking it all in, turning to look at Jack and then back again at the bullet holes in the wall.

∞∞∞∞∞∞∞∞∞∞∞∞

At the door of the apartment building, Amal scurried down from Bashira's grasp and ran up the stairs into the arms of a middle-aged woman standing in the open doorway. Behind her, Mike saw a gentleman with a stern look of concern on his face. The woman hurried Amal inside and then returned.

Bashira climbed the steps. The lean-faced gentleman gave her a quick kiss and spoke to her in Arabic, keeping everyone waiting at the door. Mike stood on the steps holding the groceries while Jack looked uncomfortable. Bashira and her father continued speaking in Arabic.

Neither Mike nor Jack knew the language. They gave each other bewildered looks and shrugged their shoulders. The gentleman then turned to them and began to speak in fluent English, with only the slightest accent.

"Thank you, my friends, for your kindness in helping my daughter, Bashira. Here, let me take those." He took the grocery bag from Mike. "Come in, please."

Her father handed the bag to Bashira, who carried the groceries into the kitchen escorted by her mother. The Americans entered the apartment. Her father followed, directing them toward the living room.

43

"Thank you again for your help. My name is Samir," he said. "Can I get you something to drink?"

To Mike, Bashira's father sounded guarded but sincere. "No thanks. We need to be going," Mike said, feeling a bit awkward himself. "We simply wanted to help."

Bashira came out of the kitchen, gave a quick smile to Mike, and nodded her head. Mike and Jack smiled back. They turned to leave, but before doing so, Mike addressed Bashira and her father.

"It was a pleasure meeting you all."

"Thank you for helping," Bashira replied.

Samir led the Americans to the front door. "Goodbye," he said.

Mike and Jack left the apartment. Once on the street, Mike looked back through the apartment window. He caught a glimpse of Amal in Bashira's arms, lifted into the air, squealing with laughter, and covered with kisses.

"Okay, let's head out," he said to Jack. On the way back to their vehicle, Mike noticed once more the bullet holes in the walls of the buildings surrounding them. They walked past the same young men who still seemed to glare at them. Now at the Land Rover, Jack threw his cameras into the back, sat behind the wheel, and started the vehicle.

"Where to now?" he asked Mike.

"Let's just drive and see what strikes us." Mike's thoughts were somewhere else.

"It looks like you're already struck," said Jack.

Mike glanced at Jack, denying any recognition in his comment. "What are you talking about?"

"The girl—and I don't mean the little one. I saw the look in your eyes when you were talking to her."

Mike gave Jack a disapproving scowl.

"That's just like you to make something out of nothing. I was helping a young woman who is trying to make it through this mess. Now drive, or would you rather stay here with our other newfound friends?" Mike threw a glance over his shoulder to be sure Jack knew he was referring to the young men on the street.

With his own parting glance, Jack put the Land Rover in gear and drove away, mumbling sarcastically to himself, "Here we go—only who knows where?"

◇◇◇◇◇◇◇◇◇◇◇◇◇

Samir closed the door behind his guests and turned to face his daughter. Bashira knew that two Americans suddenly showing up at their doorstep had presented her father with an awkward situation. She felt responsible for not being able to give him any warning, but it had all happened so quickly.

"*Habibti*, that was a surprise." Samir looked puzzled. His wonderful daughter often showed kindness to strangers, but this was different, even for her. "Where in the world did you find those two gentlemen, and why did you invite them to our home?"

"The one is a famous TV reporter with WBN, and the other, I believe, is the cameraman."

Samir raised his eyebrows as he asked again, "Okay, and how did you find them?"

"I didn't, *Baba*, they found us. Amal was upset that the soldiers wouldn't allow us to pass and go see *Sido*. In trying to console her, I dropped the bag and some of the groceries spilled out onto the sidewalk. Before I knew it, there he was picking them up and offering to carry the bag home. I told him that was not necessary. He simply held on to it and waited for me to go ahead. After he gave Amal some water and candy, I could only pick her up and come home."

Bashira felt her own bewilderment as she recalled this sequence of events to her father. Her close-knit family cared deeply for one another, choosing to believe the best no matter how strange the circumstances that surrounded them were. This incident qualified as one of the more unusual ones they had experienced together, puzzling both Bashira and her parents. She held Amal in her arms, watching the two strangers through the window as they walked down the street.

In her wildest imagination she could not have envisioned a world-famous American TV reporter coming to her home. This sort of thing didn't happen to her. She kept her life within close parameters, devoting her energies to serving her family and others by caring for their needs. She certainly wasn't in the habit of inviting strangers, especially an American newsman, into their home. This odd situation left her wondering about what had just occurred.

She and her father both turned from the window. Amal scampered down from her arms to race off into the kitchen.

"Well one thing is for sure," said Samir, "our neighbors will certainly be talking about this visit."

Bashira laughed nervously. She knew he was right. Nothing really escaped the other families in their neighborhood, especially when it involved anything out of the ordinary. *What in the world will we tell people—other than the truth?* she thought. These Americans appeared, and the next moment they were helping her to pick up her groceries.

Bashira couldn't help but notice, though, how Mike had looked at her. She was accustomed to such gazes as many other young men throughout her life had complimented her, describing her as beautiful. This always made her feel self-conscious. Her intentions were not to emphasize her looks but rather to concentrate on developing an inner beauty that reflected her moral integrity. And yet, in this case, when she had looked up at the American stranger, she sensed something different about Mike. Although his presence had surprised her, his kindness had touched her heart.

Who knows? she thought. *This might be a divine appointment to provide a little insight to someone unfamiliar with what we are going through here, in this little town of Bethlehem.*

Chapter 4

THE BASILICA

The following day, Mike and Jack returned to the Basilica. It was now surrounded by a crowd of international reporters and dignitaries. The US State Department attachés, Israeli officials, and Palestinian Authority representatives, all with their supporting staff, had arrived in full force along with other politicians and church leaders. The plaza had become a tent city comprised of makeshift headquarters.

Mike recognized most of the usual news teams in the press corral. They left sporadically to buzz around the dignitaries' staff like worker bees. From a distance, he listened to the endless instructions from staffers describing how reporters would not be able to enter the Basilica but would be able to speak with some of the dignitaries after their meetings had concluded. All the while, each news team jockeyed for position to get the best shot or quote, hoping that their description of the moment would become those few precious minutes the world would watch on their nightly news channels.

To Mike, it felt more like a feeding frenzy. The reporters seemed to sense "blood in the water." They knew that whoever could seize the most attention got the reward—fame. This was the aspect of his business he disliked the most, and now he found himself surrounded by all the fame-seekers gathered to make a name for themselves. In these situations, he became rather cynical.

Mike knew he had a similar ego and a competitive nature, yet he refused to allow these personal characteristics to compromise his integrity. Insincerity sickened his stomach. Mike knew that most of the international politicians who were present only sought to inflate their egos further by magnifying their own contribution to the negotiations. Meanwhile, the self-important staffers arrogantly ordered the news teams around by proclaiming their instructions: "This is where you will stand"; "Here is what you may film." The reporting took place amidst an endless litany of irrelevant guidance given for the purpose of controlling the message that the public would see.

Mike fought hard for his independence as a journalist. He sought to report the facts as he saw them and let the viewers make their own conclusions. At an early age, he learned the diligence necessary to get to the root of a story by watching his father maintain his integrity as a newspaper editor who built his reputation on getting the facts right. Mike consciously checked himself to avoid jumping to conclusions and refused to spin the news to the angle his producers requested. His commitment to not shaping the story gave him access to political and military leaders throughout the Middle East. His television news network eventually became willing to honor his integrity in return for inside footage of significant events. Many of his colleagues were envious of the privileged access his work ethic had provided for him.

In the crowd, Mike saw Jim Franklin, the Communications Attaché for the State Department in Middle East Affairs. Mike thought his heady title befitted this pompous idiot who thought he was the State Department. Mike considered Jim to be one of the worst story manipulators he knew. His resentment had grown personal over the years as Jim loved to get under Mike's skin by telling him what he could and couldn't do. Mike determined in his heart to prevent that from happening today.

Mike then edged closer to the group to hear the instructions for possible interviews. Everyone paid close attention. The reporters had been given clearance to talk to some of the hostages that were recently released. At the "All Clear" signal, the crowd of reporters charged toward the tents surrounding the Basilica like an invading hoard, pushing and shoving each other, showing signs of resentment anytime a more prominent member took the lead. Mike disliked this herding behavior of reporters. The commotion it generated reminded him of his childhood in Iowa when, on the surrounding farms, it became time to lead the swine to their feeding troughs. He knew this thought betrayed his bad attitude, so he chose instead not to sprint ahead and took up a position toward the rear. Jack pressed on to film what he could.

Once inside the tent, Mike saw an older nun praying in the corner at the back. She looked exhausted. Mike decided to step away from the group and approach her.

Quietly, he walked up beside her as she prayed, not wanting to disturb the holy moment. She turned to him and spoke in English with an Italian accent.

"Hello, my child. Is there something I can do for you?"

Mike immediately felt bad for disturbing her, but he was intrigued by her age and the fact that she was not paying any attention to the commotion of the lights and cameras around her.

"Oh, no ma'am. I'm just a reporter. I was wondering what it has been like for you the last few days?"

The older nun turned toward him. For a moment, she seemed to be studying his face. Although she looked exhausted, Mike felt a sense of peace about her. Then she spoke, saying, "Well, if I were to be honest, which my vows demand that I be, I would have to say these last few days have been trying."

The understatement in her answer took Mike by surprise. "I'm sure it has been. Can I get you anything?"

"Oh no, I'm quite fine."

"Are you visiting the Basilica?"

She replied with a smile on her face. "Oh no, I've been at the Church of the Nativity for over forty years."

"Oh, my goodness, that means you've seen about everything—except for what you've witnessed during this standoff."

"Young man, if you would have told me that my home here would become a place of bloodshed and death, I would have told you to see the priest for telling such tales. But today my heart is broken with what I've seen. May God have mercy—"

"Yes, ma'am, we are going to need it."

Out of the corner of his eye Mike saw his nemesis from the State Department hustling toward them. From seeing the scowl on Jim's face and the tension in his jaw, he knew he was in for a tongue lashing. With his hands on his hips, Jim moved in closer to Mike's face than anyone with a lick of sense would attempt. Jim could barely contain himself, as he shouted at Mike, "Can't you ever stick with the group? How many times have we got to tell you?"

Mike just smiled as Jim turned more red.

"You know, Jim, I guess you are worried about all the state secrets I might glean out of this precious older sister. I'm sure she's one of your more important sources in this place of conspiracy and intrigue." Mike made his eyes real big and held up his hands, wiggling his fingers as he pointed at the church and the crowd under the tent.

Mike's smirk irritated Jim to the breaking point.

"Always the smart mouth, Mike. If it wasn't for your network and your connections, you wouldn't get the time of day from me. Maybe you'll grow up someday and leave the real reporting to the professionals."

"Why Jim, I didn't know you cared that much about me or my network. Is it my reporting that rankles you so much or is it the fact that I won't follow you around like a whipped dog—or maybe both?"

Jim stormed off to engage the rest of the group. Mike watched him go, then turned back to the nun, and said, "I'm sorry you had to hear all that. I appreciate you giving me a few minutes of your time. Please stay safe. I'm sure they need you here for another forty years."

The old nun smiled at Mike. "I'll be praying for us all and lifting up a special prayer to the Blessed Virgin Mary that she will keep you safe."

"Thank you. I need all the prayers I can get." Mike gave her a quick nod and walked slowly toward the crowd of reporters. He found Jack filming and tapped him on the shoulder.

"Jack, can you spool up the footage of the fighting we shot yesterday, and let's use it as a run up to our report today."

"Already done."

Mike adjusted his mic and faced the camera, his back to the courtyard. Jack began the shot with a wide-angle view of the church, then zoomed in on Mike. Mike looked to Jack to give him the count down. Jack's hand signaled to him—three, two, one.

In the corner of the monitor, Mike saw yesterday's footage of the Basilica siege with IDF soldiers firing back at the Palestinian gunmen ensconced in the ancient cathedral.

Mike began his report.

> "Talks to negotiate an end to the stalemate at the Basilica continue today but show little progress. Minister Shmuel, the lead Israeli negotiator, and Representative Aziz of the Palestinian Authority remain locked in their historic positions. As the number of Palestinian fatalities increases, a growing outcry from the world community demands an end to the fighting. This outcry is increasing the pressure on the IDF to bring this operation to an end. Nevertheless, as these talks continue to bog down, more drastic measures will be taken, with inevitable results—further destruction and suffering for everyone.

> "While we wait, the IDF has announced a temporary lift of the curfew so that the local population can get out to acquire the meager food and supplies that

are still available to them. This relief from the curfew brings a small signal of hope for those living in the besieged city that an agreement may be reached to end this crisis. Negotiators continue to express their concerns over the obstacles before them and remain skeptical. Time is available to neither side. The death toll rises and the cry for peace appears to fall on deaf ears as each side continues to prepare for further confrontation.

"This is Mike Olson reporting for WBN from outside the Basilica Square in Bethlehem."

"That's it, Jack. Did you get it all?"

"Now you're trying to tell me how to do my job," Jack said.

"No, just asking."

"Yep, got it all, and I'll send it off to the studio. What's next?"

Mike looked around at the mixed crowd of reporters, still trying to position themselves for their interviews, and various staffers, trying to maintain their displays of self-inflated influence.

"Let's get out of here," Mike said. "With this break in the fighting, we can get back on the streets and see how things are going."

Jack started packing his gear. Mike could hear him mumbling sarcastically, "Great, back onto the streets. Just where everyone can't wait to see us."

"Quit complaining. This is what you get paid the big bucks for." Mike knew that a good-humored jab would get under Jack's skin, but they were friends after all. Mike smiled, took one more look around, then walked off towards where they had parked the Land Rover.

◇◇◇◇◇◇◇◇◇◇◇◇◇

Bashira was late. She had put on her nurse's uniform before she left the house since there was now little time to get the groceries, return home, and then get to the hospital. Focusing on her mental "to do" list, she didn't notice the Land Rover pulling up behind her and the American getting out. Mike startled her by coming up to her side.

He said, with enthusiasm, "Hi Bashira, how's Amal?"

She kept walking, thinking to herself, *I can't believe this is happening.* "She's fine," she said.

"And your family? How are they? How are your grandparents?"

So many questions so quickly, she thought. *Why is he asking all this?* Bashira kept walking, looking at the ground. "My parents are fine and my grandparents are okay, but they live so close to the fighting. This concerns us even more when Amal stays with them."

Bashira realized she had unconsciously quickened her pace. Mike had no problem keeping up with her. She looked back to see if Jack was with him. He lagged behind them both. The street became more crowded, forcing Bashira to shorten her stride and slow her pace. Mike stayed right beside her. She could now feel the eyes of some of the women on the street staring at them both. The presence of this American made her feel uncomfortable. His persistence in talking to her increased her consciousness of what these women might be thinking; but then again, she was willing to be kind. Perhaps he just wanted to know more about her family to get a sense of how everyone in the community was holding up. Despite the inherent awkwardness of their relationship, she sensed she could help him understand by allowing him to ask his questions.

"Can your grandparents move further away?"

"Not really. My grandfather has lived there for most of his adult life and has seen many of these tragic events. For him this is all a part of living here. Sharing his love with friends and neighbors, regardless of the circumstances, is more important to him than his own safety."

"Well, perhaps this cease-fire will continue. I must say though, realistically, I'm not holding out a lot of hope for it right now. Both sides have their own agendas and neither one seems willing to compromise."

Bashira looked back.

"I hope your poor cameraman can keep up with us," she said, trying to change the subject. She didn't want to delve too deep into the politics that swirled about her beloved Bethlehem. She thought Mike's questions were genuine, but politics was not her favorite subject.

Jack came around the corner behind them. His eyes moved back and forth with his steps. Bashira thought he looked uncomfortable on the streets by himself. He finally caught up with them and followed close behind, not interrupting their conversation.

Bashira had now collected her thoughts and was feeling a bit more comfortable in this situation. She recalled something from memory, speaking it softly under her breath in Arabic while clutching her necklace.

"What was that you said?"

Bashira looked a little embarrassed, thinking instead that he had not heard her, and smiled. "Just a saying my grandfather would repeat to us when I was a little girl."

"How do you say it in English?"

Bashira thought for a moment, wrestling with the interpretation, then brightened up and said in English, "Hope in the face of struggle is like a delicate flower that must be nurtured with love."

"That's profound. Is that a common saying here in Bethlehem?"

"No. It's something we've said in our family for as long as I can remember. I need to hurry now. I'm only going to the corner store."

"Do you mind if we accompany you?"

Bashira stopped to look at Mike. Her face grew distant, taking on a pensive look as she thought through her response. She knew the small store would be crowded. What would her neighbors think if she walked in with these two Americans? Of course, it would be bewildering to some and upsetting to others, but on the other hand, what better way for a reporter to gain insight into their living conditions than by seeing them firsthand? Her willingness to take this chance surprised her, but she had the feeling that she could trust Mike.

"I guess it's all right. I'll only be a few minutes."

The three of them walked on. Jack continued to follow. He took out his small camera and started filming the scene. He caught footage of some young men going through piles of rubble, some others tearing down a broken wall, and still others replacing windows using a menagerie of coverings they had scavenged from the remains of nearby buildings.

Children ran here and there all around them while their mothers hurried to get in line at the store. The presence of the children playing provided a stark contrast to the women, some young and others quite old, all carrying fatigued looks on their faces while they waited to enter.

The line to the corner store moved ahead slowly, but once inside, the women moved quickly in order to obtain whatever they needed from the meager amount of goods stocked on the shelves. Bashira made her way through the crowded store. She bargained for what food was available, purchasing what she could: some pita, a few vegetables, some fruit, a small amount of cheese, and a little coffee.

Mike whispered softly to her, "Is it this bad everywhere?"

"Yes, for now. Whenever the fighting and curfews start, many people stockpile goods, and everything becomes scarce. The fresh foods can be very hard to come by."

She finished quickly and left with her groceries and the two Americans, wondering what the neighborhood women would say about this.

She began the walk back toward her apartment in silence. Mike offered to carry the groceries. Bashira thanked him for his offer but refused.

At the point when the silence would have become awkward Mike asked, "Bashira, do you mind me asking a little about you being a nurse? I'm curious about which hospital you work at and what you do?"

This question startled Bashira before she realized that she wore her uniform with her photo ID clipped to her pocket. *Why does he want to know about the hospital and what I do?* she thought. After a few more steps she began to relax. *He's probably just curious,* she told herself.

"I work at The Sisters of Mercy Hospital. It's a children's hospital, mainly. I work in the surgery recovery ward—which is filled right now." Her eyes seemed to sparkle a little as she mentioned the children.

They continued to walk.

"Is it full due to the fighting?"

"Yes, to some degree, but even in the best of times, we are very busy. The people here have limited access to medical care, especially the children who are often the last to get the care they need."

Jack drew closer, leaning in to better hear their conversation. Bashira began to clarify her statement.

"We are understaffed, and supplies are low. With the fighting, everything gets worse. It's always a struggle, but the children are so resilient. When I see the looks on their faces—" Bashira paused, then kept walking, looking at the sidewalk. "It fills me with such love for them. They inspire me to do whatever I can to help."

"Bashira, do you think Jack and I could ever visit the hospital?" Jack jerked his head to look at Mike. Then he watched Bashira. Bashira remained quiet for a moment. Again, she wanted to think carefully before giving a reply.

"Why would you want to visit?"

"To get firsthand insight into what life is like here, how the children cope with their circumstances when fighting is all around them. It's a part of the story of this conflict that is never seen, and I'd like to know more."

Bashira stared ahead as they kept walking. Once again, in silence, she considered how wise it was to pursue his request. *What good could come out of such a visit?* she wondered. Then again, it's not every day that a TV newsman asks to visit the hospital. She concluded that her supervisors could decide.

"I could check with the head of nursing. She's a friend. If it sounds like a good idea to her, we could approach the director of the hospital. I'm not sure though. With the fighting, it may be hard to get permission for you to visit."

"Tell them that it might be a good thing to let the world know more about the conditions you face. A few minutes of coverage during prime-time TV news can often shape the world's opinion of a situation."

Bashira hadn't thought of this possible outcome. The thought intrigued her. Maybe this was why Mike had suddenly come into her life.

"Let's wait and see," she said. "Things are always more complicated than they might seem. Let me get back with you after I talk with my director."

They were getting close to Bashira's home. Bashira looked at Mike and turned the conversation to him.

"What is it like being a famous TV reporter?" she asked.

"Well, I don't know about the famous part. It may look more glamorous than it really is."

Bashira glanced at Mike and Jack in disbelief. Mike looked back at her and smiled.

"Really, it's not what you think. We're always racing around, trying to get to someone or catch something on camera that will grab the attention of a director thousands of miles away. And it's not just me trying to get their attention. These news directors are getting hundreds of images from around the world every day. They have to decide, sometimes within a moment's notice, which story is worth the precious few minutes they might allow for it that night on the evening news."

Jack chimed in, "This generates a lot of infighting among the teams of reporters competing for those few minutes."

Mike continued, "You drag camera crews around during all hours of the day and night to horrendous places, hoping that you get just the right shot or story—" Mike paused mid-sentence and looked at Bashira. She had been paying attention to his every word.

"Bashira, forgive me. That must have sounded about as egotistical as anything you've ever heard."

Bashira smiled a little. She had felt just the opposite. Mike's description of his life as a reporter and of how the news media worked fascinated her. She had to admit, as well, that she felt touched by his sensitivity to how his words might affect her. As they approached her apartment, she looked up at him, "So is it really true that such short TV news coverage can make a difference?"

Pausing before ascending the steps to her apartment, Mike looked directly at her. "Bashira, the truth is that images are being shown around the globe every day. You never know when one shot or story will touch the heart of a nation."

Bashira raised her eyebrows and pursed her lips in a look of determination. With confidence in her voice, she said, "I'll get you into our hospital. Let's see how this story turns out."

"You get me in, and we'll fight for those minutes." Mike said.

Bashira's mother opened the door, ending their conversation. Before Bashira could invite Mike and Jack in, Amal ran out the door, jumping and laughing. Bashira placed her bag of groceries on the ground and Amal leapt into her arms. Bashira lifted her into the air. Amal then squeezed Bashira around the neck, saying in Arabic, "*Did he bring me any chocolate?*"

"I heard that," said Mike. "She said 'chocolate.'"

"Yes, but you can't give her—" Before Bashira could finish her statement, Mike reached into his pocket.

"Is this what you were asking about? Can you say it in English?"

"Chocolate, please," said Amal. Bashira gave Amal a frown.

"Come on, she said, 'please.'"

Bashira continued to frown, but then broke into a smile.

"Okay, but only this once."

Amal screamed with delight, gave Bashira another big hug, and jumped down, standing in front of Mike with her hands held out.

"Here sweetie. A whole pack." Mike handed her a bag of Hershey's kisses. Amal's eyes opened wide. She grabbed the chocolate and raced to show her grandmother waiting at the door.

"That was too much!" said Bashira.

"Thank you for your kindness. I'm Miriam," Bashira's mother said, introducing herself, still standing at the top of the steps.

Mike looked up to reply, "You are more than welcome, ma'am."

He then turned to Bashira and said, "We've got to go. Let me know how things work out with the hospital. My mobile number is here on this card." Mike took out his wallet and handed Bashira his business card.

Miriam looked back and forth from Bashira to Mike.

Bashira answered, "I'll get back to you. Thanks again." She knew she would have to explain all this to her mother.

"You are welcome." He and Jack turned to go.

Miriam still stood at the top of the steps. "What was that about? Where did he find you this time, and why did you bring him home again?" Every time Bashira tried to respond to her mother, she asked another question.

"Mama, I have to go. I'm late for work."

"We'll talk about this when you get home."

Bashira gave her the groceries. Amal had taken the chocolate to her room. Bashira didn't have time to go find her.

"Kiss Amal goodbye for me," Bashira said to her mother as she opened the door to leave.

Chapter 5

BASHIRA'S APARTMENT

ashira returned late that night from her shift at the hospital. Her sleep was restless. She wondered how her director would respond to her request regarding the visit from Mike and Jack. Amal came jumping into her bed for a morning snuggle. This routine always energized Bashira. No matter how tired she might feel after working a difficult shift, holding Amal filled her soul with smiles and laughter.

Amal now sat quietly on her bed counting out her treasure of chocolate candy kisses. She divided them up into neat piles, counting the tasty treats and making sure each pile had an equal amount.

Finally, she said to Bashira, "I want to give these to my friends."

Bashira gave her a squeeze from behind. "I'm so proud of you for sharing your candy."

"I have so much. They don't have any."

"Well young lady, that's wonderful, for it is more blessed to give than to receive."

Bashira pulled Amal to her side of the bed and began tickling her mercilessly as squeals of laughter filled the house. Bashira's mother came in to scold Bashira, wagging her finger with a light-hearted smile.

"Stop torturing that little girl," she said. They all laughed with delight. Bashira jumped out of bed to get dressed. She wanted to prepare herself to receive a call from the director.

The morning passed slowly. Bashira waited to hear about the visit to the hospital, wondering if it could be possible at all. She continually reminded herself that with the Lord all things are possible. She finished cleaning up from the lunch she had prepared and stared out the window. Her mother entered the room carrying Amal.

The phone rang. Bashira hurried to answer it. Her face lit up with delight as the director let her know that they would be in touch with Mike to set up their visit. Bashira could hardly contain herself. She wanted to share the good news with Mike as soon as she could.

As she hung up the phone, she turned to see Amal in her mother's arms. Miriam was stroking her hair. Amal rubbed her eyes and yawned, still sleepy from her early afternoon nap. Bashira walked over to give her a kiss on the head. Amal then reached out for Bashira to hold her.

Bashira held out her arms to receive Amal. As Amal traded places, she now faced the window. Looking out, she saw Mike walking up the street. A giant smile lit up her face. She wiggled loose from Bashira's grip, screamed with delight, raced toward the front door, and bumped into Samir who was entering the kitchen.

Then Bashira and Miriam both looked out the window. They, too, saw Mike heading their way, talking on his phone. Miriam looked at Bashira, whose face now gleamed as she tugged at her dress to straighten it.

"Why don't you go and invite him in?" Miriam suggested.

Bashira gave her mother a little grin of thanks for acknowledging her desire. She took the apron off and almost skipped past her father to the door, handing him the apron. Samir gave her a bewildered glance, looked at Miriam, and then turned back to watch as Bashira opened the door.

Amal pushed in front of Bashira and before anyone could speak, she exclaimed, this time in English, "Did you bring me some candy?"

Bashira looked sternly at Amal, but with a loving voice said, "Have you no shame? You cannot ask such a thing. It is neither respectful nor polite."

Amal hung her head a little and then looked back up at Mike.

"Soooooorryyyyy."

Mike closed his phone and put it away. He gave Bashira a smile and slipped a sucker into Amal's hand. She ran back into the house with glee, showing it to her grandmother. Bashira widened her eyes at Mike in a message of disapproval but followed up with a smile.

Mike responded, mimicking Amal, "Soooooooor-ryyyyy."

By now Amal was in Miriam's lap, with the sucker in her mouth. Samir interrupted the moment.

"No need to stand on the steps. Come inside."

Mike entered the apartment and went into the living room with Samir. Bashira and her mother headed into the kitchen. Samir invited Mike to sit on their worn couch. Amal crawled up into Samir's lap, still enjoying her sucker. Bashira brought in a small tray of sweets.

"Coffee will be ready in a few minutes," she said. "I don't know what brought you here, but I'm glad you came. I just got off the phone with the director. She agreed to your visit. She will be in touch with you to set up the day and the time."

"That's wonderful. I hope it's soon. Things seem to be getting a little more tense. That's why I came by. We've heard rumors that the curfew is going to get more restrictive. I thought it might affect our visit to the hospital."

"It's something we've learned to live with," said Samir. "We'd hoped it would not be necessary, but we've been through this before." Bashira recognized the tone of solemn deliberation in her father's voice. She knew he was making a promise to himself and his family that they would experience provision.

She turned to Mike. "The director said you can come next week if that would work for you. She said she will be reaching out to you as soon as she has confirmed the schedule with the department heads. Is that soon enough?"

"Let's hope," said Mike.

Miriam brought in the coffee. Mike took one of the small cups and waited for Samir to take his.

Bashira, sitting near her father, warned Mike, "You may want to be careful and take small sips. It's very strong. There are grounds at the bottom of the cup."

Mike smiled, nodded, and took a sip. "Yep, that's strong all right, but very good. Thank you." He continued with a question, looking at Bashira. "Since we're talking about coming by the hospital, I've been wondering what inspired you to become a nurse?"

Bashira was surprised by Mike's question. She was not used to a man outside of her family and her circle of close friends taking an interest in what she did. She knew Mike was a reporter who probably just asked the question to get some background for the story, but this felt more personal than an interview.

"I guess I've always wanted to help others," she began, "ever since I was a little girl visiting my aunt and uncle in Nazareth. My aunt was a midwife then, and there was a hospital nearby we would visit. I saw how much the act of showing kindness meant to those who were hurting. I knew at that young age that I wanted to be a nurse."

Miriam came back into the room, joining them this time. She took Amal off Samir's lap and sat her down in hers and began to brush Amal's hair.

"Well then, how did you end up at the hospital here?" Mike asked.

Bashira took in each question, pondering it a bit before answering. She wasn't sure if Mike continued to ask these questions as a journalist or if he was trying to become her friend. The discussion they were having was so unusual; although, she and the rest of the family began to feel increasingly comfortable with him and more willing to share the details of their lives. She began to sense that Mike was someone she could trust.

"I guess you could say I'm just so fortunate to be part of this special place. The hospital has an amazing history."

"Okay? Why is it so special?"

This question from Mike caused her voice to rise with excitement as she replied. Bashira was passionate about the mission of the hospital and the work she did there; she could talk about this subject for hours. Now she was thrilled that Mike had taken the time to discover how important her work at the hospital was to her.

"The hospital was founded almost fifty years ago by medical missionaries. Since then, its vision has been to provide care for all children—Jewish, Christian, or Muslim. The hospital has served thousands of children in need over the years.

"I had a chance to volunteer there when I was young. I was forever impressed by the staff and doctors who cared so deeply for the patients. Several of the physicians are leaders in their field of specialty. They have had opportunities to leave and work in other settings that would provide more prestige, money, and benefits for their families, but they have chosen to stay here and serve the community. I've been so inspired by their willingness to sacrifice for the sake of the children.

"God paved the way for me to serve here," Bashira said with a tiny shrug of her shoulders. She felt a slight expression of embarrassment talking about herself. Yet she sensed that Mike was genuinely interested and wanted to know more. *That's why he's going to the hospital in the first place,* she reminded herself with a smile that leaked out of her eyes as she looked toward him.

Amal kept fidgeting in Miriam's lap and finally got away from her. Coming up by Mike's side, she started to check his pockets. He smiled and pulled out a whole bag of lollipops. The adults looked at him in disbelief as Amal squealed with delight. Bashira gave Mike another disapproving look.

"What can I say? We Americans have a sweet tooth and a soft spot for little kids." Amal ran across the room, clutching the bag of lollipops to her chest.

The phone rang again. Bashira looked first at Mike with hope in her eyes and then jumped up to answer.

"Yes director, this is wonderful news. Mike is here. We were just talking about the visit. I'll let him know. Thank you, I'll see you soon."

She hung up the phone and turned back toward Mike. "Oh my goodness, that was the director, and the arrangements are all set. You can come by next week!

She is going to give you a call to see what day and time works best for you."

"That's great!"

Bashira's face nearly glowed with the joy she felt inside. Her eyes sparkled. Although she felt thankful for this opportunity to get out the message of the good work the hospital did, something more stirred in her heart. She couldn't quite grasp it. It scared her a little to think about her feelings right now. She had also become thankful for this newsman who had come into her life, demonstrating interest in and genuine care for the needs of her family and friends who were caught up in this conflict. Moreover, something else tugged at her heart, something more than just thankfulness for Mike's interest in the hospital. Something was happening to her that she had not experienced before. Could it be possible that she was becoming attracted to Mike?

Preposterous! she almost shouted out loud.

Oh, perhaps as a child she might have held some slight and secret interest for someone, but it was only ever a childish whim and had never been profound. For this reason, though, she also felt troubled. This feeling sat much deeper within than any childhood fantasy, yet it seemed to be a growing affection for someone with whom she could never allow herself to share it. *This would be impossible*, she told herself. Nevertheless, she couldn't help but be excited for him to visit the hospital. Maybe that was all she needed to do—acknowledge that she had helped Mike cover a story on the hospital—and move on. She would continue to examine her emotions, but for now, she chose to celebrate this moment and cherish the warm feelings in her heart.

They all heard a knock at the door. Samir looked puzzled. He wasn't expecting anyone. He got up to answer it and invited Jack to come in. Bashira greeted him with a smile and turned to Mike, waiting for Jack to relate the news to his colleague.

Jack dropped Mike off and had been looking for a spot to park the vehicle. Only Mike had expected his knock at the door, and unknown to Jack, the timing of his arrival couldn't have been better. Mike quickly shared the news with him. Bashira listened intently as Mike described the time frame of when they would be at the hospital and some of its history that he had just learned from her.

He was about to fill Jack in with more details when Jack interrupted and said, "This is all good news, but we have to get back right away. The producer wants to have a conference call regarding the ongoing political discussions."

Mike looked around at everyone. "I'd love to stay longer," he said, "but there is always a deadline to meet. It's great seeing you all. Sorry everyone, we have to go."

He rose from the couch. Everyone stood. Amal remained focused on counting her lollipops, placing them in separate piles of different colors. Samir motioned for Mike to join Jack in the hall and shook his hand to say goodbye.

With one last glance, Mike said, "Thanks everyone. Bashira, I look forward to seeing you next week."

"Me too. Goodbye."

As Mike and Jack entered the street, heading to their vehicle, Bashira watched them go from the window. With a short sigh that only her mother could detect, she shook herself from staring out the window and then went over to squeeze Amal. They both laughed over her newfound treasure of candy.

Chapter 6

The Hospital

The week had not been easy for Mike. Gaining the permissions required by the network for the hospital visit had proven to be difficult. Within the current conflict, more officials than just his producers had to sign off. In the end, his relationship with Colonel Yakov had paved the way. Mike assured him that there was no other motive for the visit than to see what type of care was being given to children in the area and to see if there was a story to tell.

The negotiations continued at the Basilica. The ceasefire held, and the fighting had stopped for now. The IDF's decision to expand the curfew remained on hold pending the outcome of the discussions at the Basilica. It made sense for Mike to seize this moment to visit the hospital. A series of discussions with Isaac and some of the officials involved with the Basilica negotiations had cleared the way for the visit to occur.

Mike's producers at WBN finally agreed that his request could prove newsworthy. His angle, providing a firsthand story of the conflict from the perspective of its impact on the children in the area, had the news potential they needed to see in order to release their agreement. Mike had then worked out the details with the hospital director. Now they made their way through the streets of Bethlehem to keep the appointment they had set.

Arriving on time at the hospital, they parked in a pre-arranged spot close to the entrance. Mike got out of the vehicle. He turned to see a group of doctors waiting in a small courtyard adjacent to the entrance doors. Bashira was among them. He hadn't seen her since the day of the phone call at her apartment. It became nearly impossible for him to look past her. He challenged himself to get a grip and focus on the story.

As Mike collected his thoughts, he identified the director by the way she looked at Bashira. Bashira herself stood with dignity, sharing a broad smile. Mike noticed that the director responded to Bashira's smile with a little one of her own. He was trained to read the facial expressions of others during interviews. It became clear to Mike that the director held a special place in her heart for Bashira. His own response to Bashira's smile caused him to realize that he had also made a place for her in his own heart.

Careful, he told himself. *Stay focused on the story.*

Bashira walked forward to greet him. Mike didn't notice, or care at that moment, that Jack struggled with carrying the camera equipment. Bashira walked out to meet them both, turned, and then escorted them over to meet the director.

"Let me introduce you to Dr. Shifa. She has been the director of the hospital for many years."

"It is good to meet you, Mr. Olson," said the director. "Welcome to our medical facility. We're so glad you could come." The director extended her hand to Mike.

Mike took it with a gentle shake.

"I know it wasn't easy for you to make this visit possible. We're very grateful that you did," said Mike.

Mike introduced Jack to the director. "This is Jack Winslow, my cameraman. He will be accompanying us throughout the day and will be filming at times. He will try not to get in the way." Jack smiled and nodded to the director.

"We are delighted you could come," said the director, "and hope that your time with us will be insightful and worth the attention of your viewers."

The director looked toward the entrance to the hospital while sweeping her arm through the air as if to introduce the hospital itself to these two men who had come to visit today. "Although I may have been here a long time, this hospital has been here a lot longer. It's been serving the needs of the children, and so many others in this region, for nearly five decades. We look for it to stand strong for years to come. Well, let's head inside and get out of the sun. I'll introduce you to our wonderful staff in the lobby." The doctors, dressed in their sparkling white coats, seemed eager to be underway. Together they all walked through the double doors and reconvened inside.

The lobby contained some chairs, couches, and a few plants. All the seats were filled, and those who had not found a seat were patiently standing. Families crowded around the registration desk, seeking information on where their loved ones might be in the building. As the director and doctors entered the area, those gathered at the registration desk stopped for a moment to look at the sight of so many doctors in one place. The others waiting in the lobby looked on as well, but no one commented except for the children pointing at the doctors. Bashira gave them a wink and placed her finger to her lips as a sign for them to be quiet.

Dr. Shifa stepped ahead of the group. "Everyone, let's move a little further down the hall." Once the group had moved beyond the reception area, she stopped and turned to Mike and Jack.

"I want to introduce you to our senior staff." She then began to present the doctors that had been accompanying them, one by one, identifying their disciplines. Each doctor in turn greeted Mike and Jack enthusiastically, thanking them for coming. Dr. Shifa then gave the final introduction.

"This is Dr. Aziz. He is a renowned retina specialist. It's his unique gifts and care that we depend on for those with eye injuries. Now, let's begin our tour."

"Thank you all. Please lead the way," said Mike.

The director led them down another hallway filled with people. Mike's immediate perception told him there were more people in this hallway than he felt should be in a hospital corridor. The scene reminded him of being in the market with Bashira. He wondered if this crowding was normal or the result of the conflict. Although the floor and walls were spotless, he observed that the walls needed repainting. Supplies stacked in the hallway made it difficult for the medical staff to transport patients, either in wheelchairs or on gurneys. Mike also noticed that what looked a little unusual to him didn't seem to bother the director and the rest of the medical team.

"Mr. Olson, is this your first time to Bethlehem?" the director asked.

"No. In fact, I've been here on several occasions, mostly during Christmas for brief visits to report on the holiday season. This is the first time I've had an opportunity to see more than just the Basilica—and please, call me Mike."

"Before we start, may we get you anything to drink? We will gather at the end of the tour for some coffee and snacks, if time remains."

"Thank you, but we're fine. Since Jack will be filming throughout the day, is there any area of the hospital you would prefer we not enter?"

"Not really," replied the director. "There are certain areas where things must be sterile, and we'll point those out along the way, but for the most part it is your day to ask questions and film what you like.

"It is a bit more hectic than usual today since we have some desperately needed medical supplies being delivered. Please forgive some of the crowdedness. We're trying to get the supplies inventoried and dispersed out to the wards as fast as possible."

Mike had noticed that hospital staff were carrying in the boxes of supplies stacked everywhere. He now realized this wasn't the daily procedure for the hospital. Mike then noticed a tall man with a brilliant smile on his face putting his arm around one of the staff who was rolling a dolly stacked full of boxes. From the worker's response, it seemed that the man must have told him something funny. For an instant, Mike caught his eye.

The director got Mike's attention back to the tour by asking, "Mike, how much do you know about our hospital and its role in the West Bank?"

"Actually, only a little. Bashira was kind enough to give me some background, but I'd love to hear more."

"Well, let me begin by saying that it is quite rare to have a news organization such as yours show an interest in what we do with the limited resources we have, so it is an honor to have you here today. Hopefully we will be able to answer any questions you might have. Let me share who we are as an organization and what we do.

"We consider this to be the best pediatric hospital in the West Bank and Gaza. We provide health care for all children and mothers, regardless of race or creed. That translates into nearly 4,000 children admitted every year, ranging from neonatal to teenagers. We also care for about 40,000 children annually as outpatients."

"That's a lot more than I envisioned. I had no idea you served so many children and families."

"I wish we could do more. In the surrounding area of Bethlehem and Hebron, there are about 100,000 children under the age of four and over 500,000 children in Palestine as a whole. And again, our hospital is not just for Palestinian children. We care for Jewish, Muslim, and Christian children. We are here for any child needing medical care."

As the director continued to share, Mike overheard Jack speaking to Bashira. "Is it okay to start filming?" Bashira looked up at one of the doctors, who nodded yes.

"Certainly," said Dr. Aziz. "Let us know if we need to get out of your way."

"No problem," said Jack. "Thanks again for working this out today."

"You're welcome," Dr. Aziz replied.

Continuing to move forward as a group, they came to a large dormitory-style room with two rows of beds lining opposite walls and a third row of beds between them. It was a crowded area: nurses scurrying about, sounds of children crying in distress, mothers sitting quietly by their bedsides trying to soothe their discomfort.

"This is our overflow ward," the director said. "It gets like this during these occasions of conflict. Our patients here are mainly children who are not critically wounded but require some supervised care."

Mike looked around, doing his best to take it all in, trying to save the images in his mind's eye for later retrieval when he would write the copy for his broadcast. The staff moved off to the side of the room, clearing the way for him and Jack to have better access. Mike looked to Jack to be sure he was getting this footage.

"This is a good day," continued the director, "since much of the things we need—extra antibiotics, pain medication, bandages—have arrived from our friends in Nazareth. It is remarkable how quickly these little ones start to recover when they have the right care and medications."

"Dr. Shifa," said Mike, "you keep saying that you are low on supplies. Is this due to the current military operation?"

Dr. Aziz responded instead of the director. "Mr. Olson, it is difficult to have the proper supplies we need even during times without open conflict. Our funds are extremely limited. We depend upon the kindness of those who bring in aid whenever it is available. During periods when open conflict erupts, everything becomes worse."

"Dr. Aziz is correct," said the director. "When you add the curfew and limited access to utilities, the level of care we can provide is directly impacted."

"It affects us all," said Dr. Aziz. "With all the checkpoints in place, just getting ourselves here to provide care for the patients can become quite an ordeal. When you add the elderly that flood in during these times, seeking help because they are unable to access their normal medical care, it can all be a bit challenging—to say the least."

"Dr. Aziz's point is well taken," added the director. "Even during the best of times, we must be very careful, sometimes rationing our most precious medicines."

Dr. Aziz nodded at this recognition as the director continued.

"With this fighting, we are operating at a crisis level. Everything we need is scarce, from pain medication to general supplies. The staff can easily become overworked keeping up with the demand."

"It sounds like, even on a good day, it's not easy caring for your patients," said Mike.

Dr. Aziz again replied, "Yes. Just imagine ordinary health care needs; for instance, your child has asthma. Now, with all the smoke and dust in the air from the explosions, her condition is even worse. Add to this the dilemma that you can't get ordinary medical items from a local pharmacy; you then must make your way to the hospital for help. Our supplies are limited, forcing us to care only for the most severe cases. After all your efforts as a parent, your child may still not get the help they need.

"Mr. Olson, the point is that this example represents the tip of the iceberg. Add to this all sorts of trauma—broken bones, emergency surgeries, fever, cuts, and infections—and you can see we face significant challenges. Don't get me wrong, our staff does an amazing job. We have learned to cope with nearly every conceivable shortage and problem, but for the people, getting any medical care at times like this is a major undertaking."

Jack stopped filming. Everyone paused for a moment, as if to reflect on the pressing needs described by Dr. Aziz. The director broke the silence, saying, "Let's move on everyone or Mr. Olson won't be able to finish the tour."

The group continued down the hall, passing more boxes piled here and there. Mike saw the tall man he had noticed earlier coming toward them, this time with his own dolly fully loaded.

"Pardon me, delivery man coming through," he said to the group with a warm smile.

Everyone moved aside to let the dolly through. Mike looked back and saw Bashira, beaming with a smile of her own and waving to the delivery man.

"I suggest you visit our surgical wing first," said the director. "If you don't mind, I'll catch up with you when you complete your tour. Dr. Aziz will take over from here. Gentleman, please excuse me."

The director left the group. Mike paused to listen to the sound of her heels marking her footsteps as she hurried down the hall. Following the sound with his eyes, he caught a glimpse of the director. She had caught up with the tall gentleman with the dolly. He stopped to grab her hands with both of his, smiling tenderly as she spoke with him. Her face seemed to shine with gratitude.

Interesting, Mike thought, sensing a recognition he could not readily identify. His instincts told him he was seeing something familiar.

"This way, everyone," Dr. Aziz said. "Let's move along."

They continued down the hall. Mike could still see the director talking with the tall gentleman who was now pointing at him. Before he looked away, he saw the tall man give Bashira a quick wave and a wink. Bashira waved back.

"Mr. Olson," said Dr. Aziz, "I believe you said you were not familiar with our hospital. As the director mentioned, next year will be our fiftieth anniversary serving the population here, supported mainly through private donations from various charities around the world.

"We do have other medical teams visit from time to time, even Israeli doctors from Jerusalem, as well as others from around the globe. As you will see, though, right now we are quite shorthanded, to which Bashira can attest. This is one of her wards."

◇◇◇◇◇◇◇◇◇◇◇◇◇

As they walked through the door and into the surgical recovery ward, Mike's heart was moved again by the sight of how crowded things were. Bed after bed had a child in it. The mothers of these children stood at their bedsides trying to comfort them. Some of the children and mothers looked up at the camera with quizzical looks on their faces.

One child saw Bashira and sat up straight, smiling from ear to ear. Even with her eye bandaged and gauze wrapped around her arms in several places, Bashira's presence alone seemed enough to make her happy. She called out, "Bashira, Bashira!" while her mother tried to quiet her. The child pushed back against her mother, using her unbandaged arm, and shouted once again in Arabic, "Bashira, Bashira, come here! Who are those people with you?"

Bashira looked at the doctors. They nodded and she broke away from the group, rushing over to the child's bedside, giving her a big hug while her mother looked on.

"These are my friends," Bashira replied in Arabic. "They've come to see the care you are getting and to tell others about our hospital."

Many of the other mothers had big smiles on their faces too, as they saw Bashira reach out to this child. It became clear to Mike that Bashira's presence brought infectious relief to the people gathered in the room.

Bashira then turned to the child's mother, patted her arm, and gave her a quick hug. This seemed to somehow reassure the woman. She ceased to reprimand her own child's behavior. Immediately, other children began to call out Bashira's name. Their mothers continued to hold their own child's hands as Bashira made the rounds, speaking kind words to them all.

"As I said, Mr. Olson, you can see this really is 'Bashira's ward,'" Dr. Aziz continued. "She's the one they long to see—not a bunch of us 'white coats.'"

The tour group watched Bashira interact with the children and their mothers, transfixed for the moment at her effortless ability to both connect with and comfort them. The expressions on the doctors' faces did not display analytical curiosity; instead, they were expressions of gratitude, coming from their hearts.

"She's an amazing person," said Dr. Aziz. "We're convinced that her genuine love and gentle spirit provides more effective healing than much of what we doctors think we have to offer."

Mike turned to Jack and motioned him to move closer and get a better angle on the unfolding scene. There was no need for Jack to be discreet, for now Bashira, the children, and their mothers were oblivious to the camera. Bashira had become the sole object of their attention as she reached out to touch and hug each child and gave a kind word to each supportive mother.

Mike began to take a mental inventory of the condition of the children throughout the room. Some of the children had only superficial wounds; others were more severely injured. As he looked closer, he saw an increasing number of children with serious wounds—broken limbs, burns, and eyes and lungs damaged from smoke inhalation. He turned his eyes back to Bashira, watching her continue to talk to the children and mothers. He found himself admiring her with a look of fond appreciation and deep respect.

"If it were up to these children, we'd never make it out of here," said Dr. Aziz, "but for the sake of our schedule we'll have to keep moving."

Mike touched Jack on the shoulder, giving him a signal to stop filming. Everyone turned and headed out into the hallway. Mike watched Bashira, who stayed fully engaged with all those around her. She now held both hands over her eyes, playing a game of "Peek-a-Boo" with some of the children. She and the children laughed and giggled and smiled. The group had to move on. Mike wondered if Bashira had even seen them leave.

Dr. Aziz led Mike and Jack through several other wards. Jack shot more footage. Mike took it all in. He talked to other nurses and staff, making mental notes of what information he wanted to highlight in the broadcast. Mike had shifted to autopilot. His professional skills and demeanor now operated without him being fully present. His thoughts, however, kept drifting to the scene of Bashira caring for those children within her charge. He had never felt the presence of love in a room more deeply than he had just experienced. His mind's eye kept watching how the entire room seemed to light up when Bashira entered. She had become the focus of attention without ever seeking it, effortlessly dispensing joy and laughter, and touching each soul deeply. He could neither explain nor dismiss what he had seen. It seemed as if he had stepped into a supernatural, spiritual realm: a place where anything was possible because love willed it to be so.

With the tour now over and the time spent with the staff nearing its end, everyone returned to the lobby. There the director caught up with the group. Mike had succeeded in refocusing his thoughts. He knew he had to prepare to leave. This required him to concentrate on the details he would need to prepare the story.

The door opened beside him, and Bashira came out laughing with the tall gentleman at her side. He had one arm tightly wrapped around her shoulders. They seemed a bit startled to see everyone still gathered in the hall. Mike caught her eye. He felt half a dozen emotions crash over him simultaneously, none truly distinguishable from the others, all of which left him at a loss for knowing exactly how he felt—except that he felt unsure about what was happening.

The director finished facilitating the farewells, thanking her staff for offering their time to the tour and dismissing them to resume their rounds.

Mike pulled his thoughts together and added his thanks before they left. "Thank you for your time. It was an honor to be your guest today and we'll do our best to share your story." They all shook hands.

The director then turned to Mike and said, "I'd like to introduce you to Bashira's *amo*, her favorite uncle. Rashad is from Nazareth and has brought many wonderful supplies to us today."

Rashad reached out his hand to Mike. "Good to meet you, Mr. Olson. Bashira explained why you are here today. Everyone is grateful to you and your colleague," he said, turning toward Jack, "for coming."

Mike now recognized what was familiar about this gentleman. It was his smile and demeanor, so much like Bashira's. No wonder he felt like he already knew him.

"It's a privilege," said Mike.

With a proud look on her face, Bashira continued the introduction. "My uncle is authorized by the Israeli government to come periodically and bring medical supplies like he did today. It's more difficult during times like this, but fortunately my uncle has been doing this for years and is able to work with the authorities to gain approval for us when his help is needed the most."

Mike noticed Bashira give Rashad's arm a squeeze. Behind them both, down the hall, more supplies kept coming through the lobby door.

"If you don't mind me asking," said Mike, "where does all this come from?"

"From all over," said Rashad. "We collect all we can at the warehouse in Nazareth. There the supplies are inventoried and processed for distribution. We then work with the various government authorities to deliver them. Mind you, what you see today will only help for a short time, but we are grateful for being able to help."

"Rashad, you are way too modest," the director added, with a pat on his other arm. "I don't know what we would do without you."

Turning to Bashira, Rashad gave her a wink and a nudge with his elbow.

"Probably get a lot more work done," he joked. "Speaking of work, I have to leave. Please excuse me, I've got to get my team back together and sign the necessary paperwork."

"It was a pleasure meeting you," Mike said.

"It was nice meeting you too," said Rashad, "and I hope to see you again one day, whether here or in Nazareth. Feel free to contact me anytime. God bless you."

∞∞∞∞∞∞∞∞∞

Rashad and Bashira walked down the hall together toward the loading dock at the back of the hospital.

Rashad said to Bashira, "That's a pretty special young man. It will be interesting to see how his story turns out. Now, tell me how you're doing. Samir says he's worried about you. You are working too much. Do you need to come back with me to Nazareth and get some rest?"

"I'm fine." They kept walking through the corridors of the hospital, stopping at the window where they could see the newborn babies.

Looking at the newborns, Rashad said, "Time is racing by too fast, and you've been away too long."

Bashira tucked her arm though her uncle's elbow.

"You are right. When this trouble is over, I'm going to grab Amal, and we're both coming to stay with you and *Aunti* for a few days. Thank you, *Amo*, for bringing everything."

"It's nothing," said Rashad. "And now, on with the work. I've got much to do before I can go by the house and see *abu'i* before heading home."

⬦⬦⬦⬦⬦⬦⬦⬦⬦⬦⬦⬦⬦

Mike turned to the director. "Thank you for taking your time today to show us the special work you do here at the hospital."

Jack packed up his gear and started to carry it out to the Land Rover. Bashira returned from escorting her uncle back to work and came over to Mike.

"Thank you so much for coming," Bashira said.

Jack stood outside by the Land Rover with an impatient expression on his face. Looking at his watch and then at Mike, he insisted, "Mike, we have to go, or we'll never make our deadline."

Mike turned to Bashira and started to speak, but she cut him off.

"You need to go!" she said. Mike took a few steps toward the Land Rover before turning for one more glimpse of Bashira.

Jack called out again. "Mike!"

Mike struggled to decide how to respond: either go to Bashira to finish what he had wanted to say or head out with Jack. This moment of indecisiveness was out of character for him. Almost instinctively, he turned to head toward the Land Rover. He did have a schedule to keep.

"I'm coming."

Jack mumbled under his breath, "That boy's a goner."

◇◇◇◇◇◇◇◇◇◇◇◇◇

Bashira arrived home late in the evening after saying goodbye to her uncle Rashad. She was too tired to eat, even though her mother had left a note out in the kitchen telling her that she had left a plate of food in the refrigerator. Instead, Bashira silently made her way to her bedroom. As she settled into her bed for the night, she heard little footsteps coming through her doorway.

A sleepy voice asked in Arabic, "Bashira, is that you? Why are you so late?" Amal kept walking toward Bashira, reaching up to be lifted into her bed. "Can I snuggle with you?" she asked.

It didn't matter that Bashira was beyond exhausted, the request from her little angel melted her heart and called her to respond. She reached down and lifted Amal up onto her bed. Amal pressed herself into Bashira's side, getting as close as possible. Bashira wrapped her arms about her back and held her tight. She could tell from Amal's rhythmic breathing that she was already falling back asleep.

At that moment, all was right with the world. Bashira, nestled comfortably with Amal in her arms, could now take this time to lay back and reflect on the day as it had unfolded. What a remarkable time it had been at the hospital: Mike's visit, her uncle being there, everyone getting to meet Mike and telling him their stories. Her thoughts raced ahead to imagine a hopeful vision of a story that would be carried by one of the networks. Even the least coverage would be more than they could have hoped for.

Bashira gave Amal a kiss on her head. Amal stirred. A slight smile came upon her rosy cheeks. Bashira's thoughts circled back to the memory of seeing Mike walking toward the hospital. She recalled how her heart had leapt with excitement in seeing him. Surprised by how she felt, she convinced herself that it would be foolish to entertain such feelings about him. He could only be a visitor in her world. His life spanned the globe. Bashira was not accustomed to having feelings like these. She had to put them in their appropriate place.

Besides, he was there for the story . . . wasn't he? she mused.

Bashira lifted her eyes toward the ceiling in the darkness. She reached for her necklace and the reassurance she found in its familiar touch.

"Still, it was a great day," she told herself and drifted off to sleep.

Chapter 7

SIDO

The morning always seemed to come early for Mike. He had worked late into the night putting the finishing touches on his story from the hospital. He got up and started throwing a few things into his backpack, waking Jack in the process. Their small hotel room provided them little privacy. "Hey," he told Jack, "I've got to head out. I'll catch up with you later. I'll leave the mobile on."

Jack reached under his bed where he had hidden two sacks of fruit and a bunch of candy he had collected earlier. "This is for the family and the little girl. Now get out of here and be safe."

Mike threw his backpack over one shoulder. He grabbed the bags from Jack and said, "Thanks, bud, and don't forget to call my mobile if something begins to break." For the time being, he would let the politicians and negotiators do their work and take advantage of the lull in the fighting to go see Bashira.

◇◇◇◇◇◇◇◇◇◇◇◇

Mike climbed the stairs to Bashira's apartment. Bashira must have seen him coming because she opened the door before he got there.

"Mike, what a surprise!"

"I was in the neighborhood and had a few things I wanted to drop by." He felt embarrassed in saying something so trite but figured his reply didn't make much difference. What really mattered to him was that he was here.

Miriam and Samir had followed Bashira to the front door. Mike saw confusion in their puzzled looks. Samir reached out to accept the bags of fruit. Amal came rushing in from the kitchen, running past everyone, bumping into Samir, full of excitement at the sight of the grocery bags. "What did you bring me?" she exclaimed in English with glee as she jumped up and down, trying to grab the bags to look inside.

Miriam scolded her. "*Habibti*, your manners!"

Amal paused, looked up at her grandmother, then at Mike, and once more at the grocery bag in Samir's arms. "Did you bring me anything?" she asked again.

Mike reached into his pocket and pulled out the bag of candy Jack had given him, along with a package of Hershey chocolate bars he had stashed away.

"Oh my goodness, she is going to be so spoiled," said Miriam. Bashira stared wide-eyed at Mike.

"I thought maybe she could share some with her friends." Mike smiled in hopes of seeing Bashira smile back. This time he would have to wait.

With Miriam's hands draped over her shoulders, Amal looked up at Bashira.

"Amal, what do you say to Mr. Olson?"

Amal reached up with her arms and stood on her toes, trying to reach Mike. Mike knelt to look Amal in the eyes. She gave him a hug, then snatched the candy and raced down the hall, bumping into an older distinguished gentleman on the way to her room.

Mike stood abruptly as Bashira moved to support the older gentleman.

"*Sido*, are you okay?"

"Yes, my dear, I'm fine. There seems to be a lot of bustling about here today." He spoke in perfect English with a slight British accent while watching Amal run away with her treasures.

"*Sido*, this is Mr. Olson, the newsman we mentioned that you've seen on WBN. Mike, this is my grandfather, Abu Rashad."

"It is a pleasure to meet you, Mr. Olson," said Abu Rashad. "I've been hearing wonderful things about how you've treated my family with such kindness, especially my great-granddaughter, who as you know, loves American chocolate."

"It's an honor to meet you, sir. You have a very special family."

"Please sit down, *Sido*,'" Bashira said. Abu Rashad took his place in the living room chair and addressed Mike.

"Mr. Olson, please sit."

Samir interrupted. "We'll get some coffee for everyone. Bashira, would you help your mother for a moment?" He gave the grocery bags to Miriam, closed the door, and escorted Mike into the living room.

"Certainly *Baba*."

As Bashira followed her mother into the kitchen, she patted her grandfather on the shoulder. He looked up and gave her hand a squeeze. The grandfather then turned toward Mike.

"My granddaughter speaks highly of you, Mr. Olson, and she so appreciated your visit to the hospital."

"It was our pleasure. I hope our report will be picked up. The visit opened my eyes to see the scope of medical care being provided to these children and their families despite the challenges they face."

Abu Rashad continued smiling and added, "Well, I know everyone appreciated your taking the time to visit."

"What was remarkable to me," said Mike, "is how many children they care for despite the demands that increase exponentially in the middle of these conflicts. I can only imagine what you've seen over the years."

Abu Rashad studied Mike's face for a moment before he replied. Mike saw his eyes reflect the same kindness he had seen in Bashira and the other members of her family.

"My family has lived in this land since before the time of Moses. Our ancestors, and now my generation, have seen army after army invade and conquer these lands. In the 1940s, my father worked for the English. Before that he sold goods and supplies to the Turks. All the while, he ensured that his children were properly educated. I studied to be an English professor.

"My father would always say, 'Although the sun may set one day on the English empire, her language will spread throughout the earth.' I took him seriously."

Mike interrupted. "This must be why Bashira and the rest of your family are so fluent in English."

"Oh, they used to complain incessantly of having to read and recite the English classics, but now they appreciate the language."

"How many languages do they speak?"

"Not counting Arabic? Hebrew and English, of course."

"Amazing! I can barely put my words together in English."

They shared a smile. Mike realized the privilege he had received by being introduced to the patriarch of the family. He didn't take this meeting lightly. He sought to honor the gentleman before him. Simultaneously, he couldn't escape his instinct to ask some probing questions.

"Seeing that the land has changed hands so many times over the centuries," he began, "how have these transitions affected you personally?"

The smile that Mike had begun to recognize as the trademark of this special family appeared once again. Mike knew right away that he was about to get a forthright and honest answer with a trace of kindness. He paid close attention to the grandfather's words.

"Let me begin by saying that in 1948, when Israel was declared a state, my family lost its land and property not only in Jerusalem but also in Nazareth. Thankfully, my eldest son still lives in Nazareth, but my brothers left during the early days—some to Syria, others to Lebanon, and the rest to the United States. In some cases, those who left can never come back to Israel, and of course, it is nearly impossible for us to go and see them. Bashira has cousins she has never met."

Bashira entered and sat down near her grandfather.

Looking at Bashira, Mike said, "Your family has seen all this within one generation?" Bashira nodded and looked toward her grandfather, allowing him to reply.

Abu Rashad paused for a moment. "You know, Mr. Olson, when I look back over my life and consider this small corner of the earth, I am reminded that it is full of such tragedy and tearful triumph. It's been the focal point of countless acts of violence, bloodshed, and sorrow; yet, we have seen endless deeds of sacrifice, courage, and love. Today Israel, a strip of land smaller than your state of New Jersey, is the epicenter of the world's attention."

"Amazing, isn't it?"

"Yes, and full of complex cultural challenges. I'll give you an example. My son Rashad, who you met at the hospital yesterday, lives in Nazareth. He is therefore also Israeli. As such, he is afforded all the rights of citizenship, except for the fact that he is Arab and subject at times to all the suspicions of his Jewish neighbors and authorities. Whereas those of us in the West Bank are identified as Palestinian, denied any rights to citizenship, and viewed as the source of all hostility and unrest.

"The truth is that nothing is new under the sun. This is an ancient struggle begun millennia ago between two brothers, Ishmael and Isaac, that won't end until they are reconciled through their elder brother—"

Abu Rashad's last comments hung in the air, interrupted by Miriam returning from the kitchen with a small tray containing some of the fruit Mike had brought. They had cut sections of oranges, kiwi, and bananas into smaller servings and had placed them on the tray along with some dates on the side.

"Now Mr. Olson," said Abu Rashad, "tell us a little about yourself. How did you become a broadcast journalist?"

Mike sat up, looked directly at Abu Rashad, and said, "Well, there's not a whole lot to tell. My father worked for the local newspaper in our town. He started out as a beat reporter. He would come home at night telling us all about the exciting stories that would be coming out in the next day's paper. The conversation around our dinner table was like having a sneak preview of tomorrow's news. Our whole family became news hounds."

"News hounds?" Samir looked at his father and then back to Mike. "Pardon me, but what is a 'news hound?'"

Mike looked down, somewhat embarrassed he had used such an idiom, not thinking that it wouldn't make sense to everyone. He looked up at Samir to apologize. "Sorry, the phrase comes from describing how hunting dogs use their instincts and capabilities to track their prey. A 'news hound' follows a story until he discovers its significance and then brings the story to light. My dad was one of the best; I guess being a journalist runs in my veins. I can't remember a time when I wasn't involved with the news."

"So how did you come to work with WBN?" asked Abu Rashad.

"It took a while. My first real break came after college when I worked for a TV station back in Indiana. I was covering the floods in Fort Wayne that year and somehow the story caught the attention of some producers at WBN. They asked me to come join them on a couple special assignments and, before I knew it, an opening came up working for them in the Middle East. For a young journalist, it was the assignment of a lifetime. I've now had the chance to cover some of the most important events of our day."

Mike stopped for a moment. He wondered if he should better clarify what he meant. He explained. "I'm not trying to say that talking about your lives here in Bethlehem is some sort of event. It's just that we refer to our current coverage as an assignment."

Mike suddenly felt an acute sense of embarrassment sweep over his body, alerting him to the fact that his words sounded callous within the everyday struggle this family had faced for generations. His mind raced to find a way to regain the ground of the respectful discussion they had been having. He wanted to learn more about this family. To take the focus off himself, he added, "It must sound like I don't see the human element in the events unfolding here, but that's not what I'm trying to say."

Abu Rashad engaged Mike once again, setting him at ease. "Of course not," he said. "It's a privilege to have you in our home and learn more about you and your profession. And, of course, this *is* a newsworthy event. We hope more people around the world will take an interest. In the end, all of us benefit by getting to know each other better.

"Hopefully, your visit to the hospital will do just that, but whatever happens with the news coverage will be fine, for the Lord tells us, all things work for the good of those who love Him."

Mike didn't quite understand Abu Rashad's last comment. It seemed a bit odd to connect God with Sunday morning news shows, but he deferred to his gracious host and smiled.

Miriam had gone back to the kitchen and then returned with the coffee. Samir poured, first filling his father's cup and then Mike's.

Samir and Abu Rashad started talking together softly, in Arabic.

Mike looked across the room to watch Amal dividing her treasure of suckers and chocolate into piles. She had returned to the living room, apparently to be close to Bashira and the rest of her family.

"Mr. Olson, thank you for the fruit," Miriam said. Mike then heard her speak quietly under her breath. "A bountiful heart is blessed even more by giving."

Mike looked at Miriam and then at Abu Rashad. "Your family seems like a little ray of hope in this time and place. How do you do it?"

"Love, Mr. Olson," said Abu Rashad. "In and of ourselves this is impossible, but with a new heart, filled with love, all things are possible.

"A new heart?"

Just then, an announcement in Arabic came over a loudspeaker outside on the street and Mike's phone rang. Mike answered the phone. Bashira and the family paused to look at each other.

"Okay, okay, I'm on my way," Mike said into the phone.

He snapped the phone shut. "That was Jack saying I've got to get back now. The curfew hours have been changed. The army is telling everyone to stay inside."

"I know," said Abu Rashad. "That was the announcement over the loudspeakers."

"It has been a pleasure meeting you," Mike said directly to Abu Rashad and then turned to Samir and his family. "I'm sorry I must leave. Thank you all for your hospitality. I hope to see you again soon."

Everyone stood as Mike got up to make his way across the room to the door. Bashira accompanied him while Miriam held Amal. Samir again spoke softly with Abu Rashad. As they approached the door, Mike turned to Bashira and said, "I'm worried about your family, especially your grandparents. Could they leave and get a little further away from the fighting for a while?"

"I appreciate your concern, but my grandparents would never leave."

The loudspeaker in the street repeatedly blared out the announcement of the new curfew times. Its message imparted an urgency into Mike. He felt that he needed to do something to help protect Bashira and her family, but he was at a loss for ideas.

"You must go. Thank you again for coming," said Bashira.

Mike opened the door and started to leave. He paused to look back at Bashira's family. They had stopped talking and were looking at him.

"Take care everyone."

Mike raced down the steps, but before getting into his car, he took one last glance back at the apartment. To his surprise and delight, he saw Amal, held in Bashira's arms, waving to him from the window with a great big smile beaming across her face and holding a fistful of lollipops. He gave her a quick wave before he got in the car and drove off.

Driving back to the hotel, Mike let his mind drift. He could not stop thinking about this wonderful family. Every member had something special to offer that seemed to contribute to an amazing way of living life. Abu Rashad was an extraordinary person. He had witnessed so much change and experienced such great agony of loss in the region, yet he still maintained the same gentle loving attitude as Bashira and the rest of the family. *How can this be?* Mike thought. This was something he had never seen before. This family not only captivated his thinking but also spurred on his curiosity as a reporter. To be honest, he enjoyed each member of the family, especially Bashira and that sweet little Amal.

Mike had become aware that even Jack knew something was happening to him, and if it was obvious to Jack, Mike knew it was becoming clear to others as well. His thoughts led him to question himself. "How can I separate the news from my growing interest in Bashira? There, I've said it. Now what do I do?"

He made his way through the winding streets of town and parked the vehicle. Without turning off the engine, he stared for a while at the steering wheel. As he reached down to turn the key, he accepted the fact that he needed to sort this out. *How in the world can I be falling for this young woman who is trapped in this conflict? There are oceans of differences lying between me and the life she leads.*

"Wow," he said out loud, and then thought to himself, *it's too much to figure out now. I'll think about it in the morning.* He shook his head, turned off the engine, got out of the car, and headed back to his room. For the moment, he could rest in the fact that he had completed the hospital story, but then again, the increasing tensions were sure to create a new one.

Chapter 8

IDF HEADQUARTERS

M ike woke the next morning to the sounds of his phone alarm and heavy armored vehicles. He had an early morning meeting scheduled at the IDF command center. Shaking the numbness of a restless night from his mind, he looked over at Jack in the bed on the other side of the room who woke up complaining about the noise.

"What in heaven's name is going on now?" he said.

Mike pulled back the hotel room curtain to look out the window. From their location on the second floor, he could see the tents of the temporary makeshift IDF compound set up below them in the plaza.

"It looks like the IDF is bringing in the big guns. Jack, I need to get down there and check with Isaac to see what's going on."

Jack rolled over and mumbled, "I'll wait here for your phone call."

Mike got dressed and headed down the stairs. He walked across the street to the plaza that housed the IDF tents. Colonel Yakov had given him limited special access to meet with him to discuss the operation. An enlisted man met him at the barrier, cleared him for entry and escorted him to meet the colonel. Calev saw him and waved him past the guards. He led Mike to the command tent and signaled to follow him inside.

Mike walked into a hectic scene: teams of officers huddled about pointing at various locations on maps, the officer's aides scurried from team to team relaying messages and getting reports, fans whirred in the background, computer screens glowed in the dim light of dawn. Calev spoke quietly to Mike. "You can stand over here. I've got to get back to the table."

Mike could hear Isaac's voice over the murmur of the room. He turned to see him addressing some of the officers.

"The new curfew has been put in place starting at 17:00 hours. The utilities will be cut off and the lock down will begin at 19:00 hours. Reubens, what sites have you selected for the assault?"

Without looking up, Calev pointed to several sections on the map. "We've chosen these complexes near the Basilica and some further down the street."

"Show me the apartment locations again," said Colonel Yakov. Mike moved in for a closer look. A couple of the officers glared at him with concern and then looked to Isaac.

"Don't worry about Mike. He's here to let the world know the truth. Right, Mike?"

"Yeah—that all depends on how the world interprets the truth."

"That's exactly why you are here," said Isaac. "We want you to tell the real story."

Mike cocked his head and winced slightly. "Even then, truth is in the eye of the beholder."

"Men, give me a minute with Mike." Colonel Yakov looked straight at Calev. "We'll get back to this, Reubens." The other officers dispersed and gathered again a few tables away. Isaac turned to Mike.

"Mike, the reason command wanted you to have such access to the inner workings of this operation is that you at least try to get the facts straight. You don't rush to judgments or spin. We respect that. What we are planning for here is nasty business, but we are ultimately trying to save lives."

"At what cost though, Isaac? These people are barely surviving and what does the world see—the IDF coming in with tanks, helicopters, and armored vehicles against unarmed civilians? That's what gets shown all over the networks—kids in the streets for God's sake, fighting with slingshots and stones. I'm not minimizing casualties taken by the IDF, but let me tell you, the world doesn't see this as a fair fight."

"Fair fight or not," said Isaac, "I'm a soldier. Whether it's WW I rifles, AK-47s, slings or arrows, if one of my men are in the fight then I'm coming at the enemy with all I've got. I'm responsible for their lives.

When the politicians put us in harm's way, I've got to answer to the families of those in my charge. They're the ones that will ask me if I did everything in my power to keep their loved ones safe. I'll grant you that these combatants don't have tanks and armored vehicles, but they sure have more than slings and stones. You've seen the rounds fired at my men. It doesn't matter what kind of weapon delivers the bullet that takes a life. It's the job of the IDF to eliminate the threat. The truth is, Mike—"

"The truth?!" Mike exclaimed. "The real truth lies in the facts that established this bloody occupation. Everyone knows that Israel could have annexed the West Bank and Gaza just like it did with the Golan Heights. But no. To annex these territories would change the whole balance of power in the country—too many Arab citizens voting on government policy and establishing coalitions. So we remain in this state of 'limbo'—Israel occupies, the Palestinians fight for their rights, and the violence rolls on. It's an absolute mess."

Isaac stared back at Mike; his jaws clenched.

"Nevertheless," Isaac spoke with increased intensity as if doubling-down on his position, "when the fighting ends up in these apartments where families may be trapped, the press will characterize us as attacking innocent civilians. The truth is they're caught up in this conflict and we have no choice.

"So, if you want to cover the story firsthand, go with my men. See it for yourself. I'll give you all the access you need but report the whole story. Maybe the politicians will get sick of it too, and then we can end this bloody fighting once and for us all."

"I'll go," Mike said.

Isaac put his hands tightly on Mike's shoulders and looked into his eyes, as a father would when taking the time to connect with his son. "Mike, we may not agree on the reasons for all of this, but as I've told you before, it's your neck. This time be extra careful. I've instructed Reubens to keep you informed. Believe me, when it starts, you'll have to watch out for yourself and your colleague."

"Okay Isaac," Mike said.

Isaac motioned to Calev to come over. "Reubens, Mike and Jack will be with your squad. Try and keep them alive, but the mission comes first."

Isaac smacked Mike on the back. "You take care. You're the only newsman I halfway like." Isaac walked away, calling the officers to resume their meeting.

◇◇◇◇◇◇◇◇◇◇◇◇◇◇

"Okay, Mr. Olson, over here. I'll show you what we're looking at."

Calev led Mike to an adjacent area of the central command tent. A group of young soldiers huddled over tables covered with laptops, maps, cell phones, and radios.

"Guys, this is Mike Olson. He will be accompanying us on our mission. He's a reporter for WBN, so be careful what you say around him."

Calev finished his introduction with a wink and sarcasm in his voice. The soldiers gave Mike a nod. He appreciated the levity Calev had added to his introduction. He had now committed himself and Jack to whatever came next.

"All right, let's get to it." Calev pointed out areas on a map spread out on the table, then showed his platoon more details on a laptop. Mike saw that some of the locations Calev was pointing out were close to Bashira's grandparent's apartment—too close he thought.

"Take a moment to get a better view," said Calev. The squads took turns leaning in to get a closer look at the laptop screen.

"Calev, do you know any of the families in these apartments?" said Mike.

"No, these sites were determined based on the level of conflict in the area and their strategic location."

"How do you decide which buildings to hit first?"

"It's based on a combination of factors. The most important is what will have the biggest impact on the enemy's threat to our mission. Let me show you a time-lapse video taken of the area."

Calev clicked on the icon of a video on his laptop screen. The app opened immediately to show footage collected by IDF personnel.

"You see the flashes through various windows in these apartments?" Calev moved the mouse to hover the cursor over the fast-forward button. The video began to race through time.

"See how they change location? That's our problem. The enemy can move throughout the apartment complex. They have access to different locations that give them the optimum position to fire on us.

"Look at these infra-red photos. You can see in this sequence where one night they are firing from here," he pointed with his finger, "and, a little later on, from over here." Calev moved the photos around and pointed to various locations on the map. Mike nodded as he took in all the information.

Calev turned his attention to his men positioned around the table. "This operation will involve a coordinated effort between our Special Ops teams, Infantry Corps and medics. They will operate as support to secure the area and evacuate the wounded. We'll follow a rapid assault protocol. Multiple units will strike simultaneously from different directions through the access points to the buildings we've identified. We'll focus our assault on select floors and areas where we suspect the combatants are located. Our priorities are to effectively take down any combatants while reducing our losses.

"The hard part is, there are families located in all the areas where the firing originates. Whether the families are willing or not, they are caught in the middle of all this. Our goal is to isolate and remove the combatants from the civilians. It should be all over in a matter of minutes. The cleanup always takes longer."

Mike studied the images in the photos, then took the mouse and scrolled over the computer screen, zooming in on what looked like the area where Bashira's grandparents lived.

"Calev, when do you expect this to go down?"

"Soon, sir. I'll keep you informed."

"Thanks. You've got my number. I'll leave the mobile on."

Mike left the tent and called Jack.

"Well, what's up?" answered Jack.

"They're going to hit the apartments with assault teams. We're going with them"

"Whoa—when?"

"Soon," said Mike. "And it looks like one of the apartment complexes is near where Bashira's grandfather lives."

"You're kidding?" said Jack in disbelief.

"Nope. It sure looks like it to me, and we can't say a thing."

Chapter 9

ESCALATION

*L*ater in the day, Jack set Mike up for a shot out-side the IDF compound. Jack had recently edited a montage of footage that shifted between scenes of Palestinians and the IDF fighting in the streets of Bethlehem, the assaults in Nablus, and Israelis march-ing in the streets of Jerusalem demanding their govern-ment bring an end to this situation.

Mike recorded his report to be dubbed over these images.

> "What should have been a quick incur-sion into this ancient village has now be-come bogged down in political wrangling between politicians, church officials, and world leaders. As the fighting drags on, an outcry echoes throughout the streets of Jerusalem and elsewhere calling for an end to this operation. The costs of this

conflict are increasing daily. Although the IDF continues to exercise restraint within and around the holy sites, it is becoming increasingly difficult for them to counter the Palestinian's urban guerrilla tactics. According to a source within the IDF, the combination of narrow streets and the layout of apartment buildings in the old city allows enemy fire to effectively hamper the IDF in their mission to find and disarm the combatants. Progress is painfully slow. If the politicians do not create a path to a ceasefire agreement, the IDF will need to consider more drastic measures. Where this conflict is headed, only time will tell, and time seems to be running out.

"This is Mike Olson, reporting for WBN from Bethlehem in the West Bank of Israel."

Jack gave Mike the thumbs up. "Got it. I'll get everything off to the network."

"Thanks." Mike's phone rang. After a brief conversation, he turned to Jack and said, "I'll be right back. Isaac wants to talk. He's sent an escort to meet me at the entrance." He handed his microphone to Jack and hurried off to meet Isaac.

When Mike approached the barrier, an enlisted man ushered him through and escorted him to the command tent. Isaac was standing outside as Mike approached. "Wow, Isaac, you look like you could use some sleep."

Isaac rubbed his face with both hands. "When it's over." Taking a moment to pause from thinking about his ever-present duties, Isaac added, "What's so maddening is that from a tactics perspective we could end this quickly, but because of the political gamesmanship involved, it's becoming an intractable situation."

Isaac shook his head rapidly from side to side as if to shake out his thoughts of exasperation. "It's one frustration after another. Besides the numerous civic and religious interests making demands of each other, the media keeps ratcheting up the tension with their outrageous reporting—present company excluded."

Isaac paused, looking at Mike with tired eyes. "We've been put in a real tight spot. The public is screaming that any casualties are unacceptable." Isaac, again, shook his head in frustration.

Mike tried to empathize with him. "Isaac, it's what we call 'being stuck between a rock and a hard place.'"

With a slight grin, Isaac replied, "You and your American idioms. But this one works. It makes me crazy, Mike. My men are engaged in this conflict—for what? When the politicians say 'hold'—we wait. When they say 'attack'—we fight. And then we hold again. It's a nightmare for a soldier."

He paused and then spoke firmly. "But now it's on again. Tonight we'll take a decisive step with our special forces teams to root out some of the combatants' strongholds. I've alerted Calev that you and your cameraman will accompany his platoon. It's up to you though. My men are not responsible for your safety. Their focus is the mission. So, if you are going, you better get ready. Be safe."

Isaac dismissed Mike. With bloodshot eyes, he watched Mike cross the barrier and then straightened his shoulders, turned abruptly, and headed back inside the command center. Rest was a luxury he couldn't afford.

Mike walked through the barrier and crossed the courtyard to his hotel. When he entered their room, Jack was packing up some of the film gear he had used for Mike's report. By the look on Mike's face, he knew something was up. "Let me have it," Jack said.

"It looks like we'll be heading out with the assault teams tonight." Mike had a serious look on his face. His countenance signaled to Jack both the seriousness of the danger they would be facing and a determination to get the story right. Jack had seen this look before.

Jack shook his head and said, "Got it." From his tone, Mike knew Jack would be ready.

Mike's phone rang again. This time he heard Calev's voice. "Sir, the teams are assembling now. You will be accompanying me. We're heading out later this evening."

"Do you know when?"

"We'll finalize our plans at 23:00 and should have an 'All Clear' starting at 01:30. Stay close by and be ready to go. We won't be able to wait once we get the word."

"We'll be there."

◇◇◇◇◇◇◇◇◇◇◇◇◇

It had been a long day and they weren't going to get any sleep tonight. Jack had taken the last steps to make sure he had assembled everything he needed for filming the operation. He packed an extra mini camera along with some spare batteries just to make sure. Mike punched in a text message to his producers at WBN headquarters that he and Jack would be out of touch and back online in twenty-four hours.

As he typed the message, he found himself putting his thoughts into perspective. He had been drawn into this conflict at a much deeper level than ever before. His experience in covering these operations had always been focused on the conflict itself and the attempts by politicians to create a lasting peace. His experience now was becoming personal; he had started to build relationships with the people living in this setting.

He asked himself several questions: *Can I remain objective at this point? Am I allowing my relationship with Bashira and her family to cloud my perspective on covering the story as it unfolds?* Images of Bashira, Amal, and the rest of the family kept running across his mind. *This is getting complicated—stay focused.* He nearly spoke out loud.

The two men threw a few protein bars and several bottles of water into their backpacks and set their alarms for one hour. They wouldn't get any sleep but any rest would help. Soon they would enter the most intense coverage either one of them had ever experienced. Mike struggled to quiet his thoughts, but he knew he could breathe easy for the time being.

Mike might have dozed off for ten minutes by the time the alarm sounded. He saw that Jack was already awake and ready to go. They grabbed their gear and walked across the square to the command headquarters. The night was quiet and clear, a typically pleasant spring evening in Israel.

When they arrived, they found Colonel Yakov giving a final briefing to the team. He spoke in Hebrew. Calev greeted Mike and Jack and interpreted for them by summarizing the colonel's orders.

"The colonel is telling us that this phase of the operation is critical. In many apartments there will be women and children, but our focus is on the mission—to capture and take down those who are armed and obtain any intelligence that we can find: laptops, cell phones, papers. The secondary objective is to secure the area and ensure the safety of those who may be held against their will.

"Remember the twin goals: achieve the successful outcome of the mission and provide for the safety of your team. Act swiftly and decisively." Calev translated the colonel's parting admonition word-for-word.

Mike looked around at the men. These soldiers were young. He knew that every male Israeli citizen was required to serve at least three years in the military beginning at eighteen years of age. These special force commandos, as young as twenty-two, had been trained in the urban warfare school. Their training would now put them to the test. As they listened to their orders to engage in combat, Mike's thoughts returned to Colonel Yakov's words to them.

Calev continued to interpret. "Men, we have the utmost confidence that you will succeed. Alpha team is already in place. You will have cover provided by their snipers. Reinforcements are staged for cleanup and additional support if needed. Once the area is secure, the medical units will enter to occupy the targeted locations. Any questions?"

There were none. The soldiers dispersed, each one checking their equipment. They each carried an M4A1 assault rifle and a Glock 19 9×19mm series pistol designed for close-in special operations, along with night vision goggles attached to their helmet, and stun and flash grenades fastened to their tactical vest. The team then quietly reassembled, ready to fulfill their assignment.

Meanwhile, Isaac came over to Mike.

"Mike, this is your last opportunity to bow out. We want you with us, but I've told the platoon that under no circumstances are they to jeopardize the mission or risk the safety of the team for your sake."

Mike had grown accustomed to this warning from Isaac. He had heard it before, but never with the stakes so high.

"Jack and I understand. You worry about your men. We'll focus on the reporting."

Isaac gave Mike an appreciative look. "You know, Mike, you might have made a pretty good soldier." He turned to leave.

Mike and Jack grabbed their equipment and started to walk over to where the platoon had reassembled.

"Sir, we're ready." Calev said.

At his signal, the elite special forces climbed into the waiting vehicles and took their seats. Other IDF troops from the Jerusalemite Reserve Infantry Brigade loaded into their assigned vehicles and sat quietly, waiting for the operation to begin. They prepared themselves mentally to move once the order was given, saying their prayers silently and breathing out through their mouths to stay as relaxed as they could.

◇◇◇◇◇◇◇◇◇◇◇◇◇◇

The ride to the engagement zones did not take long. The armored vehicles stopped several blocks away from the apartment complex so that the troops could approach on foot without being heard.

The clear, silent night served as an ironic prelude to the operation. Everyone involved knew that the silence surrounding them would soon be broken and torn apart, along with the lives of those now sleeping in the targeted buildings. The units from the IDF Infantry Brigade took up their positions, forming a ring around the complex. The strategy decided upon earlier during the tactical planning was to swarm the apartments from every angle, with the Shaldag special forces assault team catching the combatants off guard and preventing them from accurately judging the direction of the attack.

Mike and Jack followed Calev and his platoon as it gathered at their staging point. Calev motioned to the men to proceed. They used hand signals to communicate as they moved forward toward the buildings. The special forces team now began to break up. Various members ascended stairwells or entered corridors in order to position themselves throughout the building. Mike and Jack followed closely behind Calev and his point man.

As each team leader stationed their men at the predetermined assault locations, they sent a single radio ping back to Calev who responded in kind with two pings confirming he was aware they were in place. In turn, the team leaders let the men know through hand signals that the assault was about to begin. The final signal came from Calev—three radio pings to each team leader indicating that the assault would commence in 10 seconds. The countdown began—10, 9, 8 . . .

Soldiers burst through the interior doors, tossing stun and flash grenades into the center of the rooms, charging toward the walls to gain the windows before any occupants could escape. Palestinian combatants who jumped for their weapons were shot and killed instantly. Women ran to grab their frightened children. Crying and screaming—the sounds of panic—filled the hallways of the building.

Out of one room a combatant came through the door firing his Kalashnikov automatic rifle. He hit two IDF team members who fell to the ground. The sergeant leading the squad shot the man at point-blank range, killing him instantly.

Flashes and explosions went off in the apartments throughout the building. Immediately after the operation began, the IDF had turned blinding searchlights on the buildings. The lights sent shadows fleeing, making it impossible for anyone to escape unseen. Jack swept his camera throughout the room, gaining different angles, taking advantage of the brilliant light coming through the windows. The camera captured crying children unable to be comforted by hysterical mothers.

Additional support troops entered the surrounding streets. Loudspeakers barked out commands in Arabic for everyone to stay inside.

The fight was over as quickly as it had begun. Medics now followed the cries for help throughout the corridors. Soldiers secured the hands of the Palestinian gunmen behind their backs with nylon ties and placed them face down on the floor. Another team of soldiers arrived to take the children and families out of the rooms.

Calev's squad quickly began searching for papers, notebooks, cell phones, and computers. His sergeants barked out commands to their squads to check through the rest of the rooms assigned to them for any other activity or occupants.

Soldiers walked out into the hallway, shouting in Arabic for families to stay in their rooms and commanding them to open their doors. Some residents started to step out into the hall, but soldiers raised their weapons and shouted for them to get back inside. They all complied.

The soldiers continued to move down the hallway with guns raised, entering various apartments, searching everywhere for any sign of resistance. Mike and Jack followed Calev's squad to observe the room-by-room search. Most rooms contained only stunned parents with terrified children.

Mike felt himself traveling through the scene in slow motion, seemingly detached from his surroundings. The sounds he heard caused his body to throb and ache. His vision became acute, picking up the smallest details—from the terror in a child's eyes to the lifeless stare of a dead combatant—searing these images into his memory.

Suddenly, a young gunman leapt out of his hiding place in a room the team had not yet reached, firing down the hallway as he ran headlong toward the soldiers. Mike made the mental decision to drop, but he felt his body sink slowly to the floor as if he was diving through water. An IDF team member returned fire, killing the gunman. The man's momentum carried him forward and he fell by Mike's side. The sound and vibration of the man hitting the floor jarred Mike out of his daze. Clarity returned to his senses. He smelled the warm, lifeless, unwashed body of the gunman and the blood that began to leak from the bullet holes in his corpse. He heard the commands of the soldiers telling the residents in their rooms to lie face down on the floor. He realized that he and the man beside him had already done that, but only he was still alive. It took a moment of stunned silence for Mike to recognize this. For the first time in his life, he offered up a prayer of thanksgiving.

Smoke from discharged weapons filtered throughout the rooms and hallway. The soldiers continued their search, checking each room for combatants, computers, and documents. The sergeants ordered their men to collect all the weapons found in the search. Mike got up and slowly approached Calev who was now in a room talking on the radio. He hoped to hear that the operation was over.

"Yes sir, it's secure," Mike heard him say. He still heard random shots coming from the other buildings and the screams and cries of civilians that followed them. He could see IDF troops in the streets making the final efforts to secure these other buildings. Calev looked at Mike as he replied to his commander on the radio. "Yes sir, will do. I'll get them out and back to you right away."

Calev hung up the radio. "Sir, are you alright?

"Everything happened so fast," Mike replied slowly.

"I know, it feels like traveling at hyper speed, but then again, it seems like an eternity."

"How did the rest of the operation go?"

"Some injuries, but the objectives were met."

Calev turned to his sergeant. "Sergeant, carry on with your security protocol and cordon off the area while we continue our search."

"Yes sir."

Calev turned his attention back to Mike.

"Colonel Yakov has ordered me to get you out of here right away. He wants to see the video—ASAP."

The apartments now buzzed with follow up activity. Medical teams rushed inside to care for the wounded soldiers and civilians. They set about doing their best to comfort the resident families and children. A specialized team of medics, trained to secure and care for enemy combatants, treated the wounds of the gunmen who were then taken into custody.

Calev, Mike, and Jack stepped back out into the hall. Plaster dust filled the building. The smell of blood, sweat, and spent ammunition lingered in the air. Families slowly began to move out of their apartments, escorted by soldiers in the halls who directed everyone out onto the street. Bullet casings covered the floor. Medical teams made their way through the building, carrying the wounded on stretchers and the dead in body bags.

Mike and Jack followed behind a group of women and children who sobbed quietly as they left the building. All the men were escorted out of the buildings single-file with their hands bound together behind their backs.

Calev said, "We have to leave, sir."

Mike heard him but kept staring at a wounded Israeli soldier and a young Palestinian boy, each in their own stretcher, laid side by side on the narrow sidewalk. The boy, who seemed to be in shock, looked into the soldier's eyes. Mike wondered if these two wounded individuals, opposite in heritage and purpose, lying by each other waiting for the medical care that may prolong their lives, might one day face each other again in this tragic, unending, violent conflict.

Calev tapped Mike on the shoulder, startling him. "Sir, we have to leave now."

Mike pulled out of his own thoughts to respond to Calev.

"Sure. Jack, you got everything?"

Jack moved slowly, looking weary, with his camera by his side.

"Yeah, let's get out of here."

Calev told his sergeant that he would return as soon as he dropped Mike and Jack off at their hotel.

<hr />

Mike and Jack spent the remainder of the night working on the report in their hotel room. They pieced together the images of the military operation. The unedited, raw footage told the whole story. The world would have to draw its own conclusions after the network decided how much they would show of the operation.

As the dawn began to break over the city, Mike and Jack made their way across the plaza to IDF headquarters. They crossed the barrier and were escorted once more to the command tent. The place buzzed with energy and activity. Male and female soldiers huddled over tables covered with computers. Others talked on cell phones, the sound of their voices rising louder as each one made their point. The noise level made Mike think that he had entered a beehive of sorts.

As they stood, Isaac approached. "You okay?" asked the colonel.

"Yeah," Mike replied.

"How about that cameraman of yours?" Jack nodded his head.

"He sure did his job. The guy never stopped filming the whole time."

"The Ministry wants to see what you have right away." Mike handed Isaac the compact disc with the video.

"How do you think everything went?" asked Mike.

"Overall, it went well. We'll know more later once we go through the laptops, phones, and papers we collected." Isaac replied.

"It's pretty unbelievable to be up close like that." Mike spoke as if he had not heard the colonel's reply. He was still reliving the experience. He then said, "I can tell you the network isn't going to look favorably on any effort to edit the video."

"Not my department, Mike." Isaac said. "I'm sure you and your friends at WBN will work something out. "Get some rest. We'll let you know when we take the next step. It won't be for a few days. The politicians will have their say for now."

Chapter 10

THE BARRICADE

*B*ashira awoke from her deep sleep, roused by sounds of rapid gunfire and explosions. She didn't immediately recognize what was happening, thinking at first that she might be in a dream or perhaps in a strange sort of thunderstorm, but reality set in as her phone rang. She got out of bed to take the call. The hospital dispatch told her to come in immediately. She dressed quickly in her dark blue scrubs, grabbing a jacket from the closet in her room at the last moment, and raced downstairs.

In the hallway, she ran past her mother and father, each with apprehensive looks on their faces. They, of course, had been awakened by the same sounds.

"I'm heading to the hospital," Bashira said. "I have to go now. Something has happened, and the injured are flowing in needing help."

Her mother called after her.

"Be careful, *habibti.* I put some things in your bag by the door—"

Before her mother could finish her reminder, Bashira had grabbed the bag and was out the door running down the front steps onto the street.

Bashira looked into the night. Her eyes adjusted to the darkness. In the distance down the street, an unexpected commotion caught her attention. Splashes of bright lights came from behind buildings. As she walked closer, she heard shouting. The scene troubled her; the flashes and sounds of live gunfire told her something terrible was happening.

The people she met walking toward her had anger on their faces and hatred in their voices. They looked back over their shoulders after they had walked by Bashira, shouting, "No use heading that way, they've shut down the neighborhood. Nobody is getting in or out."

She could now see an IDF patrol blocking the street and sidewalk ahead. Soldiers yelled at the crowd. The streets of her beloved hometown had become filled with tension and strife. Bashira's heart began to race. *This can't be happening*, she thought. *I must get to the hospital. The children need me. The doctors need my help. Whatever it takes, I must get there!*

She heard the Israeli soldiers delivering commands through their bullhorn in Arabic.

"This area is closed. Everyone, turn back! Leave now!"

Individuals in the crowd began to cry out, "We have to get through. We need to get to the hospital. Our family is there."

Both the young and the old pushed forward against the IDF warnings. A few members of the crowd started to throw rocks and bottles. No one could pinpoint the source of these projectiles, but they began to rain down on the squad that manned the barricade.

The soldiers raised their weapons and fired into the air. Two armored vehicles blocking the road turned their mounted M60 machine guns toward the crowd. Chaos ensued as the soldiers began to push everyone backwards, causing women and children to fall to the ground.

Some of the younger men resisted further. They tried to get closer, reaching over the barricade to punch the soldiers. Several members of the IDF squad grabbed these young men, pulled them through the barricade, and wrestled them to the ground. Fellow soldiers cocked their weapons and pointed them at the heads of these men, while the IDF squad members secured them for arrest: tearing their shirts off to look for weapons or explosive vests on their bodies, binding their hands behind their back with tight zip ties across their wrists, and pushing them to their knees behind the armored vehicles.

One soldier shouted, "Anyone trying to cross this line will be arrested."

The crowd of civilians stepped backwards in unison, responding as if they were one individual.

Bashira forced her way to the front. She had made a commitment in her heart; she had to reach the hospital, barricade or not. She fumbled for her necklace clutching it in her hand as she prayed silently, "Lord, help me."

A soldier yelled menacingly at her. "I said turn back!"

With a thin smile on her face, she said, "But I work at the hospital."

"Papers!" the soldier yelled in reply. Bashira reached into her bag. The papers showing her identity as employed by the hospital were not where she kept them. She earnestly searched through her bag looking for her identification as other soldiers continued to move the crowd back.

"Do you have any papers or not?" shouted the soldier confronting her.

Bashira's fingers fumbled through her small purse. "I—I have my hospital badge."

The soldier pressed his face closer to Bashira and told her, "I said papers—official documents?!"

"I'm sorry," said Bashira, now flustered by the fact that she did not have her credentials. "I left most of my things at the hospital. We had a special TV crew filming on my last shift. I must have forgotten to bring them home."

"That means nothing to me. You'll have to leave."

"But—"

"Did you not hear me! Leave or you will be arrested like the others!"

Another young soldier shoved Bashira with his rifle. She felt a sting of pain in her left shoulder where the butt of the rifle found its target. She stumbled backwards, stunned for the moment, then gathered herself and once again pressed forward, coming up to the soldier saying, "But sir, I'm a nurse and am needed at the hospital!"

The first soldier shouted again. "This is the last time I'm warning you. If you have no papers, you must go. Now leave!" This time a second soldier struck Bashira with the butt of his rifle on the same shoulder. Pain exploded through her arm and chest. She became dizzy and nauseous and fell to the ground, dazed. She began to taste blood in her mouth, thinking she must have bitten her lip when she fell. She resisted the urge to pass out. Instead, getting up with tears in her eyes she pleaded, "But the children need me."

"That's it, take her away."

A third young soldier grabbed Bashira and pulled her through the barrier. She clutched her bag but offered no resistance. Upon returning to the secured side of the barricade, the soldier tore the bag from her hands. He grabbed one of Bashira's arms while coming down hard on her bruised shoulder with his other hand. This forced her opposite arm to come up and behind her back. He then zip-tied her wrists together and began searching through her bag.

"I'm not a militant. I'm a pediatric nurse," she cried out from under a new flash of pain burning through her already bruised shoulder. "Check with the hospital—the TV newsman was there."

The young soldier jeered back at her, "I don't know who was there and if you're a nurse or not, but I know where you're headed tonight—to the holding cells with the rest of them." Finding no weapons or anything threatening, he threw the bag on a pile of confiscated goods by the side of the armored vehicle.

Two other soldiers grabbed Bashira and pushed her into the staging area that held the other young men awaiting their turn for transport. They looked up at her through their own pain: bruised eyes, some with bloodied noses and lips, aching wrists, and wounded pride. As if she was only one more combatant, a soldier pulled up on her bound hands and pushed down hard on her shoulder to force her to her knees.

The crowd continued to demonstrate, but to Bashira those people now seemed far away. She could not believe what was happening to her. She tasted her own blood oozing from the corner of her mouth. Smoke canisters sailed over her head, fired to disperse the crowd, but Bashira was no longer a part of that world. Alone now, and in pain, she sat there waiting to be taken away. A soldier stood her back up and pressed her against the side of an armored vehicle, apparently seeking to move her away from the young men.

She pleaded once more, "Can't you see, I'm needed at the hospital."

"We've heard enough out of you," said the soldier. He spun her around, her back towards him now. With his forearm against her cheek, he pushed her face into the side of the truck to close her mouth. Another wave of pain shot through her upper body.

She struggled to breathe. The soldier relaxed his grip to shift his position.

Bashira screamed out, "Call them, call the hospital. The newsman was filming and I—"

Another hard push sent her head crashing against the side of the vehicle. She felt pain in her eye and cheek. All the strength within her legs left the instant her head hit the sidewall of the armored carrier. She fell back to her knees. The soldier stood above her now with the butt of his rifle raised, ready to knock her back to the ground if she tried to stand again. Her head ached. The world around her began to spin.

Deliberately, she leaned into consciousness, refusing to be taken away by a black out. Slowly, she gathered her wits and commanded her body to stand. The soldier standing over her must have seen her determination; he steadied himself to deliver another blow. As Bashira willed strength back into her legs, the soldier felt the firm hand of an officer on his shoulder. The soldier turned to see the officer's face in the light reflecting off the side of the vehicle.

"Stand down!" Calev ordered the soldier.

"Did you say something about a TV reporter?" he asked Bashira.

Bashira looked up at Calev. At first, she thought she was seeing double. *Where did this other soldier come from?* she thought. Then, realizing he was not an apparition, she stuttered, "Yes."

"Was he with WBN?"

A puzzled look crossed her face. *How does this soldier know?* "Yes," she replied tentatively.

"I know one of the reporters for WBN. He and his cameraman were at a hospital this week. Was it yours?"

Bashira could barely get the words out. "Yes, yes, it was!"

Calev turned to the private. "Stand this woman up. Release her hands, get her belongings, and hold her here."

"But sir!"

Calev firmly repeated the command. "Stand her up private and release her. Then wait here." The private reached down to help Bashira stand on her feet.

Calev walked away, placing his mobile phone to his ear. Bashira stood beside the vehicle, her knees shaking, wondering if her ordeal was over, praying that she would be able to move through this nightmare and arrive safely at the hospital. She glanced around nervously as the soldier released her hands. The sting of pain in her shoulder made her wince as she wrapped her arms about herself and unconsciously reached for her precious necklace. It wasn't there.

Frantically, she began looking around. A glint of light shining from behind the tire of the vehicle caught her attention. There it was on the ground. With a grateful heart, she reached down to pick it up, tenderly wiping away the dirt.

"Thank you, Lord," she whispered through her swollen lips as she held the treasured pendant tightly in her hands.

The crowd kept pressing in on the soldiers at the barricade. Those who refused to turn back continued to be arrested. The tension escalated as the IDF released more weapons fire over the crowd. The soldiers, exasperated by the crowd's relentless push against the barricade, increased their effort to take control of the situation. With their adrenaline pumping, they shoved the crowd backwards using their weapons as clubs, striking anyone in their path.

Bashira squeezed her necklace in her hand and whispered to herself while looking out over the chaos surrounding her. "Jesus, You said, 'Pray for those who mistreat you.'"

She looked back and forth from the soldiers to the crowd to those being arrested and kneeling on the ground. "Bless those who curse you." She kept repeating these words over and over to herself. "If someone strikes you on the one cheek, turn to them the other. Bless them and pray for them."

The private continued to scowl at her in disgust. Suddenly, an uproar occurred nearby, as another group of soldiers dragged more handcuffed young men from behind the barrier into the staging area, bumping into Bashira and pushing her out of the way. She kept her eyes on the ground. From the protection of the armored vehicles, the soldiers fired another volley of smoke canisters into the crowd.

The order came over the bullhorn again, "Leave the area immediately."

She watched the women and children running in the street, choking on the fumes and crying out for help. She quietly repeated to herself, "Love your enemies." A sudden spark of hope arose within her. She saw Calev coming toward her with a paper in his hand. "All things are possible with You, Lord Jesus." Bashira stared at Calev's face with a look of desperate anticipation.

Calev gave the paper to Bashira. He spoke with a clear firm voice so that she could hear him above the noise of the crowd and the shouts of the soldiers. "You will need to hurry. I can't guarantee you won't be stopped again, but this pass should help."

With tears in her eyes, she said, "Thank you. Thank you."

The private retrieved her bag from the pile behind the armored vehicle. She grabbed it, clutching it to her chest, and turned to hurry away. Almost instantly she stopped, as if she faced a doorway she could not pass through. The choice before her became clear. She knew she had to respond to the scriptures that had begun to rise within her heart—love your enemies.

Love my enemies. But how, Lord? Such a thought seemed so out of place for the setting she was in. *Not now, I must get to the hospital.*

Other scriptures she had treasured in her heart came rising up before her: *Make peace with those while you are in the way with them—love your enemies.*

Bashira's mind began to swirl. *How Lord?* she prayed. Her sense of urgency nearly overwhelmed her. She felt that she needed to leave for the hospital before the soldiers changed their minds and took her back into custody. Yet the echo in her heart kept resounding—love your enemies. *How can I show the love of Jesus Christ in this setting to these soldiers?* she prayed.

Then she realized that she did have something to offer them—the candy and dried fruit that Amal had so tenderly packaged in little sacks to give to the children at the hospital.

"It's not much," she said silently to herself, addressing the voice she heard in her heart, "but Lord, neither were the loaves and fishes You spread among so many." Slowly she turned back toward Calev and presented a bag containing the packaged sacks to him.

"Sir, I was taking these to the hospital, but would you instead give them to your men?"

Calev looked stunned. "What?"

"Perhaps it can be a small expression of love to them."

Calev seemed incredulous, "Love? What would make you think of love at a time like this?"

She answered Calev in a tired but clear voice. "In the Bible we are told, 'It used to be said, love your neighbor and hate your enemy.' But Jesus said, 'Love those who curse you. Pray for those who mistreat you.' Perhaps, in this small way, your soldiers might see the love of Jesus."

Calev stared at her in amazement. She reached out to hand him the sack of treats. He took them from her and spoke to the soldiers guarding the rear of the barricade.

"Let her through," he ordered. Bashira held the pass tightly in her hand as she turned to leave for the hospital.

The streetlights shown like angels guiding her every step toward the hospital. Her heart continued to race, yet in her spirit she felt a calm that she knew was beyond her control. She told herself that she should be physically and emotionally exhausted, but instead she realized that a peace had settled over her that could only be understood in the way the Bible describes it—a peace that passes all understanding. This peace, and with it a sense of joy knowing that she had indeed obeyed the word of the Lord, renewed her strength, allowing her to face what she knew lay before her at the hospital. Gratitude filled her heart as she pressed on.

She quickened her pace.

"Thank you, Lord," she prayed out loud, "for making a way where there was no way."

She saw the lights of the hospital through the haze of the dark early morning. Upon arriving, Bashira moved with confidence past the small courtyard and through the entrance doors. As she entered the lobby, she heard shouts and cries from the families waiting inside.

The atmosphere in the hospital was frantic; injured children and adults crowded every available space. In crisis situations like this raid by the IDF, the hospital offered its emergency services to both young and old. Bashira had prepared for these moments. She now faced the sadness and suffering around her with strength released through love. She could not have roused this strength by her own will; rather, she received it as a gift from the Spirit of Christ within her. His compassion had brought her here and His strength would carry her through this night. Scripture she had memorized long ago came to her mind as she walked toward the recovery ward. As these verses sprang up in her memory, she felt as if she heard them for the first time: My peace I give to you not as the world gives; Let not your heart be troubled, neither let it be afraid. Bashira's gentle smile returned to her face as she received encouragement from these words of assurance.

The automatic door to the wards swung open slowly after she pressed her hand against the metal button. Before her lay both a hallway filled with deafening noise and a task that would demand everything from her, but her heart was now full.

Chapter 11

EMERGENCY

*B*ashira paused for a moment, looking around to regain her bearings and taking a deep breath. She walked slowly down the hallway toward her ward. The hospital no longer had the cheery, welcoming feel it did during Mike's visit. The IDF raid on the apartments that night had produced consequences nobody wanted—innocent victims needing medical help. That's who she was here for.

She became conscious of the activity of doctors barking orders, tired nurses caring for patients, and other staff scurrying about with bandages and medical supplies. Bashira made her way through this sea of people. She found her way to the employee locker room and put her coat and bag away. Alone and secure, she found a moment of quiet. She began to feel the ache of her bruises and the pain growing in her shoulder from the soldier's rifle, but she did not linger for fear of being overcome by soreness. She could take care of herself later. There were so many others who needed her help right now. She said a prayer before she left the room.

Back in the chaos of the hallway, several doctors called to get her attention. Pressed with the urgent need all around, they gave her instructions on where they needed her most. They seemed not to notice the black and blue welt expanding underneath her right eye and spreading through her cheek and jaw muscles. The entire hospital had become one large emergency room. Patient care had to be given almost immediately when and where it was needed. Sorting patients into recovery wards would have to wait.

Parents shouted to get the attention of the staff. Children cried, writhing in pain, looking up at Bashira for help. She delivered a kind word here, ministered medical attention there, and everywhere comforted their scared and weary souls. The pandemonium continued for hours. Doctors moved from patient to patient, bellowing her name to follow them. On and on they went—visiting beds, examining patients who could only find a spot to rest on the floor, diagnosing injuries, prescribing treatments, completing paperwork—until ultimately, the scene began to settle. At last, calm descended upon the hospital. Rest overcame the weary night as the sun rose.

Bashira found herself exhausted but continued to work throughout the day and into the evening. Only a small staff of doctors and nurses remained on duty. As the sun set, she tended to the bedside of a little girl, happy just to sit and be with this child. The child's presence comforted Bashira as much as Bashira's presence comforted her.

The director walked up behind them both, placing her hand on Bashira's shoulder. She spoke to her softly, "Bashira, you must go home."

Bashira slowly lifted her head. Until this moment, she had dismissed the throbbing pain present in her face and shoulder. Her eye had not swollen completely shut but remained puffy and sore. Visibly exhausted, her entire body seemed to ache. Her knees and elbows had crusted over with dried blood. Her mouth now seemed to be on fire from the cut her teeth had made on the inside of her cheek when she fell to the ground at the barricade. Nevertheless, she didn't move at her supervisor's directive to go home. She held her gaze on the young girl.

"Bashira, she will be fine," Dr. Shifa said. "She's in God's hands. He loves her more than we ever could. Go home. Care for yourself. Let her rest in His loving arms."

Bashira looked up at the director and once again at the little girl. She leaned over to give her a kiss on her head while patting her arm.

The director gave Bashira's scrub top a slight tug, saying, "Go home before it gets too late. It's dark. The curfew is approaching. You need to hurry."

Bashira gave a painful smile and slowly turned away from the precious child. She gave the director a hug and then walked down the hall to gather her things from the locker room. It was indeed time to go home.

◇◇◇◇◇◇◇◇◇◇◇◇◇◇

As she left the hospital, she paused to looked at her watch. The curfew was already in effect. Bashira realized that she had worked a shift of eighteen hours. She had now missed the timeframe to get home safely. She had to navigate a path that would allow her to by-pass the main barricades. Otherwise, she thought she might run into the same problems she had last night. She couldn't count on the presence of a kind lieutenant to help her this time. Nor could she trust in the pass he'd given her. It was no longer valid. She told herself to stick to the side streets and alleys and stay in the shadows. *I can make it home if I hurry.*

She took off at a brisk pace, walking through the narrow alleyways. She passed from street to street, moving like a stray cat, constantly looking over her shoulder, anticipating every potential danger, and vi-sualizing her every deliberate move. She turned a sharp corner, and to her surprise she encountered an older woman dazed and sitting against the wall, moaning to herself, and sobbing quietly.

Not expecting this, Bashira paused to think. She looked around to see if there were any others nearby. Pleased to see that they were alone, she put her finger up to her lips to motion to the woman not to speak and kneeled beside her. She operated on instinct now. Her strength, both emotional and physical, were long gone, but she found herself in a familiar setting—tending to the care of another in need.

She didn't hesitate to act, asking in a whisper, "Are you, all right?" The lady looked back at her with frightened eyes.

Bashira spoke again, ever so softly, "Can you hear me? Is there anything I can do?"

The beleaguered woman stared blankly at Bashira, and then, as though she were suddenly aware of Bashira's presence, said, "Yes. I live around the corner, but I saw the soldiers and was so frightened that I just hid."

"Can you stand?"

"I think so, but I'm not sure I can make it on my own."

Bashira looked around again, this time for help. Realizing they were on their own, she leaned down to put her hands under the woman's arms. Wincing in pain, she helped her stand. The sharp pain in her shoulder reminded her of the ordeal she had just been through.

"Let's go," Bashira said. "Show me the way."

They continued through the alleys. Bashira heard IDF troops moving about nearby and signaled again to the woman not to make a sound. A little further on, the woman pointed toward an apartment building.

"There. That's my building," she whispered back to Bashira.

Bashira looked around carefully before she helped her across the street. Once safely across, they moved quickly to enter the woman's building. Adults and young children moved about in the crowded hallways. It seemed to Bashira that they sought reassurance in the presence of others throughout the common spaces within the building. Everyone seemed anxious about the raid the night before. Applying all the strength she had left, she helped her precious cargo climb the stairs. She then led the grateful woman gently down the hall, following her instructions to her apartment.

When they arrived, Bashira pounded on the door. The door opened immediately to reveal the woman's family gathered inside. They rushed over to meet her with joy on their faces, helped her into the room, and huddled around her to kiss her cheeks as if they were one individual. Bashira looked on in wonder. A smile melted the look of fatigue on her face as she witnessed the love this family expressed to the old woman. The joy contained within the room made Bashira rejoice that one who had been lost was now found and returned safely into the arms of those who loved her.

One of the woman's family members, most likely the oldest son, came out into the hallway to speak with Bashira.

"We cannot thank you enough. My mother was supposed to be home hours ago. We've been frantic, trying to figure out where she might be, but with the curfew we were unable look for her."

The man grabbed both of Bashira's hands and held on to them in gratitude. Bashira looked back inside the room. Everyone remained gathered around their mother and grandmother. Seated on her lap, in the center of them all, was one of the young grandchildren. But Bashira no longer saw this family; she now saw her own and had to get home.

The grandmother looked up from the middle of her homecoming celebration. Seeing Bashira through the open door, she smiled toward her as if to say, "This was why I needed to get home." The woman mouthed to Bashira, "*Shukran*." Her gratitude gently raised a broad smile on Bashira's sore and swollen face. The smile returned by the woman reminded Bashira of what she knew in her heart to be true—God is our refuge and strength, a very present help in times of trouble.

Bashira looked once more at the family members by the woman's side and then spoke to the man at the door. "I'm glad she's safe. I must leave now. God bless you all." Bashira gave a slight wave of her hand and turned to make her way back through the hallway crowded with families. She reached the street, listened for a moment, and then scurried across the narrow alley to the corner. From there, still keeping to the shadows, she cautiously made her way through the narrow hilly and winding streets. At last, she reached her neighborhood. She picked up the pace of her stride as she approached her street and finally climbed the steps to her family's apartment.

Now at the door, she opened it, entered, and closed it behind her. Exhausted, she leaned back against the closed door, letting her aching head rest on her uninjured shoulder. She was home. With her last ounce of energy, she willed herself slowly off to bed. She felt a peaceful sense of how blessed she was to know that Jesus would never leave nor forsake her. She had just experienced His faithfulness.

Sleep came swiftly.

Chapter 12

APACHE

Mike and Jack followed their escort to the command center. Neither of them had had much sleep since the assault on the apartment days earlier. Mike had gotten the video and story off to the network. Now his producers wanted to know the outcome of the raid. Mike would have to wait for his answers until after Calev had briefed his colonel on the incident with Bashira at the barricade.

Turning to Mike, Isaac said, "Okay, Mike, make sure that she gets her head straight and doesn't do anything like this again. What if Calev hadn't been there? Who knows where your girlfriend would be—locked up right now most likely?"

"Isaac, she's not my girlfriend."

"All right, all right," Isaac grumbled. "Let's get on with something important. Tell your producers we may have to clear more buildings. It's not final yet, but headquarters wants us to explore our options. Calev will explain. You can accompany his platoon again. They are heading out this morning to examine some of the sites we're considering. Same rules as before; it's your neck when you are out with my guys."

Isaac turned to Calev. "You take it from here. Be sure and brief Mr. Olson while the teams get ready."

"Follow me, Mr. Olson," said Calev.

"You would think by now, Calev, you could call me Mike."

"Okay, sir."

Mike rolled his eyes.

As they turned to leave, Calev said, "For this operation water, electricity, everything will be highly rationed and limited for use to only very specific periods of time. No one will be allowed outside during curfew."

Calev led Mike and Jack to a table spread with photos of streets and apartments. He continued, "Once we provide our assessment, a decision will be made by command to launch the operation. Our part is to make sure we get the details right."

One of his sergeants came up to Calev. "Sir, the men are ready." Calev acknowledged the sergeant's interruption with a nod of his head. "Thank you, Sergeant. I'll be with you soon."

He said to Mike, "In the meantime, recon squads are going out this morning to survey the area to make sure everything is in place to proceed with the mission when the green light comes." Calev packed up his materials. "Can you leave now?"

"Sure."

As they left the tent, Mike and Jack jumped into the IDF vehicle with Calev and his driver. Before moving out, Calev looked around to see that everyone was ready to leave. The driver started the vehicle. The heavy troop carrier lurched forward toward their destination.

When the squad arrived at the targeted neighborhood, they drove slowly through the streets, looking to identify the buildings marked on their maps. They stopped periodically to verify the exact GPS coordinates. One of the buildings in the area caught Mike's eye. He thought he recognized it as the building where Bashira's grandparents lived. He couldn't be positive, but he had a strong hunch he was right.

"Calev, how do you know for sure that combatants are in these buildings?"

"We have surveillance teams tracking their locations. Even though they move about rapidly, it's the job of the surveillance teams to verify their presence before we commence an operation. Our job is final reconnaissance to verify the site is a 'go for action.'"

The driver stopped the vehicle. Calev stepped out to release the squad being dropped off at this location. He briefly returned to the cab to let Mike know that they were going to go further on to get a better view of the whole area, then went back to give his sergeant some final instructions.

Upon returning, Calev jumped in the vehicle and opened his laptop. The driver started the engine. As they took off, Calev pointed out an area on the map to Mike. "We're using an Unmanned Aerial Vehicle, called an UAV, to track our reconnaissance and to confirm we have the right site."

Mike looked out the window. He couldn't see the UAV but did recognize an Apache attack helicopter hovering nearby. He was familiar with the IDF tactics. The chopper was on standby with its full complement of munitions. The Apache AH-64A attack helicopter was known as "a flying tank." Armed with some of the most lethal weapon systems known, it could operate day or night. It carried a 30 mm M230E1 chain gun and a full complement of rockets, including Hellfire anti-tank missiles sometimes used to destroy targets inside of buildings.

"I can see, Calev, that you've got all your bases covered with that Apache overhead." Mike continued to watch the helicopter hover as he spoke.

"It's just a precaution if needed." Calev remained focused on his laptop.

The driver stopped the vehicle at their drop off point. Mike saw a different squad of soldiers actively surveying an adjacent apartment complex. A crowd of civilians also watched their activity from across the street. Mike and Jack got out of the vehicle to see if they had a good angle for filming.

Jack lifted his camera to his shoulder. He pointed at the crowd of people watching the soldiers and whispered to Mike, "Look to the left of those folks. Is that Bashira's grandparents' place?"

Mike nodded. "I think you're right. Wait—that's them standing over there with Amal. It looks like the grandfather is carrying some books or files—"

Unexpectedly, Calev's radio issued an alert, surprising everyone: "Rooftop building A1. Armed insurgents." The UAV circling above had detected movement on the rooftop of the apartment building across the street. The video images shared with the remote command center revealed armed insurgents moving about on the rooftop and through the upper stairwell of the adjacent parking garage. The threat assessment determined that the IDF troops below could not see the movement and were in imminent danger.

Calev grabbed the radio, switched channels, and alerted his team. All the IDF soldiers on the scene hunkered down behind their vehicles with their weapons aimed at the rooftop. Suddenly, gunfire erupted from one of the armored carriers. Civilians began screaming and running in all directions. Return rounds fired from the rooftop and stairwell struck all around them.

Calev shouted orders for his men to engage. The squad began firing back in the direction of the apartment building. The sharp whistling sound of high-caliber bullets filled the air. Calev then called for more support on his radio. "Alert! Recon team Alpha 2 needs immediate support. Repeat. Immediate support!" He followed his emergency call with the coordinates of the combatant's position.

The command center issued a strike order for the Apache helicopter to engage. The rapid fire of its chain gun echoed above, showering the rooftop with 30mm rounds. Combatants scrambled for cover in the stairwell of the parking garage, firing back at the IDF team from their height advantage.

Mike and Jack hunkered down behind a parked car on the street. Mike looked over the edge of the wheel well. Out of the corner of his eye, he saw Bashira's grandfather drop his books and gather Amal in his arms. He looked around for a safe place to hide. Carrying Amal, and leading his wife, they ran into the street level of the apartment parking garage. Mike followed them with his eyes until they were out of sight. He could only hope that they were now out of harm's way.

The shooting continued from the stairwell in the upper level of the garage. The Apache could no longer reach the combatants with its chain gun. The command center issued an attack order to fire a Hellfire missile.

Mike heard the sound of the missile being released. He looked up to watch as its trajectory led it straight for the garage. The missile hit its target with a concussive blast followed by an ear-splitting explosion that ripped through the entire structure, collapsing the corner of the apartment building into the demolished portion of the parking garage.

Mike stared into the void that had been the building, frozen by shock, and then yelled, "Noooo!!!" Without thinking, he raced toward the cloud of smoke and dust pouring out of what was left of the partially collapsed garage.

Calev turned to his radioman. "Eichler, get a medical team up here now! Delta squad, provide cover. We're going after Mr. Olsen." Calev ordered his men to follow him. They raced to catch up with Mike, who by now had reached what was left of the parking structure.

Calev and his squad arrived quickly, peering through the smoke and wiping the dust from their eyes. They soon saw Mike on his knees frantically trying to remove rubble away from what remained of several cars. Calev and his fellow soldiers ran up beside him.

Calev yelled, "What in the world are you doing!"

Mike never looked up. He cried out, "Help—I saw Bashira's grandparents running into the garage with Amal just before the missile struck."

One of the soldiers joined in to help clear rubble while others trained their weapons on what used to be the stairwell. The rest of the squad turned their weapons toward the partial opening that remained between the garage and the street. Mike found Bashira's grandfather under a pile of broken concrete. Working quickly, Calev and the soldier alongside him were able to pull him free.

The soldier felt for a pulse on his arm. "He's still alive, sir, but it doesn't look good."

Mike then frantically began looking around for Amal. He heard the grandmother moan. Mike turned to see her body lying off to his right. He shouted to Calev that he had found another victim and began desperately removing the rubble from around her. For Mike, time was now irrelevant; it seemed to crawl forward as if a dream sequence unfolded before him. He had, in fact, entered a nightmare. More soldiers arrived to care for the grandmother, but Mike couldn't seem to hear or recognize what they were doing. Only one question remained: Where is Amal?!

He saw a pair of little feet. He braced himself for the worst as he prepared to take a closer look. Sticking out of the rubble, a little hand still holding a sucker caught his eye.

Mike reached over and slowly lifted a small portion of the wall of the garage from Amal's limp body. At that moment he realized she was gone. Mike grabbed his forehead with both hands, gasping. He couldn't breathe. His heart pounded. He reached out to touch her.

Grief grabbed and blinded him. All he could see were the faces of those in Bashira's family who he had begun to care for and who were now either gone or fighting for their lives. Pulling her body, now empty of her spirit, free from the rubble, he cradled it in his arms. Tears streamed down his face.

Mike had no idea how much time had passed before he became aware of the shouting in the street. The crowd began to approach the structure. A squad of soldiers responding as reinforcements raced into the garage to form a security perimeter. Calev grabbed Mike to turn him around but paused at Mike's fierce gaze.

"Don't touch me!" Mike shouted.

Calev knelt beside Mike, who rocked Amal's little lifeless form tenderly in his arms. He touched Mike's shoulder and said, "Mike, we have to leave. There's nothing we can do now."

It was as though Calev were speaking to the dead. Mike couldn't move. Calev looked at his sergeant and nodded for him to take Amal so that he could pull Mike away from the scene. Mike resisted, fighting to hold on to Amal. Their struggle continued as the crowd rushed forward from the street. Shouts grew louder. The crowd, full of shock and anger, rained rocks and hatred down on the soldiers. Calev's concern was for the safety of his own team.

Calev shouted at two privates standing close by. "Help me with this civilian. Move, now!"

The two soldiers shouldered their arms, ran over and began to lift Mike from his perch on the rubble. He cursed and fought furiously but to no avail. Together, the soldiers were all able to retreat from the scene, dragging Mike with them. Amal's body lay alongside the grandparents. Ambulance sirens filled the street. More help was on the way. The medic's work was done. It was time to leave and let the local medical teams care for the wounded.

As Mike reached the safety of the vehicles, he turned back for another look. This time he saw Bashira's parents pushing their way through the stunned crowd and entering what was left of the garage.

Mike made another attempt to return to the scene. This time Jack and the soldiers held him. They took him behind the IDF vehicles. Mike saw the grandparents carried away on stretchers to the waiting ambulances. Through the haze, Mike could see one of the medical team carrying a small lifeless bundle wrapped in a blanket. It was unbearable. The nightmare kept unfolding.

Bashira's parents were no longer in sight. Additional IDF troops came rushing forward to string barbed wire across the street to cordon off the area. Other armored vehicles took up their positions, expanding the perimeter.

Jack led Mike to a Humvee where they could sit down. Mike sat dazed. Jack sat by his side. The silence within the vehicle entombed the moment. Mike began to weep. "Amal is dead," he told Jack.

Jack spoke softly, while still staring at the floorboard. "I know. All I can think of is how her name means *hope*."

Mike didn't respond. The silence returned. They sat in its timelessness for a while. Eventually, Mike began to wipe the concrete dust off his face. His tears had turned it into thin lines of caked dirt and dust that dried on his skin. He looked up at Jack. "Yeah, and in this place, we're always killing hope."

Chapter 13

FAMILY CRISIS

The sound of gun fire had awakened Bashira. Closer this time, it sounded to her as though the fighting was near her grandfather's apartment. Her first thought sent chills throughout her body. *Amal is with them.* She fought back the terror seeking to crush her heart with a thought of the unthinkable. *We've got to get to her. She must stay safe,* she told herself.

Running to the door, she met her parents in the living room also preparing to leave the house. Together they raced out the door and ran as fast as they could to the grandfather's apartment building. Rapid automatic weapon fire from the street and roof top of the apartment building echoed off the walls all around them as they approached the corner and turned toward the apartment complex. Bashira saw her grandparents run into the garage below the building, holding Amal. She frantically outpaced her parents to run after them. Out of the corner of her eye she saw the silhouette of the

IDF attack helicopter firing its 30 mm cannon. It continued to hover over the site. A moment later, a flash from underneath the aircraft signaled her worst fears. She followed the missile's trail as it sped toward its impact with the parking garage.

Time stood still. The sound of the explosion was deafening. Its concussive blast knocked Bashira backwards and her parents stumbled to the ground. A thick cloud of smoke and dust enveloped what was left of the apartment building's parking garage. The stunned crowd became speechless. Looking on in horror, until propelled by a force unseen, Bashira ran through the cloud of dust toward the collapsed structure.

She didn't hear the shouts of the soldiers. She raced toward the gaping hole left in the right side of the collapsed garage. What surrounded her made no difference to her now; her sole focus was to find Amal.

"Lord, help me," she spoke as she stumbled over the debris and entered the garage. She could see figures ahead getting up from kneeling beside some bodies. She saw IDF soldiers dragging an American away from the scene as he yelled hysterically.

Through the blur of smoke, noise, shouting and sirens, nothing mattered to Bashira now except to find her grandparents and her beloved Amal. She called out, "Amal!" *Where is she?* remained her only thought.

She made her way through the rubble to see her grandparents being treated by local emergency medical technicians. Their moans let her know that they were still alive. Then she saw Amal, her little form lay quietly in the settling dust. No cries or movement came from her lifeless body. She longed to see some sign of life as she drew closer to her beloved Amal, her eyes were closed, her tiny hand still held her candy sucker. Bashira's world stopped in that moment. She collapsed in anguish. Amal was gone.

"Oh God," she cried out softly. Agony gripped her heart in an onslaught of overwhelming fear she had never known. She knelt trembling with horror.

Then, a wail came out of Bashira from an untouched place deep within her soul, what the Bible describes as a moaning too deep for words. It came bellowing forth as a cry unlike any other, echoing off what remained of the walls of the parking garage. "NO GOD—!" she screamed and flung herself down upon the tiny corpse of Amal.

Time no longer existed for Bashira. She did not heed the voices of the medical teams that surrounded her. Nothing mattered now as she cradled Amal's body in her arms. She could only hear the depth of her uncontrollable sobbing. Her tears drenched the tiny lifeless face before her. The medical teams placed Bashira's grandparents on stretchers. "No, no, no—!" Bashira kept moaning, again and again. Wailing uncontrollably, she was swallowed up in inconsolable grief.

Mike and Jack entered the hospital, preparing themselves as best they could to meet Bashira and her family. It was a different day than the one that had graced their visit just last week. Mike wasn't looking for a story now; he was part of one. Amal was gone. The grandparents' lives were still at risk. Life as Mike had known it only a few days earlier was now shattered.

They had arranged to meet Rashad in the lobby. Cold stares from the patients and their families met them as they waited, stares reserved for foreigners who were not to be trusted within the fellowship of their present suffering. They both soon found a refuge from the painful reality that surrounded them in the beacon of Rashad's welcoming look.

Rashad had raced to Bethlehem the moment he heard the news about Amal and his parents. With kindness on his face, he grabbed Mike's arms and looked him in the eyes. *Kindness seems to be the trademark of this family*, Mike thought.

"Thank you for coming," he said. "I know it will mean a lot to Bashira and the family." He led them through the crowded hallways toward the ward where the family was recovering.

"Any word about your mother and father?" Mike asked hesitantly.

"We're still waiting," said Rashad. "But Amal—" It took a moment for Rashad to form his words. "She's gone." His face tightened as tears began to well up in his eyes. His heart, too, was broken over the loss of Amal.

Mike bit his lip, trying to hold back his own tears. "I can't believe it. It all happened so suddenly," Mike said softly.

"I know, my friend. There is no reasoning it through or finding comfort in anything else except that we know our beloved Amal is with the Lord."

Rashad led them to the ward where his parents were being treated. As they approached, Mike saw Bashira shuffling slowly down the hall towards them, held up on either side by her mother and father. She did not acknowledge his presence. To Mike, she looked more like the ghost of the woman he had come to admire so greatly. *It's as though Bashira also died,* he thought. She was the strongest woman he had ever met. *Everyone has their limits,* he told himself. He realized he had limits too. For the first time in his life, he felt powerless to help and unable to contribute.

Bashira began to weep deeply. Her mother tried to comfort her. Mike reached out to her in his mind, digging deep into his own memories to find an experience of his own he could draw on to help him understand how much she must be hurting. He simply did not have any personal point of reference. He felt any gesture on his part would be meaningless.

Mike watched as Rashad moved forward to reach out to Bashira and put his arm around her. She let go of her father and cradled her head on his shoulder. Mike saw her movement, but he could not see the spark, the light, or the life he desperately wanted to see coming from her beautiful eyes. Rashad gave Bashira back into to her mother's arms and turned to Samir.

Miriam helped her to sit down on a bench in the hallway and sat down beside her. Mike stood back in silence, not wanting to interfere in any way. He tried to figure out what he could possibly say as a word of encouragement to this family.

Rashad led his brother a few steps away from Bashira to ask, "Any further word from the doctors about *Abui* and *Emi*?

◇◇◇◇◇◇◇◇◇◇◇◇

Samir spoke. "The doctors think they will make it," he said, "but they're not sure. Their age complicates things. *Abui* has a concussion and a fractured right ulna. *Emi* has some internal injuries and a fractured left tibia and ankle. They both have some cracked ribs."

Rashad glanced over at Bashira, directing Samir's attention with a nod of his head in her direction. "What about Bashira?" he asked.

Tears came into Samir's eyes. "She's devastated."

Rashad walked back over to Bashira. He stooped down in front of her, putting his hand on her shoulder.

"Dear one," he said, "let's get out of the hallway." Bashira looked at him with her swollen eyes staring into space as though she saw no one. Rashad helped her stand. He led Bashira up the corridor, walking passed Mike and Jack.

"You two can come with us," he said to them both.

Rashad walked away with his arm around Bashira. Samir sat down to hold his wife. Mike and Jack followed as Rashad had directed. They entered a lounge used only by the medical staff. The director had given Rashad access to the room for Bashira's sake. She had given so much to the care of the patients of the hospital. The director wanted now to care for her. Just then, the director came in with some of the senior medical staff.

She addressed Rashad first. "It looks like your parents will both recover, but they will need a lot of care. We've set their fractures. Your mother's internal injuries do not appear to be life threatening, and your father should recover from his concussion, but we'll need to monitor them both for any signs of internal bleeding. We also need to recognize that due to their age, their recovery will require special attention. Both of them will be terribly sore for weeks to come.

"We will continue to monitor them closely once we remove the casts, and we will get them the physical therapy they will need. Right now, their condition remains critical, so we'll keep them a couple more days to make sure complications don't set in."

The director then took Bashira's hands and said, "Bashira, you know our hearts are broken over the loss of Amal."

Bashira did not speak. She gently nodded her head, even as she continued to lean on her uncle's shoulder. Tears welled up in Rashad's eyes and began to slowly trickle down his cheeks.

"Thank you, Dr. Shifa," he said. "We know you and your staff are doing all that is possible. Our parents are now in the best of care." Rashad regained his composure and wiped away the solemn acknowledgement of his own grief.

Samir had led his wife into the room, following the director, to hear the latest news. Rashad looked up at his brother and then turned to Mike.

"Mike, could you stay here for a few minutes with Bashira and my sister-in-law? Samir and I need to check in on our father."

"I'll be glad to."

Once again, Miriam sat down beside Bashira. Mike moved slightly closer to Bashira. Jack stood further back at a distance. Bashira continued to sob lightly, now leaning her head on her mother's shoulder. The director and medical staff left. Then, Rashad and Samir went down the hall and gently opened the door to their father's hospital room.

They edged close to his bed, side by side, and placed their hands on the bed rail. Their father slept.

"He looks so frail," whispered Samir. They both paused, staring at him with love in their eyes. Samir spoke first. "Remember how he used to lift us above his head and wrestle with both of us at once."

"He could throw us around like matchsticks."

They remained quiet for the next few moments.

"It is going to be so hard on them when they hear about Amal," Samir said, beginning to tear up again. Rashad put his arm around his brother's shoulder.

Staring at his father in the bed, Samir continued, "I can't believe she's gone. The house will be so empty without her." He and Rashad stood there without speaking, gazing at their father sleeping soundly.

"I'm worried about Bashira," Rashad spoke quietly, still looking at his father. "Last week, I talked with her about needing a break and coming to Nazareth, maybe even bringing Amal—then all of this happened."

Samir turned to Rashad. "It might still be the best thing for her," he said.

"I agree. You're going to have your hands full here with *Emi* and *Abui*,"

"They will have to move in with us. But you know how hard it will be to get Bashira out of Bethlehem now, especially since she doesn't have the right papers."

"Let's see what the Lord will do," Rashad said to his brother.

They heard the door crack open. Mike peeked in. "I'm so sorry to disturb you," he said in a soft voice. "I wanted you to know that Bashira is with her grandmother now."

Acknowledging Mike's presence, Rashad looked at his brother. "I'd like to go see her too. Samir, will you be okay?"

"Sure, I'll stay here with *Abui*."

Rashad gave his father's arm a light squeeze and walked out of the room with Mike. As they entered the hallway, he said, "Thank you again for coming."

"I'm glad we could," said Mike. "I'm so sorry for your family."

"Our parents will be okay. It's serious because they are older, but they should recover. Once they are out of the hospital, they will be able to stay with Samir and Miriam."

"What about Bashira?" Mike asked. "She's going to need care too."

Rashad paused at the door of his mother's room.

"Bashira was more like Amal's older sister, or mother, than her aunt. The loss of Amal is devastating. It's shattered her heart and it's going to take time for her to heal." Samir and I were talking about trying to get her away for a while."

"Where would she go?"

"Samir thought it was a good idea for her to come back to Nazareth with me, but there are problems in getting her out of the city."

"What kind of problems?"

"It's impossible to get papers to leave Bethlehem right now unless you have special approvals. I'm an Israeli citizen; but at times like these, even in my role of providing medical supplies, I need approvals to travel in and out of the West Bank. For those living in the West Bank it is extremely difficult to leave right now."

"Special approvals are one thing I can look in to. Give me a little time to think this through. I know some folks that might be able to help. It will allow me to do something for your family."

"We will be grateful for anything you can do. Whatever can be done, though, will have to be done quickly. I have to return to Nazareth very soon."

Mike had a new energy in his voice. In his heart, he thanked Rashad for giving him this assignment. By being asked to help, he now felt that he could at least do something for this family that had suffered so much. He sought to encourage Rashad. "Don't worry. I'll work on getting Bashira the paperwork she needs."

Rashad cracked open the door to his mother's room, peeking in to see if she was awake. Looking over his shoulder, Mike could see that her friends had gathered there. Bashira, among them, sat quietly looking at her grandmother and holding her hand. The grandmother seemed to struggle with her breathing. Rashad closed the door, remaining with Mike in the hall.

Rashad took hold of Mike's shoulders and looked him in the eye. "Thank you," he said.

Mike saw a vulnerability in Rashad's eyes that he had never seen before. He perceived that the kindness he had always known was now coupled with a deep sense of gratitude for anything that could be done to help the family in their crisis. Mike knew he was in a unique position to help. He determined to himself to follow through on his promise to Rashad.

Rashad put his hand on the door of his mother's room, took a deep breath, and entered. Mike waited in silence in the hall. He saw Jack leaning up against the wall of the hallway, resting his chin in his hands and lost in his own thoughts.

Mike came alongside him and said, "Let's get going. I've got to see Isaac."

◇◇◇◇◇◇◇◇◇◇◇◇◇◇

Mike and Jack made their way back to the IDF headquarters through the hauntingly hushed streets of Bethlehem. A solemn peace had now settled over the city after yesterday's violence. Mike noticed this as an incidental observation but remained focused on his mission.

Upon arriving, he went straight to the colonel's office. Without knocking, he entered and began to explain to the colonel the details surrounding the need to get Bashira to Nazareth. In doing so, he interrupted a conversation the colonel was having with Calev. Both men were startled by Mike's boldness and intensity until Isaac recognized who Mike was talking about.

"This is the woman Calev met at the barricade and who set up your interview at her hospital? It's her niece who was killed?

"Let me get this straight," Isaac continued. "You now want me to help you get this Palestinian woman to Nazareth. And she's supposed to be traveling with her uncle, who lives there, and they need to leave right away?"

"Yes, to all points," Mike replied.

Isaac looked up from his maps and tried to refocus his thinking around Mike's request. "This girlfriend of yours seems to require a lot of my attention."

Mike looked sheepish. "Yes—I mean no. She's not my girlfriend, but she is a nurse, and I know her family. And her niece is dead."

Isaac rubbed his face with both hands and stared at his desk. "You know Mike, no matter how much I like you, if it weren't for you and Calev vouching for this girl, there's no way I could help. I'll see what I can do. Her uncle is authorized to bring in medical supplies for the hospital where she works—and she's a nurse?"

Mike nodded. Isaac stared straight ahead into the air, not seeing Mike anymore, caught up in his own thoughts.

"I might be able to get her permission to return with him as part of his medical aid team. No promises, mind you. I'll see what I can do." His gaze returned to the paperwork in front of him. He nodded his head up and down with a slight frown, indicating to Mike his commitment to get back to him. He was a man of his word.

Mike looked at Calev, then turned away and walked confidently out of the office. Isaac looked down at his maps and then back up in the direction of Mike. Pausing at the door, Mike took a glance over his shoulder. He saw the colonel shake his head, turn away from his table, and pick up his phone.

Mike then returned to where Jack waited outside of the command tent.

"How did it go?" asked Jack.

"We'll know soon. Isaac can be a pain sometimes, but he's a fair and honest man. I think he's going to help."

A few hours later, Mike's phone rang. He answered. "Yes Isaac . . . Thank you, I'll be in touch." Mike then reached into his pocket and grabbed his wallet. He found the business card Rashad had given him and dialed his mobile number. Rashad picked up on the second ring.

"Hello, Rashad . . . Yes, we've got the approval. The paperwork is being prepared . . . You can leave on Wednesday . . . I'm assured this will get you and Bashira all the way back to Nazareth, no matter how many roadblocks you might face . . . You are welcome, my friend. I'll get everything to you . . . If you don't mind, would you let me know when you make it home to Nazareth? . . . Okay . . . Great."

Mike closed his phone and put it back in his pocket. A deep satisfaction came over him knowing that he had helped to make it possible for Bashira to now have the best of care.

Chapter 14

NAZARETH

The trip to Nazareth had been uneventful. Rashad and his wife, Dalia, had made up a room for Bashira in their home and let her know that she could stay with them indefinitely. Bashira had always loved coming to Nazareth. The city sat in the hill country, surrounded by sweeping lush valleys filled with agriculture. In striking contrast to dry and dusty Bethlehem, Nazareth could offer Bashira a place and the time to heal. Yet the pain she suffered in Bethlehem continued to smother her.

A month had passed since her arrival in Nazareth, and time and place still held no meaning for her. She left the house only to attend church with her uncle and aunt. The depth of her grief made it difficult to connect with her favorite people. She merely existed, conscious only of her breathing, alone in her emotional pain. She could have been anywhere; everywhere seemed the same—a place without Amal. Bashira's world was now hollow and empty.

A sense of hopelessness hovered over her to such an extent that even the Bible verses she knew by heart held neither comfort nor reassurance. She recounted to herself, 'For those who love God all things work together for good,' but her thoughts repeatedly reminded her that neither her faith nor anything she could do would bring back Amal. Her life seemed empty; her faith seemed void. She remained internally isolated. Depression held her in its grip. In her mind, she screamed for an answer from the God she had loved: *What good is there in losing Amal?*

A deep-seated root of bitterness had begun to wrap its stranglehold around her heart. She saw no way to escape its grip. Lying in her bed, she pulled her covers tightly around her as her lifeless thoughts sent a shiver through her body. Then she heard a voice, as if seeking to awaken her from a tormenting nightmare, calling her by name.

"Good morning, *habibti*. May I come in? I have your breakfast."

The sound of Aunt Dalia's sweet voice from behind the door penetrated Bashira's shell of despondency. The recognition of this penetration brought fear to her mind. She wasn't ready to let her aunt, or anybody else, back into her heart. There was still too much hurt lurking there, and she was afraid her grief would pour out with uncontrollable sobbing if anyone cracked open the door.

"Come in," said Bashira, gathering up her courage.

Aunt Dalia turned the handle of the door to the small room and stepped inside. She walked to Bashira's bed as Bashira began to stir. Bashira had been sleeping a lot; after all, what was the point of getting out of bed?

With loving eyes and a sweet smile, Dalia spoke. "Wake up, *ruhi*."

Bashira stretched and sat up. She leaned back against the wooden headboard that had been handed down through generations of Rashad's family. *At least I'll eat*, she thought. *I know I must keep on living, whatever that means.* Dalia laid the breakfast tray on Bashira's lap.

"You know, you don't have to do this," Bashira told her aunt. Her tone, empty of emotion, signaled the delivery of information and nothing more. She sought to protect herself from any pending emotional explosion, even stiffening against her own gratitude in determination to resist every trigger that might release the flow of tears she knew was dammed up within her.

"And why not?" said Dalia. "It's not often I get to have my favorite niece here with me."

Bashira looked up at her aunt, recognizing the love in her face and the kindness in her voice. She'd heard that kindness countless times over the years.

"Aunt Dalia, you've taken such good care of me."

"*Habibti*, we are grateful you are here. We're just so sorry it's under these circumstances."

It hadn't taken much, just a quick reminder of why she was in this bed, a bed in which she used to love to cuddle Amal in the past. Her tears began to flow. She gasped in a vain attempt to hold them back before they gushed forth as a fountain of pain, purging her of the stagnant hurt she carried within, ripping open the wound left in her heart over Amal's senseless death.

"Why Amal?!" she cried. "She was innocent, and now she's gone!" Her tears and her words were inseparable, forming the fabric of grief wrapped invisibly around her shoulders, sending shivers through her body, generating the groans of despair she had just uttered. Her sobbing continued, too deep for words. It gradually subsided into an ebb and flow, like the waves lapping at the shores of the Sea of Galilee, an hour's drive away, ultimately leaving her quiet and weak but empty still.

Bashira looked down at her food and said softly, "I wanted so much for her to be here with us *Aunti*." The hurt remained, but the tears dried up, for now.

Dalia gave her a kiss on the head saying, "I know, *ruhi*."

"What scares me, *Aunti*, is I feel like I've fallen into a deep hole. Every time I try to get out of it, I fall back in. This overwhelming despair grips me and pulls me down. I'd give anything to have her back with us now."

"You are grieving, *habibti*. It's okay. It takes time."

Dalia set aside the tray and sat beside Bashira to hold her as she began to cry again, this time softly, seeming to weep for what she had lost of herself. Dalia rocked Bashira in her arms, staring out the window with tears welling up in her own eyes. When she sensed the time was right, she stood up and smoothed the blankets surrounding Bashira. "Rest as long as you wish. You know how much we love you." She gave her another kiss on the head and walked out of the room trying to hide her own tears from her brokenhearted niece. She took the tray she had brought with her.

Bashira rolled over, turned toward the wall, pulled her pillow in tight, and with tears still slowly trickling down her cheeks, drifted back off into sleep—a sleep without dreams, without signposts marking time; an endless, aimless sleep; the sleep of sadness and pure exhaustion.

⬦⬦⬦⬦⬦⬦⬦⬦⬦⬦⬦⬦

Rashad sat at the small kitchen table finishing his breakfast—sipping a small cup of Arabic coffee and dipping pita in to some *lebane* with *za'atar*—when Dalia returned with the breakfast tray. Bashira had not touched her food. She offered it to Rashad, and he grabbed another pita.

"Mike called again," he said. "He asked how we were doing and wanted to know about Bashira. Maybe if I told her, it might cheer her up a little. Hopefully, she will get out of the house today."

"What else can we do, *habibi*?" Dalia said. "We've been praying for the Lord to lift this sadness from her heart—but nothing. It's as though the heavens are silent."

"Patience, *habibti*. We can only wait for Him to work in her heart."

"I know you're right. It's just so hard to watch her suffer."

Dalia turned back to the sink to finish cleaning up the breakfast dishes. Rashad wanted to comfort his wife, but he recognized that she, too, had to grieve the loss of Amal. Dalia knew how to carry an emotional load lightly, whatever the load might be, but now she carried a heavy load. Rashad prayed for the Lord to comfort his wife through her own grief as she cared for Bashira.

Rashad walked over to place his cup on the sink and returned to grab a stack of papers from the kitchen table, placing them in his briefcase. He closed his briefcase and turned to look at Dalia. Walking over to her, he placed his hand on her shoulder.

"I know our little dove is suffering," he said, "and it breaks my heart to see her like this." Rashad gently turned her around to face him. They hugged each other. Dalia began to weep softly. "But it's not about what more we can do; it's about what the Lord is doing. We weep with those who weep and pray, that in due time, He will turn her mourning into dancing."

Rashad recognized that the Lord had made his home a haven for Bashira. Bashira's stay with them had allowed her to begin to come to terms with her grief, but over this month in their home, Rashad had become concerned that Bashira's heart was hardening in response to losing Amal. He saw changes in her behavior he took to be warning signals that she was closing herself off to other people, even those who loved her the most. His greatest concern was that he saw her hiding from the Lord. Rashad knew that in order to work through her grief and heal, Bashira would have to open up her heart to the God of all comfort. *If not today, then soon, Lord,* he prayed as he gathered his briefcase, gave Dalia a kiss and headed out the door.

Chapter 15

THE MOUNT

For Bashira, the past month had seemed to stretch on without end. Each day, though, had steadily brought forth an incremental dose of healing. She had consistently ventured outside of the house over the last few days but never on her own. Today would be different. Bashira paused before leaving the security of her uncle's home without her aunt by her side.

Taking a deep breath, she closed the door behind her and stepped down the stairs to the street. She walked a while without focusing on reaching any particular destination. Looking down at her feet and with her arms wrapped tightly around her torso, she drifted through the neighborhood. Her body language conveyed insecurity, anxiety and a lack of self-confidence. She had lost her sense of identity and closed herself off from the world to cope with the feelings of being left all alone. *Have I been abandoned by God?* The thought tormented her. She longed for His comfort.

She didn't look at the faces of the people who passed her by, even when politely replying to those who spoke to her. She remained emotionally detached from the bustling activity in which she was now immersed. A delivery man with a dolly stacked with boxes of canned goods and cleaning supplies yelled at her in Arabic. "Watch out! Move out of the way!" His voice startled her, and she hurried to get out of his path, shaking her head to try to get a grip on her thoughts. As if waking up from a dream, she slowly began to recognize the people on the street becoming alive to her.

Proceeding further down the busy sidewalks of Nazareth, she decided to keep to the routes that were most familiar to her. Almost unconsciously, she began to walk toward her uncle's office, located in a cluster of light industrial buildings on the edge of town. Then, in a moment of conscious clarity, she challenged herself to walk the three kilometers as a test of her endurance. In her spirit, she sensed that the time had come to pursue her recovery.

Adjacent to her uncle's medical supply warehouse stood a building with a large fenced-in courtyard that housed a day care center. As she approached, Bashira saw children from the day care building playing in the courtyard. Coming alongside the property, she leaned against the fence and placed her hands on the bars to watch the preschool children playing kickball. An errant kick from one of the children caused the ball to come rolling toward her. A little girl came running to pick it up. Bashira stared at the ball as though it were some foreign object she'd never seen before. The little girl reached down to lift it and paused to look at her. Bashira froze, transfixed by the gaze of the little girl, seeing the image of Amal looking back at her. She squatted down to reach through the bars to hold the little girl's hand. Her response proved to be too slow; the little girl had run away to rejoin her friends, clutching the ball and giggling.

Bashira remained squatting with her hand stretched out. A flashback of Amal lying in the rubble of the collapsed parking garage raced across her mind. Tears began to well up in her eyes as she slowly rose and walked away from the courtyard—the laughter of the children lingering in her ears, the sting of the loss of Amal still fresh in her heart.

In front of her now stood her uncle's building. She looked up toward his corner office. Surprised, she saw him looking down at her. She didn't want anyone to see her crying, especially her uncle. Both he and her aunt had been so gracious to her, allowing her to stay with them without any conditions, giving her the time and the space she needed to work through her grief. She recognized how fortunate she was to be in their home and in their care. For the first time in over a month, she said a prayer, thanking God for his provision for her during this difficult time.

She decided at that moment to go to one of her favorite places in all of Nazareth. After all, she was very close now. The vehicle and pedestrian traffic gradually thinned as she continued to walk past the warehouse and hiked toward the top of the hill that stood behind and beyond it. She climbed the road to Mount Precipice. Newly found strength entered her legs; life seemed to return to her lungs. She was breathing hard now, but it felt good. She wondered if it could be possible that a spark of hope had begun to flicker within her heart.

She soon reached the summit. Before her lay the panoramic view she loved so much. Standing in one place and slowing spinning around she could see an unobstructed 360-degree vista. The city of Nazareth carpeted the hills directly below her to the west. She thought she could see Mt. Hermon faintly fading against the sky in the distance far to the north. Mt. Tabor, the traditional Mount of Transfiguration, stood much closer at the head of the Valley of Jezreel to the east. The Megiddo Valley stretched from east to west across her southern view. She took in deep breaths of the cool, fresh air gently blowing past her as an easterly breeze that carried the scents of dust and cultivated soil up from the valley beneath her. She then sat down on a bench next to the lone olive tree that stood as the perennial sentinel watching over this sacred spot. The bells of the Church of the Annunciation rang in the distance behind her as she stared southeast over the brightly colored patchwork of fields and villages that stretched out toward Afula.

The light wind whipped up her hair. Bashira allowed its caress to sooth her soul. She began to recite quietly to herself, "The LORD is my rock and my

fortress, my deliverer. In my distress I called upon the
LORD and cried to my God for help . . ."

◇◇◇◇◇◇◇◇◇◇◇◇◇◇

". . . He heard my voice out of His temple, and my
cry for help came into his ears," came the reply.

Startled, Bashira turned around. Rashad stood behind her; he had finished the sentence for her. A long-
lost smile came over Bashira's face as tears again began
to well up in her eyes; only now these tears contained
a glimmer of hope. Rashad sat down on the bench beside her. She placed her arm through his and leaned
against him. They sat for a moment staring out over
the valley. No words needed to be spoken. They both
simply enjoyed each other's company.

Rashad broke the silence. "How many times do
you think we've come here?"

It, of course, was a rhetorical question not needing
an answer. They both knew that this was her favorite
place. She loved to come here often, even as a little girl
who Rashad would have to carry up the final few steps
of the walkway on his shoulders; not unlike how he
would have carried Amal if she were here right now.
The thought aroused her latent pain of loss. Grief, once
again, stabbed her heart, releasing its sting. She clung
to her uncle for comfort.

"I thought you might be here," Rashad said. "From
my office window, I saw you walk by the day care cen-

ter. You looked so sad watching the children play. I drove up here to see if I could find you."

"I'm glad you came, *Amo*."

The sweet silence returned to them. They both knew that neither had to speak until either of them wanted to. "I've always wondered," said Bashira, "if Jesus might have climbed this same hill. He may even have sat in this very spot."

Rashad smiled. "Well, one thing we know for sure, whether He sat here or not, He will forever be known as Jesus of Nazareth. The question is, 'Can anything good come out of Nazareth?'"

"Only the Son of God!" Rashad and Bashira spoke this out in unison, responding to the familiar cue. They smiled at each other and then turned to look again out over the valley. Silence reached out to hold them in its embrace.

"You know," said Rashad, patiently allowing the moment to unfold, "I can see Him sitting here, looking out over this valley that He made, contemplating the cross on which He would bear the weight of the sin of the world on His shoulders. Yet He did so for the joy set before Him. Have you ever wondered what joy it was that could have possibly driven Jesus to the cross?"

Bashira cocked her head a little but didn't answer. Rashad looked at her in the way she had always remembered her uncle when he had spoken words of life and wisdom to her over the years. "I think it was the joy of His delight in seeing you, Bashira. You and countless others just like us freed from the horror of sin."

"It's this world that's so awful," Bashira said mournfully, almost bitterly.

"You're right." Rashad paused. Bashira sensed that her uncle had more to say and intended to deliver a word of kind wisdom that she had come to cherish. She knew that whatever he had to say would be filled with the wisdom found only in God's Word, bathed in prayer and delivered in love. Now she longed for any insight that could help her move forward.

"*Habibti*, when I look back over the years, I can often remember the tragedies our family, and so many others we know, have experienced in this land. At times I felt trapped in a dark pit with no escape; everything around me seemed hopeless and empty."

Rashad's statement caught Bashira by surprise. She focused her gaze on him. She had always known her uncle to be a man who lived with so much hope. "*Amo*, that doesn't sound like you."

"*Habibti*, it was me. Hope seemed out of my reach until I realized I was not alone. I remembered that Jesus promised He would never leave me nor forsake me. I was simply to cast my cares upon Him. No matter how dark things looked He had promised in His Word to complete in me all that He had begun."

Bashira also knew God's Word to be true. The Scriptures had comforted her many times in the past, but now the solace she had found in them seemed to elude her grasp. Bashira let her gaze return to the valley; although, her sense of sight became irrelevant as she pondered her uncle's words in her heart. She knew he had spoken these words to encourage her, yet she wondered if the chasm of despondency she found herself in would prove to be too deep for God to reach her.

"What if the darkness has you bound like grave clothes?" she said softly, staring out over the span of fields below.

"Have you looked deeply to try to see what binds those grave clothes to you?"

"I've tried, but I only find more pain and confusion." A tinge of sorrow edged into her words.

"Do you have any idea why?"

Bashira could hardly speak. Her lips trembled as she tried to bring order to the thoughts racing through her mind. In the end, she could only cry out, "Amal!" She began to weep, crying out in anguish, "How could He let her die? I keep calling out to Him, but the heavens are silent."

Rashad tenderly waited for Bashira's weeping to grow quiet and spoke softly. "It's in the silence, *habibti*, where bitterness and hatred often find fertile ground to grow."

Bashira lifted her head, stung for a moment by his words. "But, *Amo*, I don't hate anyone!"

Rashad paused, letting her words hang in the air. "Okay, let me ask a question. What if you happen to see some soldiers in the street or at a bus stop? What are you thinking?"

"I start to feel afraid."

"And when you see Jewish families with their children?"

Bashira stared at the ground in stony silence. Rashad, in love, had challenged her to speak the truth of her feelings. She allowed herself to trust in his care and answered, "Sometimes, when I hear their laughter, I can hardly breathe. There are moments when I see the joy in their lives and want to scream."

Tears started to flow down Bashira's cheeks. Rashad placed his arm around her shoulder. He spoke tenderly. "And—?"

Bashira responded with clenched fists, as her body unconsciously displayed her hidden emotional pain. "She was just a little girl and had nothing to do with this fighting. It's wickedness I tell you—wickedness!" Her jaw then slackened to let out a shout of agony. "How could He let her be killed?!"

She collapsed onto Rashad's lap, her arms crossed in front of her, sobbing as her words echoed off the ancient rocks of the mountain.

Rashad waited quietly once more until her crying began to soften. "*Habibti*," he said, "when you think about the evil we see around us, have you ever considered who are the wicked people on this earth?"

He waited. Bashira didn't answer.

"How about the ones who killed Jesus—the religious leaders who beat Him so viciously he could hardly be recognized, the soldiers who ripped the flesh from His back when they scourged Him and placed a crown of thorns on His head that pierced Him to the bone, the crowd that screamed, 'Crucify Him!' and mocked Him as He hung on the cross?"

Rashad spoke clearly and precisely. "Wickedness was on full display during those last hours of Jesus' mortal life. But Bashira, it's no different today. The evil within the heart of mankind stirs up the same hate and creates all the suffering we see everywhere."

Bashira moved only slightly as an acknowledgment that she was listening.

"The problem is not that you grieve for Amal; it's that you've allowed bitterness to take root in your heart, so much so that you've begun to hate."

Bashira felt as if she had been shaken by his words. She knew she could trust that her uncle loved her, yet the sting of his words wasn't the care she expected to receive from him.

Rashad gave Bashira a light squeeze with his arm and added, "The challenge the Lord presents to all of us is His commandment to not only love our brothers and sisters in Christ but also to love our enemies."

Bashira sighed. Her uncle was a good messenger. He was able to deliver a hard word in a way that did not cause her to feel judged or belittled. She appreciated how he cared for her without requiring anything from her. Yet now she faced the struggle of her life. She couldn't escape from having to look into the anguish embedded in her soul. What her beloved uncle was describing she knew to be true, Jesus said so, but the reality of experiencing this type of love seemed utterly beyond her reach. The grip of her sorrow was too much. It swirled around in her mind like a whirlwind tossing her emotions about in agony.

Rashad interrupted her thoughts. "Look out at this land, Bashira. The debate continues to rage over Who Jesus is—is He the Messiah or are we to wait for another? Yet He's the one granting us the very breath we breathe, the One by Whom all things were made in heaven and earth, Who upholds all things. And still we continually place Him on trial, making our own judgments of Him to better our circumstances and the outcomes in our lives. And even then, His cry from the cross is still, 'Father, forgive them, for they don't know what they are doing.'"

At that moment, a bright light of conviction shown upon Bashira's heart as a tender whisper of divine love came into her thoughts. She became aware that this was exactly what she had been doing—judging God! She wasn't any different from all the wicked accusers of Christ in the crowd that day. She was just like them, shaking her fist at God and blaming Him for Amal's death.

The thought devastated her. Her bitterness and hatred stood before her now, accusing her of failing and cursing God. A sinister sense of confusion tried to engulf her mind and smother her soul with its proclamation of condemnation.

How could I have betrayed Him this way? she thought. *Is there any hope for me?* Her mind raced, frantically looking for an answer.

Then, as so many times before, the Scripture flooded her thoughts, piercing through the darkness that was trying to reclaim her soul. She remembered that there is no condemnation in Christ Jesus and reminded herself, *He is faithful even if I am not.*

Bashira's heart leapt within her. She battled back against the oppression attempting to overcome her mind. Satan, the enemy of her soul, wanted her to remain unwilling to face her sin and refuse to ask for forgiveness.

Bashira spoke softly. "If we confess our sin, God is faithful to forgive us of our unrighteousness." Her words trailed off into the stillness of the moment.

Rashad gently replied. "For God, Who is rich in mercy, gave His only Son that we may be forgiven and thus reconciled to Him. This grace alone enables us to forgive one another."

A sense of newfound joy began to swell in Bashira's heart. She understood what she needed to do. She knew the commandment: 'Repent and turn to God, so that times of refreshing may come from the Lord.' All she needed to do now was simply ask for His forgiveness. The embers of hope in her heart fanned into flame, giving her renewed joy in knowing she could be forgiven and would then be able to forgive.

As new life surged into Bashira's heart, she began to bask in the reality of the great mercy of her Heavenly Father. She could sense how her heart was being transformed. Her mind was being renewed by the power of God's Word and the work of the Holy Spirit.

Bashira looked out over the horizon. Her tears, still slowly trickling down her face, now became tears of gratitude. She clutched her precious necklace in her hand, remembering the heritage of love, wisdom, and care she had in her grandfather's lineage. Memories came rushing across her mind of how her family, especially her uncle Rashad, had taught her the Scriptures as a child, and now how they were speaking to her that 'hope abounds for those who love the Lord.' Instantly, she was reminded how even the Apostle Paul cried out at one point over his sin, 'who will rescue me from my own wretchedness?' The answer resounded to her with great assurance. "Thank God for Jesus Christ," she said.

Once again, Bashira was experiencing the power of God's Word to transform her life. Her beloved uncle had spoken God's truth to her in love. His words no longer stung; they had brought liberation as the Holy Spirit applied them to her heart.

"*Amo*, I can't deny it anymore. I've been consumed with anger and hatred at everyone and everything for Amal's death, especially the Lord. I blamed Him most of all." She began to weep once more but these were now tears of contrition. The sun had recently disappeared beyond the horizon. The evening began to descend upon them. Now the world around them stood still and shadowless. In the clear dusk, they could see the distant lights of Afula beginning to shine.

Bashira stared at the sky over the valley. With the light of the day waning, a new light of God's love glowed within her heart, compelling her to thank God personally and openly. "*Amo*, could we pray?"

"Sure."

They bowed their heads. Bashira spoke. "Dear Lord, thank You for today. Thank You for the liberty Your truth brings to our lives. You tell us to come boldly to the throne of grace where we may obtain mercy in time of need. So I come to You, Heavenly Father, asking You to forgive me for my anger and rage against You for the death of Amal. I realize now how I've sought comfort in longing for vengeance rather than trusting in You and Your goodness alone. Forgive me for judging you in my sorrow. Forgive me for doubting Your love and embracing my anger as an excuse to rail at you and hate our neighbors."

Bashira paused allowing the moment of her contrition to immerse her in the firm grip of God's embrace. She continued, "You've told us that when we confess our faults before You that You are faithful to forgive us and to cast our sin away as far as the east is from the west. You tell us to whom much has been forgiven we are also to forgive, and so, dear Lord, I receive Your forgiveness and forgive those who killed Amal. Help me to press on to Your high calling, knowing that I can do all things in love through You, Lord Jesus."

With confidence now in her voice, Bashira added softly, "Oh Heavenly Father, thank you for loving us before we ever first loved You. We were Your enemies, and yet You gave to us saving grace through the suffering of Your one and only son. Jesus is the way, the truth, and the life. There is no other name under heaven by which we must be saved, and because of You, Lord Jesus, we may overwhelmingly conquer in all these things. Dear Lord, thank you for Your mercy and loving-kindness and for so great a salvation that invites us to know and love You. We're forever grateful, dear Lord, and we long to get to know and love you more. In Your wonderful name I pray, Lord Jesus."

"Amen," they said together.

Rashad gave Bashira a hug. She leaned into him to return it. "Thank you, *Amo,* for coming."

"What a blessing for us both. And now, little one, we need to get home and face your aunt. I'm sure she's beside herself wondering where we are."

As they headed to the car, Bashira knew that she was coming down from the mount transformed. She was ready now to face all that life in the valley would bring to her.

Chapter 16

THE WAREHOUSE

Rashad and Bashira opened the door to their home and prepared to face Dalia. Before they could speak, Dalia said, "You sir, there's big trouble for you for not letting me know where you both were." She then smiled to continue, "I was scared to death of what might have happened to our little dove." She gave Bashira a big hug, and before anyone could reply, she said, "Now get cleaned up for dinner."

"I'll be with you both in a minute," Bashira said.

She hurried off to her room. After tossing her purse on the bed, she looked over at the mirror. The image she saw revealed a person different from the one who had left the room earlier that day. Peace and contentment, absent for so long, now radiated from her countenance. For the first time since she had arrived in Nazareth, she recognized her love of her Heavenly Father, and she could rejoice in it. She paused for a moment to enjoy feeling God's love again and then went to the bathroom to wash up for dinner.

Walking past her uncle's room, she heard him talking on the phone. "Yes . . . okay, we'll need to speed up processing the new shipments . . . Great . . . I'll see you in the morning."

When Rashad returned to the dining room, Bashira was seated. Feeling better, she even felt hungry. Dalia began to place the salads and stuffed zucchinis and *dolmades* on the table.

Rashad sat down. "Would you like to come to the warehouse tomorrow?" he asked Bashira. "We could use the help, especially with preparing some shipments that need to get out right away."

Bashira thought for a minute. "Sure. I'd be glad to."

A big smile came over Rashad's face. "That's great! Everyone will be so excited to see you. There have been a lot of people from the office praying for you."

Turning to Dalia, Rashad said confidently and with joy, "My dear, you will have two for an early breakfast in the morning."

∞∞∞∞∞∞∞∞∞∞

When the morning came, Bashira rose early to prepare herself to head off to the warehouse. She felt as if this day would bring further healing to her heart; it was good to be moving forward with purpose. She allowed herself to smile into the mirror and recognized the face she saw. *I'm going to be okay*, she thought to herself.

At breakfast, she was pleasant and chatty. Over the years, she had always enjoyed going to her uncle's warehouse. *Today is a new day*, she told herself. *His compassions fail not.* She had decided to step out of her isolation and serve where she could; although, she couldn't help but wonder: *What does God have in store for me?*

On the way to the warehouse—about a seven-minute drive—Bashira reminded herself of the names of the staff. She wanted to be sure to thank everyone for praying for her.

"I'll walk in with you," said Rashad. "Meet me in my office when you're done saying your hellos."

Rashad pulled his car into the parking lot. Bashira took a deep breath. Even though she knew most of the employees, she walked toward the building with some trepidation. Her apprehension had its source in not knowing how she might be received by the employees after her long absence, but she did not regret her decision to come. Various staff members greeted her at the entrance. Initially embarrassed by their enthusiasm to see her, she soon realized that her uncle had alerted the staff of her visit this morning. Nevertheless, Bashira felt truly loved.

A woman with a kind voice came up beside her and reached out to embrace her. Bashira felt a special sense of love in her greeting. This woman's welcoming presence pulled Bashira out of all her remaining uneasiness.

"Your uncle said you might come today," the production manager said.

"I'm happy to be here, Noura."

"It's so good to see you. There's a lot going on. Let's see what your uncle has in mind for us to get started on."

They went up the stairs to Rashad's office and knocked on the door, but no one answered. Noura opened the door, and they walked in. Bashira let out a sigh. In her mind's eye, she saw Amal rocking back and forth in the big chair behind her uncle's desk.

"So many memories," she said quietly to herself.

"He should be right back. Let me check on a couple things, and then we'll head down to the warehouse." Noura paused before leaving the room. "Bashira, please know how sad we are about your family losing Amal."

Bashira responded to Noura with a weak smile. She felt the heaviness returning, but it no longer had the hold on her that it did before. She sensed how her heart had changed and gave thanks to the Lord for the healing He continued to accomplish in her life.

"Thank you."

Noura left the room. Bashira began to walk about the office, taking the time to run her hand over the back of her uncle's worn desk chair. On his credenza, Rashad had placed photos of her grandparents. There was also a photo of her with her father. Other photos hung on the walls—dignitaries and special guests from around the world posing with her uncle at locations throughout the warehouse and on-site in other countries where the medical supplies had been received with open arms. Bashira stopped to look at them all. As she did, she realized how proud she felt that her family had accomplished so much and had been able to touch the lives of so many people. She didn't notice when Rashad entered and quietly stepped up behind her.

"Time goes by too fast." He joined Bashira in looking at the photos.

"I know," said Bashira, without turning around. "It seems like yesterday."

"It was!" Rashad quipped, wanting to keep the conversation light.

"Okay. If I remember correctly, once the supplies are delivered, everything needs to be sorted and organized. Right?" She wanted to get busy, too, knowing she was at her best when she served others. Today she had prepared herself to move ahead and leave the past behind.

Noura returned. She spoke to Rashad. "We'll be heading down now to the staging area. Do you need anything before we go?"

"No, I'm fine. I'll see you in a bit."

Noura led Bashira down the hallway toward the main production floor. She then walked through the door and onto the warehouse floor. The floor buzzed with workers at their tables beginning the sorting process.

"I'm sure you recall," Noura said with a smile, "how everything has to be identified and categorized properly or it won't get through the inspections from the authorities. Do you remember the numbering system we use to identify the medicines, bandages, and all the other supplies? It's not that complicated, but if we deviate from it at all, the whole process slows down. The most time-consuming stage is the sorting, and that, young lady, is where you can help."

◇◇◇◇◇◇◇◇◇◇◇◇◇◇

Later that afternoon, Rashad and Bashira left for home. Rashad delighted in the change that had come over Bashira. Today, he had seen the old Bashira he knew so well. He sensed that she had come alive again. Here she was now, beside him in the car, her chatty self going on about how much she had enjoyed seeing everyone and how deeply they had all genuinely cared for her. Just as important to him was her renewed excitement over the work being done at the warehouse. As he listened to her share about her day, he remembered one more important thing he needed to tell her.

"Guess what?" He paused to let her speculate. "I got a call from Mike before we left today. He wants to come up next week to get a better understanding of the medical mission."

"Next week?!"

"Yes. He asked how you were doing and wondered if you might be at the warehouse when he comes. I told him I'd check with you, but most likely you would be."

"Oh, my goodness, what a surprise," said Bashira.

"Besides touring the warehouse, we'll take him and Jack to lunch. They probably won't have much time to see anything else."

Bashira fell silent. The thought of seeing Mike again captivated her. Rashad made the final turn entering the narrow street that led to their home and backed into the garage. Bashira exited the car and bounded up the stairs.

Chapter 17

MIKE VISITS NAZARETH

The next week, the air remained cool and fresh. The sun would soon rise to cover this unsettled land with the beauty of a new day. Mike and Jack arose early to prepare to head to Nazareth. After leaving Bethlehem, they picked up some film gear from the WBN headquarters in Jerusalem and then drove up to the Galilee region by way of the Jordan River Valley. They got an early start to arrive in time for the mid-morning appointment Mike had made to tour Rashad's warehouse.

Even though it was a longer drive, Mike preferred this route north over the coastal roads, and today he needed the extra time to think. The Jordan River ran in no more than a trickle in some places, as compared to the time of Joshua's crossing, but Mike felt more immersed into the Biblical history of the land by traveling the course of the river to its headwaters in the Sea of Galilee.

Mike enjoyed envisioning the historical battles staged in this land. He remained captivated by its ruggedness, wondering how the armies of empires mobilized throughout millenia could, or would, fight over such barrenness.

As Jack drove, Mike took the time to let his mind drift from thoughts of the long history of conflict in the land to the present moment and his upcoming meeting at the warehouse. He knew Bashira would be there. He had to sort out what was happening in him; he couldn't get her and her family off his mind. They were such an anomaly in this cruel environment of conflict and suffering. Instead, they offered love and forgiveness in the face of tragedy and sorrow.

This confounded Mike. Bashira seemed to him to inhabit a position that superseded the world in which she lived. Her innocent beauty sprung up like a fountain of pure water that flowed through the love she poured out on everyone she met. Her smile had captivated his heart and had drawn him in a direction he had not traveled before. Much more than a physical attraction, he felt something stir within his soul.

"Hey, dream boy, what's got you now?" Jack teased, pulling Mike out of his thoughts. "You've been worthless for days ever since we started planning this trip."

Mike, not wanting to reveal his thoughts or emotions said, "What are you talking about?"

"I'm talking about you, bud. You've got it bad, and a blind person could see it. That girl has messed you up."

"Back off! You're always trying to see something that isn't there."

"Yeah, you're right. We're headed up to Nazareth just to get some insights on how the warehouse works." Jack had a dry, but penetrating, sense of humor.

"You got it. And, if you could drive a little faster, we might get there on time." Jack belted out a laugh that caused Mike to smile.

"You can try and fool everybody else, bud, but not me. I know you like the back of my hand." He glanced over at Mike and added, "And as far as I'm concerned, that girl is a winner. Her family are some of the best people we've ever met; and yes, you do have a dilemma being a mid-west American Caucasian caught in the middle of a crazy mess here. So don't try and fool me. I'll try and keep you out of trouble the best I can."

The magnificent lake began to come into view as though it were a mirage set against the barren high cliffs of Jordan opposite them. Larger than the eye could take in without panning its waters, the Sea of Galilee held a wondrous beauty, like a jewel set in the desert. The quaint city of Tiberias sat on its southwest shore—a tourist destination for those who wanted to visit the sites made famous as the location of many of Jesus' miracles and sermons as well as a place to relax in the wide expanse of such a large freshwater "sea" surrounded by desert.

They could now see the city of Tiberias up ahead. The countryside suddenly changed from its barren aridness to a garden-like Eden. Water made an astounding difference in this desert land, and the Israelis knew how to use it most effectively. Endless groves of cultivated palm trees now grew along the side of the road.

Although Jack was preoccupied with driving, Mike knew all too well that if the guy had his way they'd be stopping to eat once they reached Tiberias. Jack sure could eat, and he loved the famous Saint Peter fish pulled from the depths of this beautiful lake. However, today, there would be no time to stop and enjoy either a quick meal or a moment to watch the fisherman working their ancient trade. In order to make their appointment, they had to continue on their way to Nazareth.

The traffic through the crowded streets of Tiberias increased, slowing their progress. Once past the city center, the road climbed the hill that overlooked the lake and headed west toward Nazareth.

Leaving Tiberias, they drove through Cana where Jesus did his first miracle—turning water into wine at the marriage feast. *Strange*, Mike thought. *Why would I remember some event like this from the life of Christ in this moment?* His mind had raced ahead, wondering if there was some kind of miracle in store for him and Bashira. "Get a grip man," he said quietly to himself as he stared out the window.

"What's that?"

"Nothing, but can't you get there any faster? We're going to be late."

Jack frowned and muttered to himself. "Yeah, late for a warehouse tour. That would be a disaster."

If the streets of Tiberias were a winding slow-moving turmoil of traffic, the streets of Nazareth were even more so. Mike's anxiety increased as their speed decreased. Rashad had told him on the phone that over the last few weeks Bashira had become herself again. He said that it was by the grace of God that she was healing from her grief over the loss of Amal, but Mike wasn't sure what that meant, and he hadn't been able to confirm if she would be at the warehouse today. He turned to Jack with a look of exasperation over the rate of their progress.

"Don't even go there," said Jack. "We both know we're going to be at the warehouse on time."

Mike knew Jack was trying to help him face the reality that they would get there soon enough. Finally, they rounded a corner and saw a row of warehouses on the hillside up ahead.

"That's it. I'm sure that's their warehouse. It fits the description."

Jack nodded and drove up the hill.

◇◇◇◇◇◇◇◇◇◇◇◇◇

Upon their arrival, Jack parked the car. Mike got out and waited while Jack collected the camera equipment. Jack complained, as usual, about carrying all of the gear. Bashira, Rashad, and a woman Mike did not recognize greeted them at the curb below the steps leading up to the lobby entrance.

Rashad stepped forward to reach out his hand to Mike. "Welcome, my friend."

"Thank you. It's a pleasure to be here."

Rashad turned toward the woman Mike had not met, and with the wave of his hand, invited her to join them.

"This is Noura, the production manager for the warehouse operation. Nothing could be accomplished here without her. She is at the heart of what makes everything work."

Noura stepped forward, smiling. She grasped Mike's hand in both of hers. "Good to meet you, Mr. Olson."

"Please, call me Mike."

Rashad addressed Mike while giving a big smile to Jack. "I see your faithful colleague is here too."

Jack stepped up toward the group, adjusting the equipment he carried to a more comfortable and stable position. "Yes. And doing all the heavy lifting."

Mike turned to see Jack adjusting the camera on his shoulder and the battery belt around his waist. He noticed Jack's look of appreciation for being included in the introductions.

Mike then spoke directly to Noura. "Jack is here today to shoot some video, if it's all right with you?"

"That will be fine. We are delighted you have come today."

Bashira then stepped forward and extended her hand. Mike shook it with a gleam in his eyes. He had come to see the medical supply delivery operation at the warehouse, but then again, he had to acknowledge his real interest was reconnecting with Bashira.

"We're so glad you could come," she said.

Her words and the look in her eyes gave Mike much to be happy about, but he had to maintain his composure. *Snap out of it*, he thought. *You're a professional here to cover the warehouse operation, so act like one.* Realizing he had nearly said this out loud, he pulled himself back to his senses.

Rashad started them moving. "Well, let's get going. There's a lot to see and we have a luncheon reservation already set for after the tour." Rashad's phone rang. "If you don't mind, Noura, would you begin taking our guests around? I need to answer this call. I'll catch up with you shortly."

"Certainly."

Mike, Jack, and Bashira followed Noura. As they headed toward the entrance to the building, Mike overheard Rashad answer his cell phone with a friendly greeting, speaking in Hebrew. Upon entering the building, Noura introduced Mike and Jack to the receptionist. They both signed the visitor's book and received their temporary identification badges.

Here Bashira excused herself. "I have some work to complete elsewhere," she said. "I will see you again at our lunch appointment."

Mike was disappointed that she wouldn't be accompanying them on the tour. He was looking forward to every minute he could spend with her but soon consoled himself with the fact that they would be together at lunch. Right now, he had to do his job.

After watching Bashira leave, he took a moment to look around the reception area. It was a small room set with only a few pieces of furniture. Two soft leather chairs sat at either end of a coffee table along the wall across from the reception desk. Above the chairs hung several awards given to the company by international agencies in recognition of its exemplary business practices and success. Next to them, pictures of relief operations to the West Bank and the Gaza Strip. They told the story of the company's involvement there. Mike recognized several dignitaries from other countries in the Middle East standing beside Rashad in the photos. He was surprised to also see Bashira amid so many hotspots in the wider region. Then again, seeing the smiles of the people in the background and the happy faces of the children surrounding her, he knew that's exactly where she would be.

After gaining their credentials, Mike and Jack followed Noura, who scanned her badge against the entry panel of the automatic door. The double door unlocked and swung open. They then entered a broad hallway leading to the warehouse itself. Mike paused to take in the sparkling clean and brightly lit room. Long rows of shelves containing boxes of various sizes lined the walls. His eyes were drawn to tables, lined up in front of the shelves, on which trays and sorting equipment were arranged in stations. The whole scene had the appearance of an assembly line in a manufacturing plant.

Noura began the tour with a bit of background history. "When Rashad first started, we had only a small office with a couple of folding tables and a few shelves. Our focus, then, was simply distributing what few medical supplies we could get our hands on, which wasn't much—maybe aspirin, some sterile gauze, and dressing for bandages. If we were fortunate to get some antibiotics, we were thrilled."

Mike, motioning to the large room around them, said, "You certainly have grown since then." His comment displayed his admiration of the facility.

"Yes, and by God's grace, we are recognized as one of the leading distributors of medical relief supplies in Israel. This means we're approved to provide medical aid to both the West Bank and Gaza along with other areas in the Middle East." She stopped by a line of tables so that Mike and Jack could see workers engaged in sorting bottles of tablets.

"Here's an example of how we process the pharmaceuticals. The supplies come in as contributions from pharmaceutical companies as well as donations from all sorts of private groups and NGOs. We purchase other supplies with funds we receive through international aid. Because we receive from so many different sources, the pharmaceuticals arrive packaged in various ways and carry different labels for comparable items. Each batch must be checked to see if the medicine is outdated and if the label matches the medication. The medicines are then sorted and logged into our database with our own label."

Jack edged in closer to film. Noura continued her explanation.

"Everything has to be accounted for in detail. We must be able to show where the medicine came from, when it was received, and that it can be traced to both its source and its destination. This is done by using barcodes and scanners now, but in the early days it was all done by hand. The bottom line is that when the government auditors come, we need to show them that all items are accounted for, properly labelled, and traceable. We like to joke that the government must have established a special auditing group just for us. We keep the government auditors very busy."

"How do you mean?" Mike sensed from Noura's eyes that something remained unsaid in her last comment.

"Well, let's just say our audits are more frequent and much more thorough than others."

Mike made a mental note of Noura's nuanced comment so he could later return to it for clarification. He first wanted to get the big picture of how the operation worked. He continued to look around at the tables stacked with trays. The workers standing behind the tables scanned items, packaged supplies, and filled out paperwork. Each workstation was labeled with signs in Hebrew, Arabic, and English.

"Why are the signs in so many languages?"

"Most of our staff speak and read Hebrew as well as Arabic, but many of our visitors are medical or pharmaceutical professionals. They speak English. So, having the signs in multiple languages makes it easier for everyone."

"Is it difficult to staff a facility like this?"

"At times that can be a problem. Keeping qualified people, especially in technical or management positions, is difficult." Noura moved further down the lines of tables.

"Why is that?"

Noura stopped walking and turned to face Mike. "Those with college degrees simply find it easier to live abroad."

This comment caught Mike's attention and interrupted his train of thought. His investigative intuition prompted him to pursue Noura's answer to his question. He paused to think through how to respond to what he had just heard.

He then tapped Jack on the shoulder, signaling him to turn the camera on both him and Noura and asked her, "Noura, you said it's difficult to keep qualified staff, especially those in management. Can you tell me more about why that is the case?"

Noura gazed out over the warehouse for a moment and then suggested, "Let's keep moving and I'll try to explain some of the dilemma."

They began to walk, but Mike's attention had shifted from the operation at the warehouse to his anticipation of Noura's answer.

Noura began, "Being an Arab in Israel carries a variety of meanings depending on who you are, where you live, and what is happening around you. For example, here in Nazareth, we are Israeli citizens, but often the government still views us with a suspicious eye, especially when tensions rise in the West Bank or elsewhere."

Mike stopped walking and told Jack to stop filming. Jack switched off the camera. "A suspicious eye—how so?"

"It's simple. As Arabs, we may experience a higher level of scrutiny at any time, no matter what the circumstance. The intensity of that scrutiny depends a lot on both the internal and external conditions surrounding the land."

"That I can understand," said Mike. "Although Jack and I have covered many of the events here, this is the first time we've had an opportunity to get to know what folks here face in their daily lives." Mike indicated for Jack to continue filming.

Noura turned and kept walking. "That makes sense to me. I can see that digging deeper into the daily lives of the people living here would not be newsworthy." Noura stopped walking, lifted her eyes, and said, "But for us, daily life in Israel is shaped by a myriad of circumstances over which we have very little control. Just take the existence of the state of Israel for instance. From a Jewish perspective it's a nation built for the Jews. 'Arab citizens' present a dilemma for not only those in authority but also for many Jewish people themselves."

Mike interrupted. "Can you be more specific?"

"Sure. The question that has yet to be answered is: Can we coexist? And if so, how?"

A light came on in Mike's mind, illuminating something so fundamental that he couldn't believe he had missed it. From the perspective of a visitor to the land, he had applied his own sense of community to his interactions with the people. He was now beginning to gain some insight into the true nature of the social tensions present here.

Noura continued, now moving once more. "Of course, we've demonstrated time and time again how we can live together and work alongside the Jewish community. Business and tourism provide great examples of how this can occur, but in times like these, when tensions rise, government scrutiny makes our routine operations much more difficult for us."

They continued to move further down the rows of tables looking at additional shelves of medical provisions: rows of bandages, gauze, splints, various braces, antibiotic ointments, sanitizer, and other items for basic medical care. Mike took it all in while Jack filmed.

"Noura, I'm starting to get a glimpse of what you are describing. Could you help me understand the difference between the living situation of Bashira and her family in Bethlehem and you and Rashad who live in Nazareth?

Noura continued her explanation. "Rashad's family members who live in the West Bank are, of course, not citizens of Israel. Their rights and freedoms are limited. You've seen the difficult conditions they live in. They are often without many of the resources we enjoy here in Nazareth.

"If you add religious affiliation to this geographic mix, you have Arab Christians, even Arab Evangelical Christians, like both my family and Rashad's, living in both Bethlehem and Nazareth. This creates quite a lot of separate groups, each with different experiences of what it means to be an Arab in Israel.

"To get back to your question of why we can't keep talented young Arabs here, the answer is simple. They face conflict and strife in almost every relationship and activity in their lives. It simply is more attractive for them to live elsewhere. It's perfectly understandable that they want to create a life where they perceive they will not have these difficulties. Who can blame them? The challenges we face in our lives here are very real and persistent."

As Mike listened to her answer, his intuition focused his mind on more questions that he could ask. He wanted to know more.

"If you don't mind," said Noura, "let's keep moving. We don't want to be late for lunch." They continued further down the line of tables.

Mike saw Rashad come around the corner of one of the warehouse shelving units to rejoin the group. He was glad to see that Bashira was with him, but he didn't recognize the other woman in his company.

"Hi, everyone, sorry I took so long, but calls kept coming in and I knew you were in good hands. We'll have to hurry to get to lunch. I've made reservations, but with traffic, we'll need to get started now. Mike and Jack, I'd like to introduce my wife, Dalia." Turning to face his wife, he said, "This is Mike and Jack from WBN."

"It's wonderful to meet you," said Dalia.

Mike smiled as he took her hand in greeting. "It's my pleasure to meet another member of Bashira's family," he said.

Mike and Jack said goodbye to the staff. They all walked to the parking and got into the vehicles. Rashad, Dalia and Bashira led the way. Mike and Jack followed in their Land Rover. Noura took up the rear in her own car because she had to leave lunch early to supervise the shift change that afternoon.

Mike looked forward to the meal. Eating together would give them time to all get reacquainted.

Chapter 18

LUNCH

*L*unch was scheduled at the La Fontana di Maria restaurant located across from the Baptist School in the center of downtown Nazareth, close to the site of Mary's Well. The restaurant was famous for its traditional Arab dishes. The restaurant manager met them at the door. Rashad greeted him by name; many of the business owners in Nazareth knew each other well.

As they entered the restaurant, Mike immediately felt taken by the decor of the place. They walked into a large open room with vaulted white plaster ceilings supported by intersecting stone arches. The walls were made of rough-cut, light-brown limestone blocks from the surrounding hills. Large windows ran the height of the walls. Intricately carved floor screens stood in front of the windows, diffusing the sunlight entering the room into warm tones. Arched stained-glass panels crowning the tops of the windows released the full spectrum of color from the same light source. Wooden beam rafters and hanging chandeliers finished the look and gave the restaurant an ancient feel. Mike felt like he had entered a church.

He noticed the local artifacts and photographs of distinguished guests who had dined there over the years hanging on the walls. Many of the photos bore autographs. What fascinated Mike the most, though, was the delicious smell of the kebabs and endless trays of food the waiters carried past them. He then noticed Jack's response. He had stopped in his tracks.

"Wow! This is great," Jack said, as he took in a great whiff of the savory aromas that hung in the air.

Mike turned to Rashad and Noura. "I want to thank you for the tour and now taking us here for lunch. This place looks wonderful."

"It is our pleasure," said Noura. She directed everyone to their table, a round table for six set in the corner by one of the windows. Dalia greeted the waitresses while Rashad pointed to the chair opposite his for Mike to sit in. He then held the chairs for Dalia and Bashira. Mike and Jack stayed standing, waiting on Noura to be seated. Everyone settled into their seats—Mike across from Rashad, Bashira to Rashad's left and Dalia on his right, Jack between Mike and Dalia, and Noura between Mike and Bashira.

Noura looked at Mike and said, "I mentioned to Rashad that you might have a few more questions."

"I'd be happy to answer any that I can, Mike. Do you mind if we first thank the Lord for our meal?"

"Not at all. Please do."

Everyone bowed their heads. Rashad prayed, "Heavenly Father, thank You for this wonderful day. Thank you that we are able to visit with Mike and Jack. We are so grateful for Your loving care and endless mercy. May You bless this food and our fellowship together that we may glorify You in all that we say and do, in Jesus' wonderful name. Amen."

Noura had called in the order for the lunch ahead of time. The table had been set beautifully with dishes and cutlery. Immediately, servers brought various salads, falafel balls, and a basket of fresh pita. The salads were small but came in such a variety: *tabbouleh*, *fattoush*, *mutabbel*, and *malfouf.*

"Gentlemen," Noura said. She held her hands out palms up, sweeping them over the table as an invitation for Mike and Jack to help themselves to whatever was laid on it. "Let me describe what we have ordered for you: *tabbouleh*, bulgur and parsley; *fattoush*, a fresh salad of seasonal vegetables; *mutabbel*, roasted eggplant, like baba ghanoush; and *malfouf*, a cabbage salad. Start with what is in front of you, and please pass the plates of salad around."

Mike and Jack surveyed the array of salads set before them along with plates of hummus, baba ghanoush, tahina, and olives. Jack's eyes lit up. He took some of each salad on the table. Mike and Rashad dished a small amount from several options onto their plates.

"What would you like to drink?" Noura asked. "There is lemonade, water, and soft drinks."

Jack told Noura that he would have water. Mike requested lemonade. Noura poured the bottled water and Rashad poured the lemonade.

Then Bashira took her glass of lemonade and turned to toast Rashad. As she did, she lowered the lip of her glass beneath his. Rashad did the same, trying to position his glass lower than hers. Bashira countered by quickly moving her glass even lower. He adjusted his glass in response to her move, spilling a little of his lemonade on the table. Bashira giggled at this.

Mike wondered what they were doing. With a quizzical look, he said, "Obviously, there is something more behind what we just saw."

Bashira smiled. "It's an Arab custom for offering a toast to another. It's taken as a sign of humility to have your glass lower than your friend's glass. My uncle and I are always trying to be the lowest and sometimes— well, we get a little carried away."

"Whoever has the best technique ends up being the humblest," said Rashad. "Or humbled," he added, "depending on how much we spill. So, Mike, tell me; have you ever seen so many medical supplies?"

"No, and I must say the process for getting them organized and ready to distribute was a lot more complex than I imagined."

Rashad looked at Noura and Dalia with a smile. The gleam in his eye seemed to Mike to be a grateful recognition of their presence in the business over the years. It became clear to Mike that Rashad knew their contribution was essential to the success of the medical distribution operation.

Rashad turned back to Mike and said, "I remember the first carton of supplies that we sorted out on an old folding table. It was a jumble of abandoned Red Cross surplus. And now—well, the Lord has been good to us. But now, Noura said you had some questions?"

"Yeah," Mike began, "during the tour, Noura got me thinking about some of the challenges of living with the conflict here. She spoke of the pressures you feel as a Christian Arab in Israel. My question is: How do you prioritize your identity as an Arab Israeli Christian?"

Rashad cocked his head slightly. Mike sensed from his look that he was considering how to share his perspective. "Well, actually, it is a bit complex. To be frank, I would have to say I identify myself first as a Christian and second as an Arab Israeli citizen."

"What does that look like?"

"There are so many layers. First and foremost, my identity is in Christ. Which means as a born-again Christian my life centers around being a disciple of Jesus and a member of the body of Christ—His universal Church. As a citizen of Israel, though, it's more complicated. My race is Arab, and I am a Palestinian.

"Whoa," Mike interrupted. "That already sounds crazy complex. How in the world does this work?"

Rashad placed his hands together with his fingertips touching each other and pressed them to his lips while resting his elbows on the table. His face took on a serious countenance with kindness reflected in his eyes.

"Let me put it this way, the first aspect of my identity is the result of God's grace, while the other three are God's choice for me."

Mike shook his head, his eyes wide in bewilderment.

"What I mean by that is God selected these identities for me with a purpose. I was not born here by accident. It now becomes my responsibility to discover God's plan for my life as a Christian who is an Israeli citizen with Arab ethnicity and a Palestinian heritage."

Rashad paused before he continued. "We don't choose our family, country, culture, or the heritage we were born into. Yet it's these factors that often determine who we perceive as our friends or our enemies. Consider the most extreme Palestinian. If God had chosen for him to be born into a Jewish family, he might have been the most extreme Jew. The same goes for Jews who could have been born as Palestinians. Without Christ, these complex identities are a source of rivalry and hatred, culminating in the suffering we see around the globe."

"So you're blaming God?"

"On the contrary, it's our inherited nature as human beings who sin that drives us into conflict with God and each other. Let me put it this way, our earthly identities become assignments rather than measures of value. My value as a person is secured in Christ's love for me. My mission as a Christian is to share His love with all those around me. I want to understand what

God wants me to accomplish with this identity and how I can fulfill His purpose for my life."

"Okay, I get it. Your faith allows you to be more accepting of others. I admire that. But how do you live as an Arab citizen of Israel?"

"The truth be told, the flag of Israel does not represent Arab citizens, and it's impossible for me to connect with any sentiments expressed in the national anthem. To be candid, my existence in the land of Israel represents a problem for many people. To most of the Jews and the Israeli government, I am an Arab, whether Christian or not, who does not belong to the Jewish state of Israel. To the Muslim Arabs in the land and throughout the region, I am a Christian who they consider to be an infidel and a polytheist. And to the rest of the world, I am a foreigner who they may not trust.

"So maybe to summarize in the best way I can, as an Evangelical Christian Arab living in Nazareth, I am a minority, within a minority. I'm neither wanted in the country of Israel, nor welcomed among the Arab nations."

Rashad paused to lift his head a little and then turned his eyes toward the wall on his left. On that wall hung photos depicting colonial Nazareth placed beside images of national politicians. Rashad turned back to Mike and said, "In many ways, as Arab Christians in the Holy Land, we live without a place on this earth that can truly be called our homeland. In reality, our only home is heaven, where Jesus went to prepare a place for us."

Rashad's penetrating sincerity touched Mike's heart. He had expected a more cagey, theoretical response, the kind of answer he had received in much of the time he had spent in Israel. Rashad's response disarmed him, leaving him full of respect for the man in front of him.

Mike sat back to look at Rashad with admiration. He seemed to have an answer—a response that Mike couldn't seem to anticipate. He could only wonder where Rashad and his family had gained such hopeful expectations. Mike was impressed with the fact that this was not wishful thinking on Rashad's part. This was his reality. This Jesus, of whom he spoke so freely, was real to him.

Mike knew that Rashad could easily be filled with resentment and anger or self-pity. But instead, somehow this man possessed a generosity of heart and love that Mike saw as genuine. Mike sensed that Rashad carried a liberty within himself that seemed unbound by governments or people and their prejudices. In this moment, he realized that he had much to learn from this man and his family.

As Mike processed his thoughts, the servers came in and out, continuously exchanging the empty salad plates with full ones and bringing more pita. Mike appreciated their expertise in quickly disappearing, balancing the empty plates on one arm, and reappearing with more plates filled to the brim.

Mike and Rashad both took a moment to scoop some hummus onto the pita they had torn into smaller pieces with their fingers. With his fork, Mike took a few more bites of his salad selections, thoroughly enjoying the savory tastes he experienced but wanting to reengage Rashad rather than focus on eating. He took a sip of his lemonade to clear his throat. "It sounds like you're pretty isolated in the midst of all this."

"You could say that." Rashad seemed to Mike to be perfectly at ease in his response. "As Arab believers in Christ we're a bit of an enigma for many in the world. Especially for the western church, particularly when conflict arises in the Middle East that is perceived as a threat to the nation of Israel."

"Wait a minute. I thought the church in America loved coming to Israel and supporting the—" Mike paused as new insight lifted the veil covering his own understanding. A slight smile shown on his face. "If I'm hearing you right, you're saying that the focus of the church in America is on Israel and the Jewish state. The problem is, they're not quite sure what to do with Arab Christians?"

"Exactly. It's hard for Bible-believing Christians living in the West to reconcile the promises given to Abraham about the land with us living here in it."

"So how does that work?"

"Let's take church tours for an example. When they come from the West to visit Israel, they focus on visiting the sites where Jesus taught, and they celebrate that the Jews have a homeland to call their own. If they encounter Evangelical Christian Arabs here, their minds must then wrestle with how to include us in the

Church universal. Usually, they begin to ask where we stand in God's covenant with Abraham and the land. What is ironic is that *we* point *them* to the Bible where the Lord speaks clearly about this issue."

Mike responded with a look of amazement. "Wait a minute. You're saying the Bible addresses this somehow?"

"Absolutely. The prophet Ezekiel, in the Old Testament, is used by God to tell the people of Israel, 'You are to distribute this land among yourselves according to the tribes of Israel. This is the land God promised to Moses.'

"But then he adds, 'You are to allot it as an inheritance for yourselves and for the aliens,' Arabs and others, 'who have settled among you and who have children.'" With a broad smile, Rashad added, "And here's the part that many people don't recall. God then told them, 'You are to consider them as native-born Israelites.' And get this, He then says, 'Along with you, they are to be given an inheritance among the tribes of Israel.' He even adds, 'You shall not mistreat them. The stranger who dwells among you shall be to you as one born among you, and you shall love them as yourself.'"

"Let me get this straight. You just said that the Jews are to consider non-Jews, Arabs in this case, as fellow citizens? Is that right?"

"That's what the Bible says."

Mike chuckled. "Rashad, you have to be kidding. Nobody I can think of talks about this. So, where do *you* stand about the land?"

"We have no dispute over the land as God describes in His Word."

Mike stared at Rashad in dismay. "I'm not doubting what you just said, but it sounds so counterintuitive to what is happening here."

"I know it does. The promise in the Bible is that, through Abraham and his lineage, salvation would come to the entire world. This promise is fulfilled in Jesus Christ. And for those who believe in Him there is neither Jew nor Arab—we are all one in Christ Jesus, His body, the Church."

Mike looked over at Bashira.

She nodded in agreement. Her smile beamed with the radiance of kindness. Then she spoke. "There's a saying about the church tours that come to Israel: They come to see the *dead stones* but they fail to see the *living stones*, the Christians who live here. Don't get me wrong; we are delighted that they come. They see firsthand the sites they've heard of in the Bible and become so enamored with the ancient ruins. What they often miss, though, is us, their Arab brothers and sisters in Christ who are still living in this land."

"It's a dilemma for them, for sure," said Rashad, "but look at us here; we are talking so much you've barely touched your food. I apologize, everyone. I'm getting so engaged with this conversation that I'm not being a very good host. How's everyone doing? Do you need anything?"

Jack appeared to be enjoying every bite. He spoke up, after quickly swallowing, "I'm doing great."

Mike hadn't yet eaten much of his food. He had concentrated instead on listening to Rashad. "We're fine," he said, glancing at Jack, shaking his head with a look of wonder regarding how the guy could eat so much.

Mike took a bite of his salad and looked up at Bashira who smiled back. Her smile nearly took his breath away. *She is so lovely*, he thought and wondered if there would ever be a time where he could talk with her alone?

Then Mike wondered what he had gotten himself into. He could see that Rashad held a tremendous confidence in what he believed. He wanted to hear more but felt uncomfortable engaging with Rashad's honesty. He wondered if he could maintain his objectivity.

Mike fell silent and leaned back from the table. He needed a moment to soak in what he had heard. The servers scurried about preparing for the next course of the meal. This gave Mike his moment—a moment of contemplation in which he tried to process all that Rashad had shared. He knew in his gut that he was about to enter a story he had never heard before.

Chapter 19

ELDER BROTHER

Mike was puzzled. Preferring to enjoy the company of friends and a good meal, he instead felt uneasy. A disturbing intensity had settled upon him and left him wondering where this conversation would go.

Noura broke into Mike's train of thought by asking if he or Jack would like more to drink. "The next course is arriving," she said.

Servers placed on the table a platter of kebabs, barbecued meats, and chips (thick French fries). The kebabs of lamb and beef were arranged with their metal rods piercing a center stand. This gave the effect of the meat forming a grand, round, flowering display. Jack's eyes bulged with delight. All Mike could think about was how he would be able to take another bite. He just wasn't hungry, but he didn't want to offend anyone. *Perhaps another question could buy me some time,* he thought while making some room on his plate to at least sample the kebabs.

"Enjoy!" Dalia said to Mike and Jack.

Jack's eyes remained bright. "What a feast."

They all joined in to help move the plates around to accommodate the variety and quantity of the meats on the table. Everyone made their selections. Jack sampled a bit of everything.

Mike looked past the new setting of plates and food. He shook his head a bit. His voice took on a tone designed to bring the conversation back to the sort of reality he could comprehend.

"Rashad, I hear you saying that God can make everyone in this land get along, but from what Jack and I've seen, there doesn't seem to be much evidence of what you're talking about. It's a mess on both sides, wouldn't you agree?"

With a twinkle in his eye, Rashad responded without hesitation. "You know, Mike, my grandfather had a saying in our family that we cherish. You may have heard this from the time you spent with my father. The words describe the hope we carry in our hearts. It goes like this: The only way for Ishmael and Isaac to find peace together is through their elder brother Jesus Christ."

Mike looked a little puzzled, and Jack stopped eating to hear more.

"Let me help explain what he meant. God promised to give Abraham a multitude of descendants—one of whom would be the Messiah. We believe this is Jesus

Christ. The issue was that Abraham's wife, Sarah, was barren. So he took his wife's handmaiden to bear his first child and named him Ishmael. The problem now was that Abraham had acted on his own volition to receive a divine promise. However, God came to Abraham years later, in his very old age, to give him the son of His promise. Abraham named his second son Isaac. The Jews trace their lineage back to Abraham through Isaac. God, though, also promised to protect Ishmael who began the lineage of the Arabs.

"What this saying means is that there is only one means of true and lasting peace between the descendants of Ishmael and Isaac. It comes solely through God's one and only Son, Jesus Christ, their elder brother, Who broke down the wall of separation between Abraham's offspring through His atoning sacrifice upon the cross. From that moment on, everyone who believes in Jesus is a member of His Church universal where Christ reigns supreme as the Prince of Peace. There is no longer Jew or Gentile. We are all one in Christ Jesus."

Mike couldn't deny that Rashad believed what he just said, yet this miracle of unity seemed to him so improbable as to be a pipe dream. He raised his eyebrows to concede. "Well, to be frank, the Son of God is about the only one who could make this kind of unity possible."

Rashad leaned in closer to the table, and, with excitement in his voice, said, "We've experienced this firsthand."

Mike responded incredulously. "You're kidding?"

"Before this Second Intifada began, the Messianic Jewish community, those who believe Jesus is the Messiah and Arab Evangelical Christians gathered together for fellowship, worship, and the teaching of God's Word."

"Messianic Jews?" Mike sat back as he repeated this phrase, emphasizing each word. "Wait a minute. You mean there are Jews who believe that Jesus is the Messiah?"

Jack looked up at Mike after swallowing his most recent bite to give him a shrug of his shoulders that indicated he wasn't familiar with this term either.

Rashad's excitement had now become sheer joy. "Oh, how I wish my good friend Yosef were here. Yosef is a Messianic Jewish believer in Jesus. We met years ago at one of the outdoor gatherings in the Lavi Forest. During those times, those who followed Jesus from all walks of life would gather there to worship the Lord.

"On one of those occasions, I kept hearing this young Jewish man respond to the guest speaker with such enthusiasm. Afterwards, when the meeting began to break up, I decided to introduce myself.

"Here we were, two young men whose lives—separated by race, culture, and history—were suddenly thrust together, acknowledging a common bond—the Savior of the world. After only a few more minutes of conversation we exchanged phone numbers and shortly thereafter met again.

"Over the next several months, he told me his story—how he had been traveling after his time in the army, reflecting on what he'd seen and done in the service and wondering what the future might hold for him. It was a time of wrestling with who he was and of deciding what he could do with his life. He then met some Jews in Turkey on holiday. They struck up a friendship, and Yosef discovered that these Jews carried a marvelous joy and peace about them that made him curious.

"He was shocked to hear them talk about Jesus as the Messiah. They referred to Him as Yeshua Hamishiach and to themselves as Messianic Jews. At first, Yosef couldn't believe what he was hearing. He resisted everything they said. In his mind, he fought back with his logic and reasoning until a young believer simply said, 'Yosef, you can't come to Yeshua with just your mind. You must give Him your heart.'

"Yosef describes the moment as though the words pierced his soul and destroyed all his resistance. The next thing you know, he's a born-again believer in Yeshua, sharing his testimony of receiving the good news of saving grace with everyone he knew."

Mike stared at Rashad as though he was hearing a strange tale set in a reality totally unfamiliar to him. *This just doesn't happen*, he thought.

"Over the years we continued to get together. In fact, Bashira would accompany me on many of these occasions. She patiently listened as we talked about our lives in Christ and the challenges we both faced living in the land as believers in Christ."

Mike glanced quickly over at Bashira who smiled, nodding her head in acknowledgment.

"You'll have to meet him one day and let him tell you the whole story." Rashad had a glint of tears in his eyes. "Those were times of sweet fellowship in the Lord," he said softly. "We lived it, Mike. It was an amazing time of unity. We long for more."

Mike became uncomfortable with this unexpected show of emotion from Rashad. He desired to get back to the facts at hand. "But it sounds as though this gathering was something that happened in the past. Are you not meeting now? What happened?"

A look of sadness came over Rashad's face.

Bashira spoke. "It's the Intifada." Mike turned to listen. "It split us apart."

Mike's heart leapt for a split second as he looked at Bashira. He heard her voice, but it was difficult for him to comprehend what she had said. Each time he looked at her, he could barely take his eyes off her. Now he felt his own emotions rise, wanting to carry him away. For a moment he was lost, absorbed in her beauty, and had to pull himself back to keep from staring at her. Acknowledging what he felt taking over his heart, he glanced at Bashira once again. *Are my feelings toward her more than attraction? Am I in love?* he wondered. This thought made him nervous. He had to get refocused. Recovering his senses as best he could, he said, "What a shame."

He immediately realized his words seemed an unfitting response to the look on Rashad's face and certainly for what he could see in Bashira's eyes. He tried again to recover. "What I mean is—I would have loved to have seen one of those gatherings. I can only imagine what it must have been like to have everyone together—out in the forest."

His words felt like dribble containing nothing of real value. He wanted to learn more about what drove Rashad and his family to live their lives the way they did. He could tell that Rashad held a genuine belief, something that he couldn't fully understand but did respect. His upbringing in a nominally Methodist home had not prepared him for the living faith that Rashad and Bashira possessed.

Mike glanced around at all the people at the table. He realized he had dominated the conversation by engaging with Rashad and wondered why the others were not exasperated with his endless questions. He was grateful to see in their faces that they appeared to be enjoying every moment, especially his colleague who was preoccupied with another helping of kebab.

Rashad then said to Mike, "You've hardly eaten. I feel bad about keeping you away from the food."

"No," Mike said, "thank you for putting up with my questions. We have a saying in the states when something powerful is coming our way: It's like drinking from a fire hose."

Rashad displayed a large grin. "I apologize for turning the valve on full."

Everyone chuckled.

"The problem is once I get started asking questions it's hard to stop," Mike said.

Jack nodded his head vigorously. "You got that right."

A scowl crossed Mike's face as he looked over at Jack and then back at Rashad. "Well, you certainly have been more than patient."

"My pleasure. I hope some of it is making sense."

"It does, but I must admit that even though I struggle with the terrible things Jack and I have seen reporting the news, we've also witnessed some good—people sacrificing themselves for others despite incredible danger. Doesn't this count for something? Few people here agree on who God is in the first place. So where do we start?"

Rashad took his time to respond. He looked at his plate and took a sip of his drink. After setting down his glass, he said with compassion in his voice, "You're right. We've all witnessed extraordinary, selfless deeds. The issue, though, from a Biblical perspective, is that mankind's inability to live in peace with one another begins with the fact that we've offended our creator, God Almighty. We continuously disobey two of His foremost commandments: to love the Lord God with all our heart, soul and mind and to love our neighbors as ourselves."

Mike interrupted. "Are you saying there is nothing good in us that merits God's favor or approval?'

"Only if we could follow His commandments in absolute obedience. Don't get me wrong, I agree that we can act at times with kindness from a sense of duty to others. Yet none of these acts by themselves measure up to the standard of perfect obedience that God, in His holiness, requires."

"That sounds impossible." Mike allowed his cynicism to show.

"It is."

"Well then, what's the answer?"

"God's incredible mercy and love. I heard a pastor once say that God's holiness permeates every aspect of His character. This means He must act in accordance with His holiness, yet God cannot think, speak, or act in any way that is not loving."

Mike winced a little, shook his head slightly to indicate his confusion and took another quick glance around the table. He lifted his left hand upward with his fingers extended outward in a gesture to indicate he was baffled by the last comment. "But if God is so offended, and we're so corrupt, then there's no hope."

"That's right if it weren't for Jesus. He is the perfect representation of God's love. He gave His life so that we could have peace with God and with one another. He is our only means of gaining this living hope. That's the whole point of my grandfather's saying."

"So, if you don't mind, let me try and get this straight. It sounds like God is this supreme judge who declares that we're all guilty of disobeying Him. And because of this, we turn on each other and face the judgment of a penalty we can't pay. Right? Yet, because God loves us, He gives His only Son to pay the penalty so that we can obey Him and love one another?" Mike's eyes grew wide as he finished his last statement.

"That sums it up about right," said Rashad. "It's a matter of eternal consequences: either life eternal through the grace of God by receiving Jesus as our Savior and being able to love God and one another, or eternal suffering in hell for rejecting so great a salvation."

Mike bristled at Rashad's statement implying that God required something of him. Yet he knew his host and those around the table were sincere about their beliefs. It was an uncomfortable moment. He had heard, and had discounted, this message before. But now, something about how Rashad spoke captivated him. His thoughts began to swirl. His reporter's instinct usually led him to listen more objectively to what he heard. Although when it came to religion, which he saw as personal, he could quickly become defensive. In matters of believing in God or not, he lived by the motto: To each his own.

His objections centered around the thought of there being a place where people suffered forever. He pushed back against the whole idea. *Even if all this is true, it still makes no sense that God would punish those who do good*, he thought. This proposition stood at the core of his thinking: There must be some good in the earth that merits a reward in and of itself.

Mike tried to keep his emotions in check. He believed strongly that human beings all had some form of goodness within them, even though in his own experience he had seen very little of it. He believed that bad people simply existed because of their own choices. His pride rose to defend his own philosophy of life. He was a reporter after all. His mission was to cover the atrocities of war by informing others of the facts surrounding these horrors. In doing so he looked for acts of kindness and sacrifice to share with others so that they might become inspired to see the humanity within it and support those who were being oppressed.

Rashad had just told him that what he venerated as "goodness" had no real value. This thought both alarmed and disheartened him. Much of his life's work and thinking were being challenged at a level he'd never experienced before. Yet it seemed to Mike that this understanding brought a deep sense of peace to Rashad and his family. *Could all this be true?* he wondered.

Mike didn't believe that the nature of mankind was predisposed to suffer for eternity, but Rashad was his host, and there was Bashira. He certainly didn't want to appear argumentative, so he resisted the urge to disagree with Rashad. It was clear, though, that Rashad and his family had discovered something deep and secure in their own lives that addressed this dilemma of sin as Rashad described from the Bible. They had already discussed more of the Bible than he ever had. He certainly couldn't ignore how Rashad and apparently everyone else at the table, except Jack of course, had a genuine love and respect for the Bible.

Mike took a few bites of the barbecue he had hardly touched. He smiled at Bashira and Noura and commented how wonderful the food was. Jack continued to devour what was left in front of him. The atmosphere around the table remained cordial as Noura spoke softly to Dalia in Arabic and Rashad called a waiter over to clear his plate. Mike seized the moment to explore one more question rising in his mind.

"This whole time you have constantly referred to the Bible. I mean, to accept what you are saying, a person has to believe that the Bible is true, right?"

With a giant smile, Rashad responded, "Yes, absolutely."

In a curious way, Mike was enthralled with the fact that Rashad and his family actually believed the Bible contained the words of God Himself. He took another bite of the meat sitting on his plate from which he had removed the skewer. The taste reminded him that in all their talk he was missing out on an amazing meal.

Rashad touched his lips with his napkin and returned it neatly to his lap. "The reason we believe God speaks through the Bible is that He tells us heaven and earth will pass away but God's Word will last forever. Let me put it this way, God places the Scriptures at the core of His reputation and is committed to abide by what He has said and promised; because it's impossible for God to lie."

Mike realized now that the Bible not only formed the bedrock for what Rashad believed but also served as the foundational guide for how he conducted his life. Mike could not grasp his commitment to God's Word, but he felt respect for Rashad. Mike's doubts about who God is and what He has said in His Word could remain but clearly none existed for the man in front of him. Mike could sense envy rising within his heart as he began to consider what life would be like if he held such conviction. Nonetheless, his nature was to question everything. He looked around the table, resting his eyes upon Bashira for a moment and then turned back to Rashad. "So, if one were to ask, where is the evidence for what you are saying?"

Without a moment's hesitation Rashad said, "The resurrection."

"The resurrection? Wait a second, why the resurrection? Sorry I don't get it."

"If there's no resurrection, there's no Christianity. The resurrection is essential to the gospel. Without the resurrection, Jesus is just a man and God's Word is not true."

Rashad's enthusiasm brought a smile to Mike's face. Mike could not deny that he saw something utterly real and life changing in this family, yet something remained bewildering to him. "Well, one thing for sure, I would have loved to have been around and reported on that event."

Everyone around the table nodded in agreement. Even Jack stopped eating for a moment to say, "And man, if I could have caught that on film."

A peaceful air of silence settled over the luncheon table. Mike became aware of the sound of the conversations at other tables throughout the restaurant. Rashad took a sip of his water and a few more bites of the meal.

Mike looked around again at the photographs on the walls displaying the history of this city through the memories of significant events. He needed another moment to take in all that Rashad had shared. Rashad's description of God seemed illogical to him, but what he knew of and had seen in Rashad's life proved that he was a man of integrity.

Mike's appetite had picked up while he listened to Rashad. He finished his kebab and French fries. He pushed his plate toward the center of the table, took his napkin off his lap to wipe his mouth, and set it on his empty plate. *What a luncheon this has been*, he thought to himself.

Noura interrupted. "If everyone is done with their meal, we would like to move to a great place right around the corner near Mary's Well for dessert and coffee. It has wonderful outdoor seating."

"I'd love to walk a bit," Mike said. "I'll see if I can possibly find room for dessert. But coffee for sure."

Jack added, "I'm game and looking forward to both."

Noura said, "Gentlemen, I have to get back to work since we have some deadlines to meet. It has been wonderful spending time with you. Please do come again. Rashad, Dalia and Bashira will be your hosts from here."

Chapter 20

MARY'S WELL

Stepping out into the bright sunlight awakened everyone's senses. They walked past rows of outdoor cafés. The savory smell of flavored tobaccos produced by several groups of men smoking hookahs on the outdoor patios drifted through the air. Sounds of laughter from small groups of young people mingled with the tobacco smoke and gave a sense of light festivity to the atmosphere. They soon came to the site of Mary's Well. In front of them, on the opposite side of the open square, stood the Greek Orthodox Church of the Annunciation.

Of course, the area had changed dramatically since the time of Jesus. Back then, Nazareth was a small village inhabited by subsistence farmers. Now the city bustled with small shops, tourist attractions and thousands of visitors from faraway places who had come to see where Jesus grew up and to honor the Virgin Mary.

Rashad led his guests to one of his favorite cafés. Once again, the owner greeted him on the patio with great affection and beckoned him to have a seat. Rashad motioned to the group to enter and stepped aside, allowing everyone to find their way to the table made available for them. They all took their seats around two tables that had been pulled together and began to look over the desserts on the menu.

"This café," said Dalia, "is known for its great variety of desserts. If you like, we can order an assortment so that you can try several of them."

Jack answered quickly. "Sounds great to me."

Mike heard Dalia, but he was more concerned about whether he'd worn out his welcome by asking so many questions of Rashad. Rashad ordered several desserts from memory and Arabic coffee for all.

A few moments later, the waitress began laying out before them a fabulous assortment. Each dessert looked delicious to Jack who couldn't wait for the others to make their choices. He piled up a bit of fruit and slices of various pastries and cake on his small plate. "These look awesome," he said, finding a spot on his plate for one of each variety.

Mike looked at him and rolled his eyes. "Where do you put it all?" he asked.

Jack took his first bite; a giant smile of gleaming satisfaction came onto on his face, spanning from ear to ear.

Mike selected portions of a few desserts from the table. He then set the plate down and looked once more to Rashad.

The waitress brought water for everyone. She began clearing some of the small serving plates. Dalia helped by handing several of them to the waitress.

Rashad took a bite from his own plate of desserts. He turned toward Mike and said, "I'm thinking that it's no wonder you do so well in your profession. Your questions are fascinating. It's a challenge to do them justice."

"I don't know how good the questions are, but it's not every day that Jack and I get to be with someone that's as patient as you in answering them."

"Thanks. I hope you at least get to enjoy some of your dessert. I kept you talking way too much over lunch."

Mike looked down at his plate and took a bite of the *kanafeh*. Its rich sweet taste was remarkable. He found himself immediately reaching for another bite as the sugary texture melted in his mouth. The sun, temporarily hidden by the large cumulous clouds floating above, now covered the square and its surrounding buildings with warm clear light. For the moment, everyone delighted in savoring each bite of their delicious pastries.

Mike's focus shifted to the indistinct conversations of the people walking about the plaza. The sound of their voices filled the air around the café with a pleasant sense of place and peace. He was enjoying his time with Bashira's family. He felt comfortable with them. Somehow their presence caused Rashad's answers to make sense.

Mike continued to wrestle with the contrast between what he was hearing and what he had experienced in the region. He remained troubled, though, that he did not understand how Rashad and his family could have such peace and confidence amid the daily turmoil in which they lived. He had to ask, "Okay, Rashad, so as we say in the States: How does the rubber meet the road? I mean how do you live out your faith in this environment?" Mike caught himself feeling more frustrated than he wanted to be.

"Only through the love of Jesus, Who told us to love our neighbor," Bashira said.

Hearing Bashira's voice caught Mike off guard. He turned toward her, losing himself in the beauty of her soft eyes. He remembered how she had faced all the trauma in Bethlehem—the struggle with the soldiers, the demands at the hospital, the loss of Amal, and the fact that her grandparents were still recovering from their injuries. She seemed to him to be a living example of the words she spoke.

"Your neighbor?" Mike's eyes studied Bashira's face, looking for any hint of possible feelings she might have toward him. The pause only took a moment, but his gaze remained transfixed until he came to his senses and said, "I wonder in this setting, who is your neighbor? Everyone around your family seems not too neighborly." Bashira's eyes showed no reflection that he could interpret other than her kindness.

"That's true," said Rashad, "and it was no different in Jesus' day. In fact, He asked the same question to those around Him: 'Who is my neighbor?'" Rashad left this question open, suggesting that it still needed to be answered.

At the sound of Rashad's voice, Mike forced himself to tear his eyes away from Bashira. "Okay, then how do you define who is a neighbor?"

"Imagine if Jesus were speaking today, which neighbors would He be talking about—Jordanians, Syrians, the Lebanese? They might be our neighbors. For those living in the West Bank, whose neighbors are they?"

"You got me," said Mike with a grin. "I can't imagine what Jesus might say now?"

"The same thing as He did back then; He would tell a story—a parable. Let me retell the one He shared as an answer to this question in the context of today. Imagine a Jewish man injured and lying by the side of the road. Everyone passes him by, including pastors and rabbis, until a young Palestinian comes along. He takes the man in his arms, carries him to a hospital, tells the staff to take care of him and that he will return soon and pay the bill in full."

Jack blurted out, "That's the story of the Good Samaritan."

"Exactly!" said Rashad. "The point is that Jesus makes very clear that even our worst enemy is our neighbor. This is the love of Christ in action, or as you said, 'Where the rubber hits the road.' Those who once hated each other can now love one another. Not because we loved God but because He first loved us. Through the life of His Son living in us we're made new and able to love one another."

＊＊＊＊＊＊＊＊＊＊＊＊＊

Mike let silence reply for him. He needed time to allow Rashad's words to sink in. He saw that what Rashad and his family understood about God allowed them to possess a remarkable depth of love. They showed no hesitancy in their explanations, only confidence in what they understood to be true. Mike had never seen a group of people who could live their lives with such liberty to love others. Now the thought that this way of living was possible tugged on his soul. He could only wonder how someone like himself could have such assurance.

He took another bite of his dessert. The exhilarating taste continued to simply amaze him. The waitress had served the coffee. He took a sip to complement the rich flavor. A slight breeze circled about the café table caressing each one in its cool embrace. As he sat basking in the stillness of the afternoon, he felt the sun's warm rays on his shoulders. He didn't know what a holy moment might look or feel like, but he thought that in this setting something sacred had unfolded. It felt to him more like what he imagined church would be if silence was the only proper response from a person who stood in the presence of a holy God.

He knew that his feelings were real. He also knew that if he allowed himself to go much further, he would have an opportunity to discover the nature of the God who Rashad had described. The reality of Rashad's faith warmed his heart, but he was still hesitant to believe that such a declaration of good news could be available to everyone. He did not accept Rashad's claim that he, along with so many others he knew, were without hope except in Jesus.

Mike had nothing more to say. He knew that Rashad and his family had some special understanding of who God was and how a person might come to know Him. That knowing remained distant from his comprehension, yet he could appreciate fully the way in which they shared their beliefs. He could not deny that their faith in Christ was at the core of their being and that the Bible was the instrument that guided their thoughts and actions. Mike felt that he had been talking to people who had actually been with Christ, the Jesus of the Bible. For him, one thing was sure; this was a pretty special family.

Mike looked at Bashira. She smiled back at him. Certainly, from the moment he first saw her, he had seen something special in Bashira that had caught his attention. His attraction to her had grown steadily since the day they first met. He tried to grasp any connection between the reality of what he had heard from Rashad and the feelings he had toward Bashira. He knew he couldn't sort it out in this moment.

The waitress came back to see if they had any further requests. Rashad gave her his credit card to pay the bill.

Mike looked at his hosts and said, "This has been delightful. Thank you. I can't speak for Jack, but I've learned more about being a Christian during our time together than I have in a lifetime of living back in the States. Don't get me wrong; that's probably my fault for not listening very well, but one thing is for sure, it didn't sink in, certainly not with the impact it's had on your lives. If you and Bashira keep this up, you'll be making Christians out of us yet; although, I don't know about Jack, he may be too far gone."

They all laughed, except Jack, who gave Mike a hard stare quickly followed by a grin.

Jack's phone rang. He placed it to his ear and his face became serious. "Okay, I'll tell him. It looks like he had his phone off while we were at lunch . . . Yeah, we'll be careful . . . Okay, I got it. We'll call you back."

Jack leaned toward Mike. "Mike, that was Dennis. A suicide bomb was detonated in the cafeteria at the Hebrew University today. The place was packed with students studying for their final exams. Dennis says it's awful. A bunch of folks are injured and many are dead. He wants us there right away."

They all heard Jack's message. The reality of the world they lived in had come crashing down upon them and would now bring an end to their time together. Mike reengaged with this reality. He thought, *Peace and good will among men. Not hardly, not where I'm headed.* He and Jack had to be on their way.

The news brought a solemn end to a delightful day. They all walked in silence back to Mike and Jack's car. Mike spoke first. "It's been wonderful being with you all, and I'm sorry we have to leave." Mike had a clear sense of sadness in his voice.

Rashad put his hands on Mike's shoulders and said, "Thank you for coming. It's been our pleasure."

With a look of concern on her face, Bashira said, "Be careful. We will be praying for you both."

Mike looked at Bashira. "Thanks. We'll be in touch."

Mike opened the car door on the passenger's side and got in. Jack started the car. They both waved and pulled out into the street to head back to Jerusalem.

Chapter 21

TROUBLE IN IRAQ

ashira, Rashad and Dalia watched in silence as Mike and Jack turned the corner. Bashira let out a sigh. Rashad said to Dalia, "I have some things I need to get from the office. Are you okay driving home from there? I'll drive the van home when I'm done."

"Sure," Dalia said. She looked at Bashira with concern before getting into their car. Rashad held the door for her. Rashad then opened the door to the back seat for Bashira.

They drove through the busy streets in silence. Rashad looked at Bashira in the back seat through the rearview mirror and said, "Are you okay, little one? You were pretty quiet during the lunch."

Bashira turned her head from looking out the window. Her face portrayed the concern she held within. "I was praying nearly the entire time. What you shared, *Amo,* was amazing. Then, this horrible bombing." Bashira fell silent.

Rashad continued to maneuver the car through the winding streets. "I feel the same way, *habibti.*"

They soon arrived at the warehouse. Rashad asked Bashira to stay to help him. "We'll see you in a little while," he said to Dalia, giving her a tender kiss on the cheek before she drove the car home. He and Bashira entered the warehouse, walked through the front reception area, and went directly to Rashad's office.

Once inside, Rashad gathered various papers on his desk and put them into his briefcase. He paused to look up at Bashira. "Do you mind my asking— is there something else troubling you? Is there more regarding Mike?"

Bashira looked as though a bright light had suddenly exposed her deepest thoughts. Although she felt safe with her uncle, she was embarrassed to realize that she may have somehow revealed her feelings even while they still confounded her.

"I don't know what to think. I'm confused by my feelings about Mike, except for my desire for him to be saved. For some reason, another emotion keeps growing stronger. I mean it's crazy to even be the slightest—" Bashira paused. Her words hung in the air as though she were about to say something so private that only the Lord and her trusted uncle could hear.

She continued hesitantly. "He's a world-renowned journalist and I'm a nurse in Bethlehem. I know it's not right to think of Mike in some romantic fashion, especially when he's not saved. I'm trying to sort all this all out, and I sure don't want anyone to think that Mike has indicated anything to me that warrants these thoughts and feelings."

Rashad took a seat behind his desk in his high, worn-leather, wingback chair.

"Why don't you sit down, *habibti*." Bashira sat in one of the chairs in front of his desk. "Let's face it. Mike is a nice person. I like him a lot. He's reached out to our family and helped us in so many ways. And of course, it's obvious he's fond of you. How could that not be the case?" Bashira blushed. "It's hard to not get caught up in the emotions of all this. My point is you don't have to worry about the outcome or even what comes next. God is faithful to direct you and we can trust Him to have His way, both for you and Mike."

Bashira's eyes glistened with tears. "*Amo*, if anyone could tell what is going on inside of me, it would be you. I feel so foolish. The last thing I want to do is get drawn into some romantic fantasy that, God forbid, interferes with His saving Mike and Jack. So, like you said, I'm going to cry out to the Lord that His will be done and follow Him wherever He leads."

Rashad began to straighten a stack of files on his desk. He looked up once more at his beloved niece. Bashira drew comfort from the kind expression on his face. "You know," he said, "you can speak to me at any time about this or any other thing that might be on your heart.

"Are you going to be okay?" Rashad asked. Bashira sat up straight with her head raised, revealing the broad smile he so often saw on her face. He rejoiced in knowing that she was at peace.

"I'm fine," said Bashira. "We better get going, though. I don't want to be late for dinner and in trouble with Aunt Dalia." Rashad came around the desk as Bashira rose to give him a hug.

"Get your things and I'll meet you down by the van," he said with his own trademark smile.

∞∞∞∞∞∞∞∞∞∞∞

Just then Rashad's mobile phone rang. He looked down at the name on the screen and back up at Bashira.

"*Habibti*, it's Faraj in Iraq," he said with a quizzical look on his face. "I'll have to take this."

"Sure," said Bashira. She waited to find out why Faraj had called.

Rashad answered the phone with enthusiasm. "Faraj, what a pleasant surprise. It's been so long since we last spoke. It's great to hear from you."

Bashira could hear Faraj's soothing voice coming through the phone. His name meant "joy after sadness" and his personality fit his name. Bashira and Rashad had spent many days and nights at his home in Iraq with his lovely family. They had hosted Rashad and Bashira on their trips to deliver medical aid over the years. He had not only looked after their comfort while they were with him, he and his wife had also escorted them to meet the Christian leaders and many of the villagers in the surrounding area, all of whom were struggling to survive.

Today, Faraj had not called to get reacquainted. "Yes, my friend, I wish it were better times and I could give you a friendly call, but to tell you the truth, things are getting much worse than when you were here last. I need to talk with you."

"Please, my friend, it is good to hear your voice no matter what the circumstance. Bashira is with me, also."

"Oh, give her our love. Every time she is here, she brightens so many lives, especially the children."

"I will. In fact, I'll put her on speaker phone." Rashad pressed the button on his phone and held it out toward Bashira.

"Hello Faraj."

"Oh my, Bashira. It's so good to hear your voice. I wish we were all together."

"Me too."

"Now, my friend, what can I do for you?" said Rashad.

Faraj described to Rashad the current conditions they were facing in Iraq. "I'm sure you may have seen some of this on the news, but questions about the regime developing WMDs are growing each day. The West is convinced that Saddam Hussein is hiding them. The UN inspectors are not allowed into certain sites, which only heightens their suspicions. Rumors are everywhere that it won't be long until America tries to force the hand of the Iraqi leadership to open more inspections. It looks like we're heading into another war.

"In the meantime, Christians are becoming scape goats for the animosity people feel from their losses in the Gulf War. It's becoming outright persecution. Christians are leaving in droves for Jordan, Syria, and elsewhere. There is no telling how many of us will be left if we don't begin to bring in aid before another war begins. When you were here last, we were barely able to carry on from the last war, and now the West and the regime are locked into an intense standoff. I fear for our brothers and sisters in Christ."

"I'm so sorry, my friend," Rashad said. "We are getting some news, but nothing like this. How may we help?"

"That is why I called. I know you have been focused on your own problems, but with your international connections we could use your help organizing some medical relief for those in the North. You've been in the area before. In fact, that's where Bashira has done most of her work with the children. If we could get some supplies in to replenish what is either gone or remains at extremely low levels, it would at least prepare some of us for the worst to come. I'm not asking you to bear the burden yourself; rather, could you contact some of those you know who are able to care and get them in touch with us? We would welcome anything you can provide, but most of all we need your support in getting the word out to others. Then, perhaps, some folks may be willing to come and help disperse what supplies we can get. We can work with the Red Crescent, as we've done before, to get items into the country. The other issue will be getting our people some medical help and possibly training."

At hearing the need for medical staff, Bashira tried to get Rashad's attention. He continued to concentrate on the call; the connection proved to be weak, causing Faraj's voice to cut in and out. Rashad didn't see Bashira's efforts. She tried once more and then passed him a note. It said: I'll go. How soon would they need me?

Rashad read the note while listening to Faraj. When it registered on him that Bashira was offering to go, his eyes crinkled with a smile. While continuing to listen to Faraj, he shook his head and mouthed, "Not this time. Your mom and dad would kill me."

Bashira slumped back into the chair, her arms crossed and her head cocked slightly to the side, listening intently to every word Faraj said.

"Faraj," said Rashad with confidence, "let me get to work on this. It will take me a while to contact some people, but I'll start right away. We may be able to contribute some items ourselves and spare some help."

At his words 'spare some help,' Bashira pointed vigorously to her chest, saying with a big smile, "Me!" Rashad did not acknowledge Bashira this time. He concentrated on the voice at the other end of his mobile phone.

Faraj said, "My friend, I knew I could count on you. May the Lord guide you and bless you in whatever you can do. I will be out much of next week in areas where the cell service may not be so good, but don't hesitate to reach out with a text or call or leave a voice message. I'll get back to you as soon as I'm in a service area with good coverage."

"No worries, my friend. I will be in touch. By God's grace I look forward to seeing you soon. Many blessings to you and your family. Please give my greetings to everyone."

Bashira tried frantically to get Rashad's attention. This time he looked at her. She mouthed, "And me!"

Rashad added, "And Bashira sends you all her love and will be praying."

"Give her our blessings," Faraj said. "We'll talk soon. Goodbye."

The call ended. Rashad pursed his lips and stared at the phone. Bashira had not seen this look often, but when she saw it, she knew it was not a time to interrupt his thinking. By the look in his eyes, he was preparing to act.

Rashad looked up at her as though waking from a dream and realized once again that they might be late getting home for dinner.

"*Habibti*, we have to hurry," he exclaimed. "I lost track of the time. Let's go!"

Rashad grabbed the remaining stack of files, stuffing them into his briefcase as they both raced out the door and scurried down the stairs. They jumped in the van and drove away with a slight squeal of the tires as Rashad accelerated anxiously.

Bashira giggled. Her uncle caught her eye. They both laughed out loud.

Rashad worked his way through the winding streets as quickly as possible. Arriving at their home, he skillfully parked the van in their narrow garage. He turned off the vehicle and opened the doors. Grabbing his briefcase, he spoke under his breath, "Well, here we go."

At the top of the stairs, they found Dalia, her arms crossed, a frown on her face, and a stern look in her eyes. The scowl upon her face dissolved into a broad smile as Bashira gave her a big hug. Rashad followed them inside, watching Dalia hold her niece tight around the shoulders.

Chapter 22

THE UNIVERSITY

Mike and Jack made their way through the crowded streets of Nazareth. Due to the urgent need to return to Jerusalem as quickly as possible, they decided to take the more direct coast route south through Afula on Route 65, connecting with Highway 6 and merging onto Highway 1 that led into the heart of downtown Jerusalem. Fortunately, traffic would be light as they approached Jerusalem; at this time of day, most people would be exiting the city.

The drive normally took about two hours, but Dennis, the WBN producer, had directed them to get there as fast as they could. Jack took liberties that pushed the limits of both their speed and their safety. Mike and Jack were fully aware that, because of the bombing, tensions would be heightened and surveillance by both the Israeli military and the Jerusalem police would be increased. Fortunately, their press credentials gave them the ability to move through the city to the university even if they were stopped along the way.

Mike made the entire trip lost in thought. He tried to process the great conversation he had just had with Rashad in light of the trauma that he knew awaited him. He recalled how Rashad had said something like "sin is at the heart of all evil and suffering in the world." *This bombing sure proves evil exists,* Mike thought. *And we're about to see it firsthand.*

This assignment was not going to be like the war correspondence he had previously covered in the region. The battles he'd seen, even the raid on the apartment with Calev's platoon, were gruesome all right, but these operations were sanctioned by the government of Israel. They were an official act, undertaken by soldiers trained and committed to carry out orders. In the face of battle, the loss of life and all the horror surrounding war was to be expected. Covering war became part of the newsperson's professional objective experience— reporting on outcomes from a strategic point of view.

This event was altogether different. The lives and well-being of innocent students, staff, and faculty, along with their families, were now unwillingly thrust into the endless cycle of violence and retribution. Mike felt a sudden surge of bitterness and anger rising in his heart. *When will this all end?* his frustrated mind screamed within his head!

They continued on their way, welcoming the silence that had settled upon them. Mike knew that Jack was steeling himself for filming what would be a horrific scene. Filming carnage required a certain amount of detachment to capture on camera what the viewer would see to experience the horror for themselves. Jack performed well in these situations, and Mike didn't want to disturb his mental preparation.

As they neared Jerusalem, the traffic seemed to grind along more slowly than they had expected. Entering the city center, they could see the flashing lights of military and police vehicles ringing Mount Scopus and the university. They would be there soon. Their job would be to report the facts, no matter how gruesome the details might be, so that the world might know what had happened. Mike clenched his jaw in anticipation of what lay ahead.

◇◇◇◇◇◇◇◇◇◇◇◇◇

Mike thought he had prepared himself for the scene at the university, but he was wrong. Combat was bad enough; randomly targeting university students was beyond the pale.

This site was intended for learning, designed to be a center for the discovery of life and identity surrounded by others who shared similar dreams of accomplishment. Here young adults from nearly every corner of the world invested themselves in the next phase of their lives, gaining the knowledge necessary to move forward with hope for the future. But now, this place had become a reluctant battleground, a funeral pyre upon which those hopes and dreams had vanished in the flame of an explosion. In its aftermath, only the ashes of sorrow and mourning remained.

Jack, in his stoic professional manner, let the camera capture the awful scene. It was as though they had entered a hallowed space where words had lost their meaning. The cries of those around them rose into a cacophony of languages that became one single voice of anguish.

Amid the torn bodies of Arabs, Jews, and Americans, the distinctions of color, race, or creed no longer mattered. Only hours before, the students had been sitting together in laughter and study. Now, they were an indistinguishable mass of bloodied body parts. The sights and sounds and smells of the scene offended the senses. In the continuous wail of sirens and flashing lights, the cleanup crews searched to find and collect all of the bodily remains. The smell of flesh and blood nearly overwhelmed Mike. *This isn't an act of war,* he thought, shaking his head in sadness and disgust. *This is terrorism at its worst.*

Mike then gathered his composure and collected himself.

He said to Jack, "We have to go on air, bud. Are you ready?"

He knew the question was unnecessary. Jack would be ready. He asked it only to remind them both to focus on their job—to report from this horrific site what needed to be seen and heard. Jack shook his head "yes" and turned toward Mike.

"Ready," he said as he counted down silently with his fingers—three, two, one.

⬦⬦⬦⬦⬦⬦⬦⬦⬦⬦⬦⬦

Now that Rashad and Bashira were home. Dalia could recognize something more was on the mind of her beloved husband. Her admiration for him shone in her eyes. He could be late for dinner at times, but he always had a good reason. Today was special enough that she didn't care all that much. "Let's sit for a few minutes while a couple things are heating in the oven. I made a light dinner after all that lunch."

Rashad placed his briefcase near the door and walked into the living room. He sat in his favorite chair. Bashira sat on the couch. Dalia sat next to her and put her arm around her. "So what do you two think?" she asked. "I thought the lunch went well, and *habibi*, what you shared was wonderful."

"Thanks," said Rashad.

"I wanted them to get saved and baptized right then," said Bashira.

"That's exactly the way I felt," Dalia responded. "I was on the edge of my seat at one point thinking, oh my, this is the moment, they can't help but respond to the gospel."

"By God's grace, we sow the good news; the Lord reaps," said Rashad.

Dalia squeezed Bashira's shoulders. "Yes, and He will do a great work." Dalia got up from the couch. "I'll check on the dinner. Bashira, *habibti*, after you get cleaned up, could you help me set the table?"

Dalia left the room. Bashira sat for a moment, and then, before heading toward the kitchen to help her aunt, she asked Rashad if he would like her to turn on the TV.

"Yes," he said, "that would be great."

The devastation they saw on the television screen left them speechless. The scene at the Hebrew University in Jerusalem, filled with medical emergency workers treating the wounded and carrying away the dead, startled them. They could only stare at the TV in shock over what they saw. The commentator indicated that Hamas had laid claim to the suicide bomb and confirmed that the bomber had detonated himself during lunch time in the crowded university cafeteria while the students were on campus for their final exams. The deaths now included four Israeli nationals and five foreigners from the United States. Over one hundred people were seriously wounded.

Bashira clasped her right hand across her mouth as the camera panned over the destruction. Rashad sat, gazing at the screen, his furrowed brow the only outward sign of the grief he felt rising up within him. Dalia came back into the room. She gasped as she stared at the TV in horror and placed her hand on Bashira's shoulder.

The commentators ran through a litany of condemnation from the world's leaders including the UN Secretary and President of the United States. One statement from the university president summed up the shock felt by everyone in the room as he said: "Diversity lies at the heart of the Hebrew University, a model of co-existence between Israeli, Arab, and other students from around the world since it was founded in 1925. But this bomb did not discriminate, and more than a dozen nationalities, including Arab students, were among its hundred or so victims."

The news coverage was on every channel and echoed the sentiments of the UN Secretary who called upon "all concerned to end the cycle of violence, revenge and retaliation."

"Bashira," Rashad said, "would you change the channel to WBN? I want to see if Mike and Jack are covering the scene?"

Bashira quickly changed the channel. The video cycled through individual scenes of the event as the camera panned across the destroyed cafeteria and then focused on Mike. He began his report:

> "I am on the site of the suicide bombing at the Hebrew University in Jerusalem where an explosion today took the lives of Arab, Jewish, and American students. Other students from around the world were severely wounded in the blast and have had their lives changed forever. Israeli medical emer-

gency teams have treated the wounded and taken them to nearby hospitals. Several are in critical condition tonight while their families await news of their recovery.

"Hamas has claimed responsibility for this act of terror that took the lives of six women and three men. The explosion injured nearly one hundred other students from all over the world, all between the ages of eighteen and thirty. The bomber detonated the device in the crowded university cafeteria during lunch time while students were on campus for their final exams.

"Nations around the globe have condemned today's act of terror. The government of Israel vows to hold accountable those who committed this abhorrent act. The Palestinian Authority has also condemned this bombing, while blaming Israel for pursuing a policy they describe as destructive.

"While governments condemn, cleanup crews remain working through the night gathering what bodily remains they can find. This site where learning is exalted and inclusion is cherished will now retain memories of the sorrow of this day as people bury their loved ones along with the hope that a resolution to this conflict will come soon. In the meantime, more anguish and suffering has been heaped upon this region as many pray for the peace which seems a long way off.

"This is Mike Olson, reporting for WBN from Mount Scopus at the Hebrew University in Jerusalem."

The camera swung wide over the decimated site, which only a few hours earlier had been the scene of youthful enthusiasm. The report then switched back to the studio for its own commentary on the horrific event.

"'More anguish and suffering,'" Bashira spoke softly. She struggled to process the events of the day. The recent memory on Mount Precipice with her uncle came to mind like a flashback. In helping her work through the pain of Amal's senseless death, he had also helped her understand that these acts of hatred emanate from the heart of mankind. She shook her head in an attempt to tear herself away from the scene on the TV before her. Time would determine how much more agony this land would have to endure until the people turned their hearts to Jesus.

Have mercy, Lord Jesus, she prayed silently.

Bashira slowly rose to help her Aunt Dalia prepare the table while Rashad sat silently before the TV.

Chapter 23

CONVICTION

After dinner, Bashira helped Aunt Dalia with clean up, said goodnight and went off to bed. Rashad walked into the kitchen as Dalia put away the last set of dishes. He reached into the refrigerator to retrieve a bottled water and sat down at the kitchen table. Dalia noticed from the way he sat that there was something more on his mind than his thirst.

She turned towards him and said, "Obviously, there's something you want to talk about. It's probably not anything I'll want to hear, so let's get on with it."

Rashad said, "Sit down, *habibti*."

Dalia pulled out a chair across from Rashad at the table and prepared herself to hear what was on her husband's heart.

Rashad recounted for Dalia the phone call with Faraj. Dalia was familiar with this region of Iraq since Rashad and Bashira had been there several times before. She knew how fond Rashad and Bashira were of Faraj and his family along with many others in the community. It became clear to Dalia, though, that the burden Rashad felt was not only for the plight of Faraj and the community in Iraq. She sensed Rashad carried something more.

Then Rashad spoke of Bashira. He shared how excited she became at the thought of being part of the team to deliver the supplies to Faraj.

"Initially, I was against her going," he said. "I thought it was too soon after losing Amal. But, as I thought about the expression I saw on her face and the excitement in her voice, I could tell she wanted this opportunity to serve the Lord.

"I know the final decision will be up to her and the family. The problem is I'm going to be tied up with the preparation and coordination of the aid. Someone needs to be on the ground in Iraq to assess the need and help organize the transfer. Bashira is perfect for the job."

Dalia knew that her husband was processing his decision out loud and needed to express the thoughts of his heart. Over the years, this was the way they worked best together when facing important decisions. In this case, though, the risks Bashira would be taking would not only affect her but the whole family as well. She wanted to be a good sounding board for her husband so that he could examine his thoughts before the Lord and make his decision for Bashira's sake. Dalia learned a long time ago that if she would just let him think and talk, the answer would come.

Rashad took a drink of his water and, staring at the table, added, "Frankly, there is no one else I can turn to right now who knows the area and the people like Bashira does. What troubles me is not whether she is capable. The issue for me is the timing. I don't want to stand in her way if she has faith that the Lord is calling her to do this."

Dalia could see how this decision weighed heavily on Rashad. She knew he would examine and prepare the best he could for all the risks regardless of who went; but in this case, the candidate was his beloved niece. She realized that whomever he sent would have to travel alone until he could follow shortly thereafter.

Dalia continued to listen. Her desire was to support her husband. To accept a decision by Bashira to go would be a challenge for them all, but the real question now was: Is this the right time for Bashira? *It certainly would be wonderful for the people,* Dalia thought. *But is she ready?*

They both loved Bashira more deeply than a niece. To them, Bashira was the daughter they never had since children were not one of the blessings Dalia had received from the Lord. Rashad continued to stare at the table. Dalia gently reached out her hand to grasp his.

"Beloved, we've been waiting for this moment for a long time. It looks like our little dove is ready to fly once again. I don't pretend to know all that God has in store for her, but if He wants Bashira to go, then God forbid that we would get in her way."

Rashad placed his hand over hers and gave it a tender squeeze. He looked up at her and said, "I was probably more concerned to mention this to you than to my brother. I know how much you love her. I needed to hear what you thought first.   God knows that He gave me the greatest gift in you—and then in this lovely niece of ours."

"Well," Dalia said, "one thing we know is that God loves her more than either of us. We've seen her heal in our home, and we know He is faithful to complete in her what He's begun. We have to trust in His perfect will for her life."

Dalia slid her hand away from Rashad's tender grasp and got up from the table. She turned back toward the sink, folded her dishtowel and laid it on the counter.

"I'm off to bed, *habibi*. Don't stay up too long."

Dalia knew Rashad had much to pray about and would come to bed when he was through seeking the wisdom of the Lord.

<hr />

Once comfortably tucked underneath the covers, Bashira still could not get the shocking images on the TV out of her head. A deep sigh of grief over the incident at the university came rolling out from her spirit as she contemplated the individual lives taken and the crushing impact their families would feel at their loss.

She grasped the necklace her grandfather had given her and held it loosely in her fingers, gently rubbing her thumb up and down the pendant. She had worn the image of the ichthys smooth through the years of holding it in this way as she prayed. This early symbol of ancient Christianity served as a constant reminder of God's love for her and for others. She wore it constantly, even as she slept. As she held the pendant now, she couldn't help but recall her own pain and sorrow of first losing her sister and then Amal. Grief tried to rip open her wound. This time, though, rather than spiraling into an abyss of sadness and despair, she welcomed the relief of knowing that they were both in God's eternal presence. His love both exposed and cast out the fear that tried to make its way back into her heart. Instead, a peace beyond understanding gave her the strength to pray for those suffering through this most recent tragedy.

She looked over at the lamp on the nightstand beside her. It shined its light on her Bible lying at its base. A small hand-written journal lay underneath her Bible and a pen lay beside it.

The scenes on the television kept playing out across her mind. She felt an intense connection with those young people and their families.

She knew exactly what it felt like to be in such pain and sorrow. Her longing now was for their agony to not imprison these families as her own agony had imprisoned her. She knew that this endless cycle of anger and hatred would trap many others into seeking vengeance while being caught in the merciless grasp of bitterness. A shudder shook her body as she recalled the pain and sadness that had gripped her soul over the loss of Amal. She then imagined herself back on Mount Precipice, looking out over the Valley of Jezreel, wishing she could have these others share in her liberating experience.

Bashira stared silently into the stillness of her room. She knew what liberty felt like. *How many more like me could You set free if they only knew of Your mercy and kindness, dear Lord? But how can they know if no one tells them?* The treasure trove of scripture she had stored in her heart began to open. She recalled what the prophet Isaiah had said when he heard the voice of the Lord asking, 'Whom shall I send, and who will go for Us?' Isaiah had responded, 'Here am I Lord. Send me!'

As if a sudden shock awoke her senses, she thought, *Are you sending me, Lord?* The question was sincere. Was she being asked to go somewhere to do something? She thought of Faraj and the call that afternoon. Of course she was willing to go to be with him and their friends, and hoped that would be the case, but was that the issue now? Was there something more?

Bashira whispered with a slight glint of tears in her eyes, "Oh Lord, that I may be willing to go wherever You wish—to the ends of the earth, if that—"

"Oh my," she caught herself saying, "to the ends of the earth. That sounds so grand. What about right here?" *Lord, am I hiding out here in the safety of my uncle's home while others are suffering around me?* she thought.

Peace, like a warm blanket, settled over her as she answered her own question in her mind. *We're to be ambassadors of Christ and commanded to take up our cross and follow Jesus.* The reality of these words of scripture made it abundantly clear to Bashira that it didn't matter where He would lead her; she was to follow with the assurance of His promise that He would never leave nor forsake her. This promise emboldened her resolve to obey and honor Him.

Chapter 24

RECONCILIATION

*L*ooking up at the ceiling, now too excited to sleep, a smile born of profound insight beamed across Bashira's face. How could she not be His ambassador, especially now that His love had set her free? She was now free to share the love of Christ—the only love that matters and the only hope for humanity.

Bashira sat up in her bed, grabbed the notepad on her nightstand and wrote: For this is love, not that we loved God, but that He loved us, even when we were His enemies.

She continued to write: God is love and there is no fear in love. We love because He first loved us and nothing can separate us from the love of God.

A singleness of mind and clarity settled over Bashira. She knew that God had a calling for her life, but He was now leading her into something more specific. If she was to be His ambassador, was there something in particular He wanted her to say and do?

She wrote in her journal again: Ambassadors of Christ. She paused to think and added these words: Ambassadors of Reconciliation for Ishmael and Isaac through Jesus Christ.

She set the journal down and thought about how God had reconciled her to Himself through Christ and committed to her the work of reconciliation. This was the hallmark of unity in Christ that the world might know Christians by their love one for another. *We are baptized into Christ. There is neither Jew nor Greek*, she thought.

Now with a sense of urgency, she grabbed her journal and wrote: All who are baptized in Christ are one in Him.

She knew the Lord was speaking to her. Her heart and mind stirred with excitement as she began to explore what God would have her do.

She recalled when she was first baptized. It was a day to celebrate how old things had passed away and all things had been made new. She remembered how excited she was to publicly declare that she was born again and how wonderful it was to openly indentify with the death, burial and resurrection of Christ. Her only desire had been to tell the world about the hope that flooded her soul through the love of Jesus.

Suddenly, like a flash of lightning, the thought came across her mind. *That's it! What if I could publicly rededicate my life to You, Lord, like when I was baptized.* The idea was exhilarating. *I could invite my family, friends and other believers in the area.* Her thoughts burned like a fuse racing ahead to ignite the explosion of joy building in her heart. "It could be a day of unity celebrating Your love for us all, Lord," she said out loud.

Bashira then leaned back against the headboard of her bed, basking silently in the thoughts of what such a celebration might look like. She smiled, remembering her uncle at lunch describing the times in the forest when he and Yosef and their friends would assemble in one accord to worship the Lord. Then she spoke out her next thought. "But wait a minute, I've already been baptized. What am I thinking?"

Bashira knew that the baptism she had experienced as a young girl was genuine. It had been an outward expression of her faith in the inner work Jesus had done in her heart. She knew that the Holy Spirit had sealed her salvation and that His sanctifying work would continue in her life until her last breath. Forgiveness from the Lord was not based on her being rebaptized. He had forgiven her once and forever on the cross, and her forgiveness of her enemies on Mount Precipice restored her fellowship with Him.

Bashira found herself talking out loud to the Lord—a natural, prayerful conversation knowing that He was listening to every word she said. "But Lord, this wouldn't be a baptism in the traditional sense. That baptism was once and for all." She stopped speaking for a thoughtful moment and stared into the night. "This could be a rededication ceremony—an event where I proclaim how You restored my soul by setting me free from my bitterness and anger." Scriptures echoed in her mind: *For those the Lord sets free are free indeed. Free to love one another so that those around us may know we are Christians by our love.*

Then, as if the crest of the wave that had overtaken her was now retreating, she uttered a realization of practicality. "But how and where could this occur. Who could perform the baptism? This gathering would need to represent the Body of Christ, not just my family." She thought about this dilemma for a minute or two. "Of course," she exclaimed, nearly shouting. "*Amo* and Rabbi Yosef could do it. They could perform the baptism together. They're perfect for this. Rabbi Yosef and, God willing, his congregation could join us at the Jordan River."

A smile beamed across her face as she thought how well these two men would represent both communities in the church. A furrow came to her forehead as she pressed her lips together in determination. *I need to go talk to Rabbi Yosef,* she thought.

Bashira felt closure had come to her. The Lord's spirit of wisdom and revelation had brought her peace. She tenderly placed her Bible and notepad back on the nightstand, settled back against her pillow and turned off the light.

Gazing out her bedroom window before drifting off to sleep, Bashira imagined the setting on the banks of the Jordan River where she was first baptized. She tightened the covers around her and envisioned a bright sunny day with young and old alike gathered by the river.

Who knows what God might do, she thought. But for now, she knew what she must do—reach out to Rabbi Yosef. She could hardly wait. Blessed sleep welcomed her into a restful night as she dreamed of the day to come by the water's edge.

∞∞∞∞∞∞∞∞∞∞

In the morning, Bashira awoke to hear sounds already coming from the kitchen. Dalia bustled about, preparing breakfast. Rashad read his Bible at the table. Bashira got up, raced down the hall, turned the corner and embraced her uncle from behind, saying breathlessly, "*Amo*, you won't believe what happened last night."

Rashad stopped what he was doing and turned to face her.

"Okay. Sit down. Let's hear all about it."

Bashira's face gleamed with excitement as she recounted for him what the Lord had revealed to her during the night. A look of joy came on Rashad's face as he listened intently to every word his niece was saying.

Bashira could barely contain herself. "I know it sounds outrageous, and I'm not sure what Rabbi Yosef will say, but *Amo*, I know this is what I need to do. And, if he agrees, it would be such a witness to the community. Think of it—a young Arab woman surrounded by her family as she rededicates her life to

Jesus with the blessing of a Messianic Jewish rabbi who also loves Jesus!"

Dalia gasped, grabbed her head and turned toward the table. She cried in a loud voice, "You and your uncle are talking crazy."

Bashira and Rashad looked up at her as though they suddenly realized there was someone else in the room.

"Seriously you two!" continued Dalia. "Do you realize what you're saying? You are asking our dear friend to call more attention to himself and his congregation by having him baptize you. He already has enough problems with the Orthodox Jewish community. On top of that, you want the rest of your family and our church to be there?"

Both Rashad and Bashira looked at each other and then back to Dalia.

Bashira sheepishly replied, "Well, it seems like an opportunity to publicly proclaim how Ishmael and Isaac—"

Dalia turned her head, looking first at Bashira and then directly at her husband for some sign of support. Their silent stare was her only response, to which she replied, "I know, I know—Ishmael and Isaac will come together only through Jesus."

Everyone was silent for a moment. Dalia stood there, wringing the dishtowel she held in her hands.

Rashad reached out to take his wife's hand. "*Ruhi,* what if, in this ceremony, everyone gets a small glimpse of how we are all really united in Christ?"

"Yes, but at what risk for everyone?" she answered. "And think of all the pressure this would put on our family as well as Yosef and Bashira."

Rashad drew his wife in closer, putting his arms around her. Bashira looked down at the table. There lay Rashad's Bible, opened to one of the verses she had read last night. Dalia started to tear up. She reached her hand out to rub Bashira's shoulder. Bashira placed her hand on Dalia's.

"It sounds like this could be something special for us all, but is it wise at this time?" Dalia said.

"The timing is not ours," Rashad replied. "If it's God's will, we simply need to obey."

Dalia pulled a delicately embroidered handkerchief out of her apron pocket and used it to dab the corners of her eyes. She kept her other hand on Bashira's shoulder. Rashad leaned in toward the table and grasped Bashira's hand. She looked up at him.

"Bashira," he said, "this won't be easy for any of us, but go ahead and reach out to Yosef. See if you can get together and share your heart with him. Let's see what the Lord does. In the meantime, I'm planning to go to Jerusalem this morning to see how Mike is doing. I'm sure he could use a friend right now after what he's seen. Let's pray for Mike and your time with Yosef, believing that God can do exceedingly abundantly beyond all that we may ask or think."

They closed their eyes. Rashad led them in prayer.

Chapter 25

THE AFTERMATH

Rashad left after breakfast. He had called Mike the night before, and they had planned to meet at the Christ Church Coffee Shop near the Jaffa gate in the Old City of Jerusalem. This was one of Rashad's favorite places to meet, having hosted many guests from around the world here. He loved to stay at the guest house across from Christ Church—the first protestant church in the Middle East—on trips that required an overnight stay in Jerusalem. Fortunately, Mike was also familiar with the coffee shop. Even with the heavy traffic in the area both he and Mike would have an easy time getting there.

Mike arrived first and ordered his coffee while he waited for Rashad. He hadn't slept much after reporting on the scene at the university the day before. Rashad arrived shortly thereafter. He walked up to Mike, bearing his kind smile.

Mike stood and said, "I'm glad you came, but I'm sorry it's under these circumstances. Please sit." He pointed to the chair across from him.

The coffee shop hosted a contemplative, open-air atmosphere—small tables set up in a courtyard adjacent to the ancient walls of the city. Jerusalem was quiet now, tentatively resting in an air of unsettled peace. The aroma of fresh baked goods and coffee filled the air.

"Thank you. I'm glad we can meet. Everyone sends their love and prayers." Mike hoped to hear that Bashira had mentioned him. His experience of the bombing had left him disconnected from even his own emotions. He had fallen into an emotional stupor. Grasping for a touch of humanity that might bring him hope, he thought that hearing of Bashira's concern for him might be the lifeline he needed to pull him free from the despondency and despair he felt. He wondered if he could ever feel again without this taint of sorrow and anger hanging over him.

"Would you like some coffee?" Mike offered in a monotone.

"Sure," said Rashad as the waitress walked up. She spoke to him in Hebrew asking what he would like. He responded that he'd love to have a cappuccino and a piece of poppy seed cake. "What about you?" Rashad asked. "I see you have a coffee. Would you like another one?"

"Another coffee Americano, please," Mike told the waitress.

Rashad smiled and nodded toward the waitress as she retreated. "So how are you, Mike? After watching your broadcast, I can't imagine how awful it must have been for both you and Jack."

"Yeah. Jack keeps things inside and does his job, but I could tell he felt this one was tough."

"And you?"

"Me?" He looked up at Rashad. Then he looked away, giving himself a moment to collect his thoughts and wrestle through how he could possibly describe what he had seen.

"To tell you the truth, it tore me up inside. I mean, I've reported on a lot of awful things, but this one has been the most difficult—such a senseless act of terror. I can't get the scene out of my mind."

∞∞∞∞∞∞∞∞∞∞∞∞

The waitress brought their coffees and set them on the table. Taking Mike's empty coffee cup, she went back to get the cake and a fork for Rashad.

Rashad spoke softly. "You know, Mike, it's not far from here where Bashira's sister and husband were killed in another suicide bombing."

Rashad paused to honor the sobriety of the moment. He felt it was important to let his words sink in so that Mike would know the family was intimately familiar with this kind of tragedy. "Their deaths tore at our souls for a long time. It became especially difficult for my brother and Bashira. It fell to them to raise Amal."

Mike shook his head, looking down again at the table, and responded, "It's as though this country knows no end to bloodshed. Like Amal—just another example of this endless killing."

Rashad focused his gaze on Mike. He wanted to assure him that he was not here to give glib answers to horrific problems. Speaking softly, he said, "I don't envy you having to report on what you saw. Frankly, I don't know how you do it. I know it's your job, but it has to be—" Rashad let the sentence hang in the air and shook his head. He couldn't place himself in Mike's shoes and there was no reason to try and imagine what Mike had seen. It was simply too awful. He came to offer healing to this young man's heart. They both sat in silence, sipping their coffee.

Then Rashad spoke. "As I was driving down today, I couldn't help but think that the evil carried out on that campus is exactly the reason Christ came to this very city."

Mike winced and looked aghast. Rashad could see that he had touched a deep nerve in Mike. He sensed Mike struggling to try and keep his emotions under control as both the tone of his voice and his demeanor changed. "How can you bring Jesus into this mess? If you were to say that God is anywhere in the midst of this, I'd have to challenge you to show me. Give me, and all the families who have lost so much, some proof that He somehow cares."

The anguish on Mike's face was palpable. Rashad recognized the look. He understood the feeling of sorrow he saw in Mike. He'd experienced it himself and witnessed it many times before in others. He knew that the weight of agony felt by those who suffered through these tragic events could cause them to fall into a bottomless chasm filled with anger and bitterness. Suffering could consume a person's soul with hatred, making it impossible to climb out of the pit under one's own power. Rashad knew that his response in the next few moments would have a crucial impact on Mike. He had to choose His words carefully and yet speak the truth in love as the Scriptures demanded. In that moment, Rashad prayed a simple, short, silent prayer: *Lord, help me.*

"The proof," said Rashad, "is the cross. It's why Jesus came—to save us from sin like this barbaric act of terror. It's evil that stems from our deceitful hearts."

"Wait a minute. You're saying that what Jack and I saw on that campus is an act that reflects what's in *our* hearts?" Mike's look revealed a deep anger rising out of him as he raised his voice. "This is terror at its most vile level. Innocent people were killed and others were maimed for life. I don't know what was in the suicide bomber's heart, but I do know that families are suffering, some of them thousands of miles away. They sent their kids here to learn. They learned all right. They learned that in this place no one is safe."

Rashad chose not to respond right away. This moment called for his utmost sensitivity. He looked at his coffee, took a sip and set his cup back down, silently praying for direction from the Lord.

Rashad could hear the turmoil in Mike's voice. He knew this feeling all too well in his own life. Rashad's dilemma was how to console Mike in the midst of this tragedy while giving him reason to hope. He knew Christ was the only hope for Mike. Christ's love was no mystery to Rashad. His own circumstances had demanded a similar rescue. He wondered if this could be the time for Mike to come to terms with his own need for the Savior, Who would set him free from the pain of this sorrow. He couldn't know how Mike might respond, but he remained determined to share the only good news Mike could afford to know.

He pressed in. "You asked where God could be in the midst of this horror." He took up Mike's challenge in a somber tone. Mike stared at him with a glassy look in his eyes. "God is in Christ reconciling the world to Himself."

Mike kept his eyes focused on Rashad. His look seemed to demand more of an explanation. "What in the world does that mean?"

"It means God only gives us a few simple commands. He tells us: Do justly, love mercy and walk humbly with your God. Instead, we fail in every way. We deny Who God is and willfully offend His supreme holiness by disobeying His commandments in either word, thought or deed."

Mike just stared at Rashad. He continued, "The problem is the very nature we're born with. Out of our hearts come every evil thought and sinful action. The Bible tells us no one is good. The consequence is that we are separated from God forever if we reject the salvation offered to us by grace through the life, death and resurrection of Jesus."

Mike leaned forward. "You're saying that the only hope for mankind required more suffering, more death and pain, born by God's own Son?"

"Short answer—Yes," said Rashad emphatically.

Mike leaned back in his chair and looked around, shaking his head from side to side, seemingly looking at nothing. Rashad looked down at his plate and back up at Mike. They experienced an awkward moment of silence together.

Then Rashad said, "But, Mike, it's God Who is rich in mercy. As the Bible tells us, it is because of His great love that He sent His Son Jesus into the world not to condemn it but to save us from our sin so that we could love God first and then love one another."

These words seemed to ignite Mike's feelings of agony and despair, producing an explosion of indignation, escalating the intensity of the conversation. He nearly shouted, "That the world might be saved? What was the world being saved from in what I saw at the university? If it's true that humanity is enslaved to our own passions, then there is no hope. We're all doomed."

"True. That really is the point. Doomed, yes, but not without hope. Eternity hangs in the balance for everyone; God Himself provides the only answer."

Mike clenched his jaw and looked down at the untouched coffee in his cup. Rashad recognized the look of pleading for answers that woud not come. He'd seen it so many times before. He had experienced it himself as he had tried to grasp the unfathomable love of God.

Rashad spoke softly and confidently. "Mike, our sense of doom is met with the assurance of hope, an everlasting hope that all who believe in Jesus receive God's forgiveness and that our lives are made new. It's a blessed hope given to us in the reality of Christ's victory over sin, death and the grave. His hope liberates us from the tyranny of sin and enables us to love Him, our neighbors and even our enemies as ourselves."

Mike did not respond. Rashad gave him time to think through what he had spoken. He paused to take a bite of his cake, savoring its flavor. He then placed a heaping teaspoon of sugar into his cappuccino and stirred the mixture slowly.

<hr />

Mike could see by the look on Rashad's face that he shared his last comment with sincerity. He knew this was not some fanciful thinking on his part. Mike could not deny that Rashad and his family both believed and experienced something that was utterly real and life changing to them.

Yet he remained bewildered; he could not understand. Nevertheless, he had begun to envy the perspective that Rashad and his family shared. They all reflected some sort of deep-seated peace and confidence of hope in the face of tragedy that now, considering what he had just reported to the world, seemed so unattainable.

What he had heard from Rashad cut against the grain of his life's experience gathered through reporting the news over the years. His professional obligations required that he sort out the truth from fiction. Over the course of his career, he had developed the ability to recognize genuineness in a person's tone of voice. He could not deny the sincerity in Rashad's voice and the integrity he saw in his life.

Rashad's words, though, sounded foreign to his ears and their meaning seemed impossible to grasp. He knew that mankind could be full of wickedness, yet he thought human beings were capable of doing good things too. But, according to Rashad, without Christ these good deeds were meaningless and the outcome, even for good people apart from Christ, was some terrible judgment and endless punishment.

In light of the horror he had witnessed, Rashad's perspective proved too perplexing for Mike to grasp. What he had seen at the university certainly reflected evil at its worse and deserved some form of judgment. But he heard Rashad implicating him, along with all of humanity, as accomplices of this evil. And furthermore, it seemed to Mike, that Rashad's course of action was to forgive those who had intentionally shattered the lives of so many innocent people. Rashad's words had provoked Mike to defend himself, but he didn't have the strength to respond. A bitter cloud of anguish continued to hover over him.

Chapter 26

ALL THINGS MADE NEW

Mike looked about the courtyard. The sounds and voices of the shopkeepers opening their doors for business demonstrated an act of their hope for the day, hope that business would again flourish after the fear from this tragic bombing was laid aside on the pile of tragedies stacked up over the centuries in this war-torn land.

Hope, he remembered, was the meaning of Amal's name. Mike wondered if all this talk about hope was only sourced in vanity or wishful thinking. The idea of "a living hope" sounded as foreign to Mike as the languages that surrounded him here and was just as impossible to grasp.

He then looked straight at Rashad and said, "Don't get me wrong, Rashad. You speak of hope and good news, but I just don't see much of it here. You and your family are special. I mean, I see the hope and life you espouse, but the good news you talk about may not be for everyone. It's something you all have because you are good people." Though the anger in Mike had subsided somewhat, it remained present in the tone of his voice and his clenched jaw. Rashad responded with a serious look Mike had never seen before.

◇◇◇◇◇◇◇◇◇◇◇◇◇◇

Mike's words "good people" stung Rashad. They hung in the air like the echo of a strident gong, making it clear to him that he had failed to help Mike understand that nothing good resided in him either. Only the miracle of saving grace made him a new man. Rashad was aghast and knew he had to seize the moment to shatter this image of him that Mike carried so that the truth could prevail.

The firm tone in his voice left no doubt of the seriousness of what he shared. "Mike, let me be perfectly clear. What you saw on the campus yesterday is not foreign to me. I've seen it and lived it. I've felt it. My family lost everything in what many Palestinians refer to as *Al-Nakba*. When Israel was established as an independent state, our homes, our property and our way of life were taken from us. The lives of our family and friends were destroyed as the land we lived on for centuries was pulled out from under our feet.

"It may be hard for you to believe now, but then, if you mentioned Jesus to me, I would have cut you off. I cared less. The Jews, along with all those in the

West that supported them, were my enemies. And if you would have asked me then, I would have told you that Jesus was a Jew and that I didn't want anything to do with Him. I was a bitter, angry young man until that great day when, in His lovingkindness, Jesus confronted me with the sin in my own heart."

Rashad saw respectful wonder in Mike's face as he responded, "Rashad, I've not known you long, but it's hard for me to believe you were this other person."

Rashad's eyes glistened with a slight mist of tears; this time the smile on his face reflected a faint memory. His face gleamed with gratitude as he said, "I was that guy all right. I was the perfect example of the one Jesus tells us is guilty of murder when anger and hatred fill his heart. I'm telling you; it consumed me. All I wanted, and all I could think about, was getting vengeance on my enemies and retribution from them for the things we had lost.

"Oh, I never acted out those feelings, but I was still guilty before God and accountable to Him for every thought and feeling of hatred I held in my heart. I knew Jesus taught that anyone who hates his brother is a murderer; I just didn't care. I longed for them to suffer. I wanted revenge."

Mike shook his head slightly, displaying what Rashad understood as disbelief. Rashad felt he needed to press his point further. "It's a fact. Let me tell you, my life was riddled with the same passions and anger that you see all around you. I would tell myself, 'I've not harmed anyone or taken revenge for our loss, so

I'm not guilty of anything.' But I knew deep down that even though I had not acted out the vengeance I longed for, I carried the stench of its bitterness within me and wanted nothing more than retribution. Oh, I was good at hiding my feelings from others. Self-righteousness and pride can put on a good mask. Only God's Word can effectively confront us with the truth that sin reigns in our hearts."

"Rashad, Jack and I have seen our share of sinners and let me tell you, you sure don't seem to fit the mold." He raised his eyebrows in emphasis.

"Well, let me smash that mold for you. In many ways, I was worse than others. I felt I was better than the sinners you are speaking of since I wouldn't carry out the acts I imagined in my heart. But I took the offenses personally. The more loss and bigotry my family experienced, the more calloused and hardened I became. Any injustice only added fuel to my anger. For my father, though, injustice was an opportunity to share the love of Christ.

"He was the real example of godliness in our home. No matter what happened, he was always bearing the fruit of love in Christ to those around us. He believed in the reality of God's promise that our real home is waiting for us in heaven where Christ went to prepare a place for us. And here, as He promised, all things work together for good to those who love the Lord.

"My father could tell what was happening to me, and in his loving way, he told me my real need was for a personal relationship with Jesus. I would bristle at the thought. His words made me angrier. He had raised me in a Christian home. I went to church with him, sang the songs, read the Scriptures and prayed. No one could tell me that I didn't know who Jesus was."

Rashad paused and slowed his pace. He rested his elbows on the table while tapping his fingertips together. "Then it happened," he said softly. "One evening, a traveling evangelist came to our church as a guest speaker. As usual, I really didn't want to be there. But something special happened that evening. The speaker read from God's Word describing how Jesus spoke to the religious leaders who were confident of their own righteousness and who looked down on everyone else, offended by other people's unrighteous behavior. Then he read the parable in which Jesus spoke about two men who went up to the temple to pray—one was a Pharisee, a religious leader, and the other a tax collector. The Pharisee stood by himself and prayed, 'God, I thank you that I am not like other people—robbers, evildoers, adulterers—or even like this tax collector.' The tax collector stood off at a distance. He wouldn't even look up to heaven, but beat his breast and said, 'God, have mercy on me, a sinner.' Jesus said, 'I tell you this tax collector, rather than the Pharisee, went home justified before God. For all those who exalt themselves will be humbled, and those who humble themselves will be exalted.'

"Instantly, I knew that speaker had just described me. I was the Pharisee, decked out in my religious acts, thinking I was justified in hiding my feelings. Yet deep down, I knew that my resentment and anger ruled me. Pride sat enthroned on my heart, leaving no room for anyone else."

Rashad hadn't planned on opening his heart in such a way, but he felt compelled to let Mike understand the man who sat before him now was not the man who he had been. He had become a new man through Christ's gift of salvation.

With a new sense of urgency Rashad continued. "Mike, it wasn't anything in me that night that caused me to change; it was only God's grace that allowed me to begin to see that my pride stood between me and God Almighty. God opposes the proud. Pride goes before destruction, but He gives grace to the humble.

"Here I was in my pride justifying the anger seething within my heart and hiding under a façade of self-righteousness. The words of the evangelist became a blinding spotlight exposing the murder I hid in my heart. I realized I was guilty before God. I could try to continue to hide my heart from others but I couldn't hide from God Almighty. That's when I was able to see Jesus for the first time as God hanging on a cross, paying the debt I owed for my sin. I finally realized I was destined for eternal suffering, and yet, in His great mercy and grace, Jesus had paid the price I owed to obtain the forgiveness I so desperately needed.

"God poured His love into my heart and the chains of anger and hatred simply fell away. I realized then that since I had been forgiven by God, I could now forgive and love others. I experienced the miracle of saving grace. The man I was passed away and everything became new. It was amazing. His life came to live in me. I was born again."

Mike replied, "It sounds so simple when you say it, but that's because it's you. I mean look at this—" Mike waved his hand in a gesture designed to indicate the whole geographical area. "Folks here have been killing each other for generations."

"You're right. Because of the wickedness in our hearts, we've been killing each other around the globe since Cain slew his brother Abel."

Mike's countenance appeared to soften. Rashad sensed that perhaps his words were beginning to make a difference for Mike, as if the weight he carried was being lifted.

The waitress came by once more and asked if they would like anything else.

"Not for me," said Rashad.

"Some water, please," Mike said. "Well, if anything, what you describe is certainly some kind of miracle. New life, as you call it, or at least a new beginning. It certainly stuck with you and your family." Mike shrugged his shoulders. "The problem it seems to me is that we still have to live on this planet where there is plenty of evil and a whole lot of suffering."

"True, believing in Jesus doesn't mean we will have a life without pain or sorrow. You've seen it in our lives. As long as we exist on this earth, there is no escape from the suffering that exists all around us.

"We are no different than those who came before us. The apostle Paul describes his life as one in which he was hard-pressed on every side, yet not crushed. He was persecuted nearly everywhere he went, but He was not forsaken. At times he was perplexed, but not despondent. He tells us he was struck down, but not destroyed. The man was whipped repeatedly by the Jews. He was beaten with rods by Gentiles, stoned and left for dead by his own people, shipwrecked and spent sleepless nights in peril from robbers.

"The point is, he had an eternal perspective. He tells us that his light affliction—Can you imagine what I just described as a light affliction?—existed for a moment and was working to produce a far more exceeding glory, a glory that will be revealed one day in the blink of an eye, and we will be with the Lord forever."

Mike stared at Rashad, nodding his head slightly up and down, signaling he had been listening. "I appreciate what you've said, Rashad." Mike's words seemed soaked in sadness and sincerity. "It's what makes me admire you and your family the most. You have a perspective on life that I wish I could possess. One day, perhaps, I might see things like you do. You have faith. I only have sight for reporting on the reality of the fearsome pain in this region. At times it grieves me to no end."

"Well, you are in good company. Jesus wept over this city. He, too, was a man acquainted with sorrow. He told us to weep with those who weep. He wept at Lazarus's tomb. But then He said, 'I am the resurrection and the life.' He then called out to his friend Lazarus to come forth from the tomb—and he did!

"The point in all this, Mike, is that eternity is a split second away for all of us. It's in that moment that we will face Jesus. We'll either, by His mercy and grace, be received into heaven with His embrace and hear, 'Well done, good and faithful servant, enter into the joy of your master' or be told 'I never knew you' because we rejected so great a salvation and suffer forever without His presence. In either case, every tongue will confess that Jesus Christ is Lord, for there is salvation in no one else and there is no other name under heaven by which we must be saved.

"The question remains: Will we receive the gift of God's love? It's the only essential question in life. The fact is that He's gone to prepare a place for us where there is no more death, sorrow, mourning or tears. The alternative in responding to God's gift with disdain is too horrific to contemplate."

Rashad could see that their conversation had come to an end. He hoped that the Lord would use what he shared to reveal the love of Christ to Mike. Perhaps the seed he'd sown would be watered by others, but for now he prayed silently, *Lord have mercy upon him.* He smiled and sat back in his chair.

Mike struggled with the idea that a person's life could change so dramatically by simply believing in something or someone. But he had to acknowledge that the man in front of him had changed. Rashad clearly was not the same person he had just described. *How remarkable*, Mike thought, *that such a thing could be possible.*

Mike now felt calm but empty. He felt himself in the presence of the inaccessible. The signs of his anguish had been absorbed into the recesses of his professional demeanor. He could not give himself over to believe what Rashad said was true for him.

Mike was silent for a moment. "Rashad, thank you for coming today. I know I've been pretty raw about this whole thing. I promise I'll think about what you've said. And I must say, even though I don't possess the hope you have, your friendship and the life your family lives brings me comfort. Please say hello to Bashira and your wonderful wife for me. Perhaps I'll get to see you all again."

"Yes. You are welcome in Nazareth at any time. Please come. Just give me a call. Let that cameraman of yours know we're praying for him too."

The waitress returned. Mike quickly grabbed the bill as Rashad reached for his wallet.

"No way, my friend. This one is on me."

They both smiled. Rashad stood and reached out his hand to grasp Mike's hand in both of his.

"Until the next time—let's get together soon."

Mike replied in a more formal tone, "I hope it will be soon." He watched Rashad walk away toward his car and then he turned to go.

Chapter 27

NAZARETH VILLAGE

After seeing her uncle off to Jerusalem for his visit with Mike, Bashira raced out the door, feeling like she had been granted new life. She hoped that whatever her uncle might share with Mike would be life changing for him. She could hardly wait for the end of the day to hear how things went, but now she had to get on her way to Nazareth Village. She didn't want to be late.

Bashira had kissed her aunt goodbye and had walked, almost skipping, to the nearby bus stop. When the bus arrived, she got on board and took a seat. Looking out the window at the multi-story homes passing by, she recited Scripture to herself. "'This is the day that the Lord has made, and I will rejoice and be glad in it.'" She felt a new day dawning in her life. She couldn't wait to see what was in store for her.

The bus stopped with a screech of its worn brakes. She got off, thanking the bus driver with a word and a smile. Then she walked up the hill through the parking lot towards the entrance steps to Nazareth Village.

At the landing near the entrance, she turned and looked at the sweeping view of the surrounding neighborhoods below. She paused to look out over the familiar landscape of this city she loved. It seemed as if it had been quite a long time since she had felt this good about herself and the world in which she lived. Squaring her shoulders, she turned and hastened up the steps to the second floor of the building where the Nazareth Village offices and gift shop were housed. At the top of the stairs, she bumped into the director of the village.

"Whoa! I should have known it was you—always in a hurry," said Mary, with a beaming smile across her face.

Startled, Bashira collected herself to apologize. "Mary! I am so sorry. I got excited about seeing everyone and—"

The director chuckled out loud and gave her a kiss on both cheeks. "And they can't wait to see you. They're getting ready for the tour group Rabbi Yosef is hosting today."

They both went into the gift shop together. Mary continued, "It's been a good season for tours this year. This church from America is one of the many groups we've hosted and has been quite a blessing to Rabbi Yosef and his Messianic congregation."

"I can't wait to see everything and everyone," said Bashira. "It's been so long. Uncle Rashad told me about the synagogue being completed and the new olive press."

"Yes, and maybe we can get you into wardrobe. You can be that young maiden waiting at the well once more," Mary hinted with a smile.

Other staff entered the gift shop excited to see Bashira. Three young girls dressed in first century clothing came racing over, giggling with joy and giving her big hugs. Mary stepped inside the checkout area to talk with the cashier. The girls, along with Bashira, made their way toward the back of the gift shop. Bashira looked all around, complementing the staff on the beautiful look of the recent expansion.

In a corner towards the back, an older woman placed items on the shelves. She turned and saw Bashira. Stopping her work, she walked across the room to greet her, giving her kisses on her cheeks.

As they held each other for a moment, Bashira said, "I hoped I would find you here, Adela. How are you?"

"I'm fine—and look at you! As lovely as ever." Adela held a special role at Nazareth Village. Her job was to manage the wardrobe and see to it that the characters were always ready and in position throughout the grounds when tours arrived. The costumes had been designed to replicate the dress in the times when Jesus would have been in Nazareth. She enjoyed her work; it allowed her to interact closely with all the young people and volunteers. In her spare time, she helped out in the gift shop.

Mary heard the two women laughing together. She looked up from behind the cash register. "Ladies, I know you all are glad to see each other, but we have guests coming soon."

Adela spoke. "Come, girls, we'll have plenty of time to visit. We need to finish here and to see if Bashira is willing to help host our group today." Adela gave Bashira an inviting wink.

"Of course. I'm looking forward to it."

"Do you remember where the dressing room is? I'll meet you there. Choose a costume while you wait for me."

The girls giggled again and ran off. Bashira took a last look around the gift shop and headed out the door, following the girls and turned toward the dressing rooms. When she arrived, she began going through some of the wardrobe choices. Adela soon came in behind her.

"We'll have to hurry." Adela started browsing through the costume options too. She selected a simple maiden's costume and handed it to Bashira. "How do you like this one?"

"Very much."

As Bashira started to change into the costume, Adela asked, "How is your family? When we last spoke with Rashad everyone was doing a little better."

"They are, but we miss Amal so much."

Saying those words helped Bashira to realize she had truly begun to celebrate the memories of Amal while accepting the reality of a life without her. She continued to feel the Lord releasing her from the pain of her loss and trusting once again that His plan for her life was good, even in the midst of sorrow.

Bashira finished dressing. She looked into the mirror to adjust the headpiece of her young maiden's costume and moved about freely to check if the garment fit well. She thanked the Lord for the reflection she saw in the mirror, seeing the evidence of His joy springing up inside her once again. Reconnecting with how good it felt to be alive, she celebrated His lovingkindness while she beheld the image of herself transformed by the costume.

Adela opened the door of the fitting booth, placed her hands on Bashira's shoulders and peered into the mirror. "No wonder Boaz didn't have a chance when he saw Ruth. You couldn't look lovelier, *habibti.*"

Bashira smiled. She leaned her head onto Adela's hand. Together they stared into the mirror for one more moment, relishing the strength of their enduring friendship. Adela had been like a second aunt to Bashira during the many years Bashira had spent time in Nazareth.

"By the way, who is this Boaz in your life? I've heard all about some reporter."

Bashira's cheeks began to blush. *How does she know?* she thought.

"You'll have to tell me another time. We've got to be going. The buses are about to arrive."

Glad that Adela had changed the subject, Bashira pulled the garment down lower toward her ankles and tightened the cord around her waist.

"Where do you want me?"

"Where any beautiful young maiden should be— waiting at the well for a reporter. I mean, a possible husband. Oops!"

Bashira blushed again. She knew that Adela could be a persistent tease. Adela laughed out loud, putting her hand over her mouth like a teenager would when caught in the act of revealing a secret. Bashira didn't want to talk about Mike now. She picked up her clothes, hung them in a locker, and hurried out the door heading up the path toward the well.

On her way to her staging point, she saw several large tour buses arrive in the parking lot below.

∞∞∞∞∞∞∞∞∞∞∞

To get to the well, Bashira had to pass by the new Nazareth Village synagogue, an exact replica of a synagogue from the time of Jesus. She stopped to look in. The bright light of the day prevented her from seeing the interior clearly. The only light in the room shown through thin vertical openings in the upper reaches of the wall, designed as windows not to see through but to allow light to enter.

As her eyes adjusted to the dim light, she saw a rabbi wearing his prayer shawl, with phylacteries wrapped about his arms and a kippah on his head. He was davening while reciting in Hebrew, "The Spirit of the Lord is on me, because He has anointed me to preach good news to the poor. He sent me to proclaim freedom for the prisoners and recovery of sight for the blind, to release the oppressed, to proclaim the year of the Lord's favor . . ."

Bashira entered the room quietly and softly, walked up closer to the rabbi and began to speak, finishing his sentence, ". . . then he rolled up the scroll and sat down saying, 'Today this scripture is fulfilled in your hearing."

The rabbi slowly lifted his head and turned toward Bashira. "I know that sweet voice, but I think my eyes betray me." Looking at Bashira, a cheerful smile spread across his face. Rabbi Yosef walked up to her and placed his hands on her shoulders. "The child has become a young woman, and look at you, you've not only grown, but you've also gone back in time." They both chuckled at the thought.

"My uncle sends his love and misses being with his friend."

Yosef nodded. "I miss him as well." Yosef's eyes showed the joy of recalled memories. "What great times we had in our talks together. They were so special. It's these troubled times that have robbed us of such sweet fellowship."

"I miss hearing two wise men as they talked for hours about the Scriptures, the land, and the settlements."

"Yes, and our talks would always end when one of us would say, 'My brother, peace comes to Ishmael and Isaac,' and the other would reply, 'Only through their elder brother, Yeshua Hamashiach.'" As a Messianic believer, Yosef referred to Jesus as Yeshua or Messiah, instead of Jesus Christ, and to the Church as the Body of believers; although, in their conversations, in deference to one another, they both might interchange the names, depending on who was speaking.

Yosef looked down for a moment shaking his head side to side. Then, with a pensive smile, looked up at Bashira to say, "Please give your uncle my warmest greeting. Now, my dear, what in the world brings you here today?"

"To see you." Yosef looked at her quizzically. "I've been talking with my uncle about the loss of Amal. Do you have a moment to talk?"

"Yes, of course. You didn't interrupt me. I've done so many of these tours that I'm as prepared as I'll ever be. We grieved for you and your family when we heard of Amal's death."

"Thank you, and that's why I'm here." Bashira lowered her eyes looking at the floor of the synagogue. Her voice became softer as she explained, "When Amal died, my grief grew into a suffocating bitterness. I was consumed with hatred for those responsible for her death. But Rabbi, by God's grace, I finally realized that my hatred was not only directed toward those who had killed Amal. I also held a deeper anger in me directed toward the Lord for allowing her to die."

Bashira paused and took a deep breath. This confession brought back to her a sense of sadness over how she had allowed her grief to overcome her. And yet, she also felt sweet relief in the knowledge that she had followed through on her commitment to the Lord. She wasn't demanding a response from Rabbi Yosef; she only hoped that he could see what the Lord had done in setting her free from the bondage of hatred.

Yosef looked at her with kindness. "Sorrow has engulfed many of us during this time. Love and forgiveness have become casualties on both sides of this endless conflict."

"That's the point, Rabbi. I want to ask for forgiveness."

Yosef cocked his head. "What do you mean?"

"My anger, Rabbi, festered in me like a cancer. It ate away at any love that I felt for those outside my family. The experience was terrible. I became so consumed that I resented not only the soldiers responsible for the death of Amal, but all other Jews, and I turned my back to the Lord, blaming Him for her being killed."

A flood of emotion welled up within Bashira. Even though it was difficult to share her heart, she had come today to deliver this confession. Sharing this sad truth with Rabbi Yosef was only the beginning of what she believed God wanted to do in and through her. She had to press on.

"The bitterness and resentment grew within me so much that I withdrew from fellowship in the church. Finally, with the help of my uncle, I realized that I had become entombed in what seemed like a sepulcher of bitterness and despair."

Bashira felt relief as she turned the corner on her story. She then told Yosef how the truth had set her free on Mount Precipice and how, by God's forgiveness, she had experienced the wonder of His great love once again.

Yosef set his eyes firmly upon Bashira. "Bashira, of course He forgives you. He loves you, *yakirati,* with an everlasting love."

She could see that he had focused and listened intently to what she had said. This attention gave her even more strength and courage to continue. Tears began to glisten in Bashira's eyes and with new vigor in her voice, she said, "Yes, Rabbi, and in His forgiveness, He reminded me that we are to confess our faults to one another and to ask forgiveness. I couldn't think of anyone better to ask for forgiveness than you. You've been a dear family friend for so many years, and I betrayed that friendship in my heart."

Bashira paused before she continued. She wanted Rabbi Yosef to be able to take in all that she was telling him. Yosef nodded, waiting for her to speak.

Bashira knew she was on solid ground. She felt confidence growing within her. "Rabbi, you know how His Word tells us we are commissioned as ambassadors of Christ. I had forgotten the mission or even the message of the good news. I couldn't be an ambassador of His love while bitterness and hatred ruled me. Yet, when He confronted me with what was in my heart, He not only forgave me; He set me free.

A smile rose across Yosef's face as he said, "Whom the Son sets free is free indeed."

Tears filled her eyes. "That's exactly the way I feel. All I can think about is how I want everyone to know that Jesus is more than able to break the chains of hatred. He can make us able to love each other. We don't have to see each other as our enemy. Today I want to ask you to forgive me for using Amal's death as an excuse to hate the Jewish people."

Bashira let out a sigh and stared into the kind eyes of her uncle's dear friend.

Chapter 28

SYNAGOGUE

People began off-loading from the buses that had just arrived at Nazareth Village. Mary greeted them as they spilled out into the parking lot, pointing them in the direction of the steps. Most of the tourists were Americans. Some were older and had difficulty exiting the bus due to their age and physical limitations. Yet this did not deter them. They displayed a sense of anticipation on their faces; the cameras hanging around their necks and slung over their shoulders swayed back and forth as they made their way up the steps to the reception hall outside the gift shop.

Soon the lead Nazareth Village guide introduced herself to the group and began explaining the layout of the grounds, specifically identifying the sites they would see. Everyone paid close attention to her explanation.

"Nazareth Village was established to replicate a village from the times of Jesus. Based upon historical records and archeological findings, everything—from building construction to apparel—has been designed to recreate, as close as possible, the original look and feel of ancient Nazareth. The intent behind everything developed here is to immerse you in a setting reminiscent of the times of Jesus. Enjoy your experience and let us know if you have any questions."

The lead guide then broke the large tour into smaller groups to give the visitors a more intimate experience as they made their way through the village. A different host led each team along a different route through the grounds.

Each group first saw the audio-visual presentation of the history of the site before starting the tour. Stepping out from the dark theater into the bright sunlight gave the impression that they were transported back in time. They saw people walking about in ancient dress. Sheep grazed in the fields. Shepherd boys watched over them while escorting small donkeys. The tourists looked around to see recreations of ancient buildings rising up from the landscape.

The guides gathered their groups together and directed them toward the path that they would take through the site. During the tour, each group would hear many scriptures within the context of this historical setting. Each host began their group's journey with a recounting of the parable of the sower and the seed.

Yosef looked thoughtfully into Bashira's beaming face. Her words were no longer from the child he had known; rather, these words came from a young woman whose heart had become a fountain of love. As he listened to Bashira, something began to stir deep within him; he wasn't sure if he was prepared for what the Lord was doing.

Is her visit about more than just her asking for my forgiveness? The thought caused him to evaluate the state of his own heart. *What about me?* he wondered. *Are old prejudices and fears driving my behavior? Is this why we've cutoff fellowship from our Arab brothers and sisters?* Yosef lowered his eyes and shook his head with a growing sense of shame. *This is the bride Yeshua died for, and we're tearing her apart.*

Yosef had witnessed the conflict first-hand and knew how the tentacles of pain and suffering had reached out to pull apart the body of believers. This moment became a revelation for him. *Out of the mouth of babes*, he thought. He felt as though a two-edged sword, the revelation of the Lord, had cut through his own insensitivity, revealing a lack of empathy that had made him deaf to the cries of his Arab brothers and sisters in the Lord. He now faced this truth that pierced his soul.

How could this be? He couldn't help but wonder. *Yeshua is to return one day for His bride. Will she be torn apart as we are today, or will He find us loving one another in unity as He commanded us?* Yosef felt a chill come over him at the thought.

What was he to say to this sweet young woman who managed to summon the courage to come and ask for his forgiveness? This was not what he came to Nazareth Village to do today, but he couldn't help sense that this was a divine appointment, a time set aside by the Lord designed to confront him with his need to repent for turning his back on the rest of the body, the Church. Yosef saw that the same resentment, anger, and bitterness had crept its way into his own life, and not only his, but also into the lives of so many others within his congregation.

Am I the one now that needs to ask her to forgive me and all those whom I represent? The moment seemed to hang in time and space. He thought about the circumstances that surrounded him—the dispute over the land and the daily prejudices that arose from this conflict. Had he allowed himself to justify building walls between congregations, breaking down the bond of unity the Messiah had paid for in His death? Yeshua had said, 'By this all men will know that you are My disciples, if you have love for one another.'

The reality behind Bashira's confession resonated within him with such conviction that it could not be ignored. Her words echoed within him, declaring that she was no longer the only one who needed to ask for forgiveness today.

This flood of conviction also brought with it memories of harmony with his Arab friends and gratefulness for what the Lord had done in their lives together. He remembered the beauty of the fellowship he had

had with Rashad, and how sad he felt to realize now that these circumstances had torn them apart

Yosef now knew the Lord had created this special moment for him to see his own reflection in Bashira's face, a reflection that allowed him to accept the truth that he now saw in his own heart. He could no longer escape the reality that he had contributed to this separation between believers that was an affront to the love and sacrifice of the Messiah. Yosef shook his head in regret. He could now see how this fruit of the conflict had poisoned his soul and created the enmity that had brought division.

What a special day this is, Yosef thought. He had begun his day at Nazareth Village simply with the intention of greeting a church from America. He had set aside this day to enjoy the richness of fellowship with the American church on his native soil. But the Lord now required more from him. This day had become the crucible God would use to liberate him from his own sin and renew the fellowship with the Arab believers who lived right here in his community.

Astounding! he thought. He looked at Bashira with gratefulness. He, too, felt the invisible chains that bound his heart in judgment released as the love of Yeshua poured into his spirit. He felt a great relief.

With a sincere smile and kindness in his eyes he said, "Thank you. Thank you for coming and reminding me of the fellowship your uncle and I cherished. This conflict has taken its toll on all of us. We've allowed it to tear away at the bond of fellowship we used to celebrate. How ironic it is that a burden on your part to ask for forgiveness has allowed me to see my own guilt."

Yosef could see the bewilderment upon Bashira's face as he spoke. With a glint of tears in his own eyes, Yosef looked straight into hers. "Bashira, of course, I forgive you," he said. "The question is: Will you forgive me and my congregation for shutting you and your family out of our lives? Oh, how I wish your uncle were here with us today to enjoy this moment."

Silence filled the air within the synagogue. The sounds of the active village were all about—the bleating of the sheep, the braying of the donkeys, the chattering of the tourists as the tour group leaders escorted them up the stony path toward the synagogue.

"Rabbi," said Bashira, "I don't know what to say. I came here only to talk about my own heart and what I needed to do. I'm stunned. Of course, how could I not forgive you? So much has been forgiven of me. I'm overwhelmed that you would ask."

The synagogue proved to be a perfect setting for what had just transpired. They both took a moment to realize that they had participated in an event that only the Lord could have orchestrated.

Bashira then looked at Yosef in earnest. "But there is one more thing I came for today."

Yosef couldn't help but smile at this young woman who stood before him now as a champion for the faith. "What else is on your heart?" he asked.

"I want to ask if you and my uncle would oversee a ceremony where I rededicate my life to the Lord."

"What type of ceremony?" Yosef expressed with some bewilderment, wondering what he and his friend could participate in together.

Bashira said cautiously, "I want you to baptize me in the Jordan River."

Yosef recoiled, dropped his jaw, and stared at her. "But you've already been baptized." Yosef shook his head. "Forgiveness is one thing, but why would you want to do this? It's not necessary to be baptized more than once."

"I know," she said. "It's not a baptism for the remission of sin. It's a rededication ceremony."

"A rededication ceremony with a baptism?" Yosef stated back to her with some bewilderment.

"Yes, a baptism of sorts. It would be demonstration where I proclaim that this separation is over with, the walls between us are buried beneath the shed blood of Yeshua, we are one body and joint heirs according to the promise given to Abraham's seed that we may love one another."

Yosef stared past Bashira. For him, time had paused. *What would this mean for me and my congregation?* he thought.

Her simple confession had resonated within him and brought the conviction he had felt to ask for her forgiveness. But this request required more from him and the members of his assembly. It was one thing to agree in principle that we are one in the Messiah but all together another thing to stand publicly with such a declaration, especially now as the conflict raged.

It only took a moment for him to see that he had become self-focused in his perspective. He pondered the words of Yeshua: *'He who loves his life will lose it. If anyone serves Yeshua, he must take up his cross and follow him.'* These scriptures came alive within him as Yosef now realized his response to Bashira's request could not be about him or his congregation. This decision could only be made by following Yeshua and obeying Him as Adonai—the Lord.

Yosef could see that Bashira had already made her decision. She had stepped out to become a witness for the Lord even as she stood before him, modeling a profound posture of humility and tender love, embracing a steadfast resolve, willing to face the world with the joy she had found in the liberating love and forgiveness of Yeshua.

Yosef turned and walked slowly toward the corner of the synagogue where multi-level benches lined the wall to accommodate the tourists. He stopped before a set of clay jars and said, "Bashira, do you know why I'm here today?"

"To host a church group from America?"

Yosef reached into a clay jar, removing a scroll. "Yes. I've known them for many years. They love to come to the Holy Land."

Yosef lifted his head as though he was trying to remember something. "How does your uncle put it? 'They come to visit the *dead stones* but leave without seeing the *living stones*.' They spend time with us, and I rejoice that we have this opportunity to fellowship together, but they leave without seeing the whole family of God."

Yosef walked back toward Bashira as he continued, "They love coming, particularly during the feast days of Passover and Easter. I take the time to share some of our history with them and read from these scrolls, as it would have been in the days of Yeshua. I'll remind them of the time when He came to a synagogue, maybe one just like this and read from the scroll of the prophet Isaiah, like we were reciting earlier. I'll close the scroll and sit down, telling them, as you recited earlier, that Yeshua said, 'Today this scripture is fulfilled in your hearing.'

"Usually, I pause at this point and let the words sink in. Then I say, 'Can you imagine 400 years of silence from God—no prophets to speak the word of the Lord to the people, silence while the entire nation of Israel waited for the Messiah and offered up centuries of sacrifices. And now, the Living Sacrifice, the Word of God Himself stood before them declaring, 'Today, the Scriptures are fulfilled.' And yet, they said, 'Who is this? Isn't this the son of the carpenter?'

"The question is: Are we any different today? The world thinks that Jesus is a good man, possibly a prophet, surely not the Son of God, and certainly not the one by Whom all things were made on earth and in heaven."

Yosef drew closer to Bashira holding the scroll in his hand. "We are no different. It is only by God's saving grace that we can realize that Jesus of Nazareth is God in the flesh. He is the Messiah, the Son of the living God, the One Who upholds all things by the Word of His power and now sits at the right hand of the Father to judge the living and the dead."

From the windows above, a ray of light shone on Bashira and Yosef, illuminating them in a shower of dust particles floating through the air.

"Today, my dear, you've brought this clarity once again to light. Judgment begins in the house of the Lord, and now His light is shining on my own failures." Yosef cocked his head to the side slightly. His face radiating kindness in his eyes. "Bashira, I realize now how I've excused my own prejudice to justify withdrawing my fellowship from your family and so many other Arab brothers and sisters. We've raised a wall of separation that the Lord would have us tear down. It's time to recognize that all who are baptized into Yeshua have clothed themselves as His Bride. We are all one in Messiah Yeshua."

Tears welled up in Bashira's eyes.

"What you ask is no easy thing. My congregation is also dealing with the loss of friends and young ones. A ceremony like this one will become a focal point for even more accusations to be laid on us for being traitors to our nation and lovers of those who want Israel destroyed."

Bashira started to speak, but he interrupted her. The kindness in his voice reminded her of the many conversations between him and her uncle she had overheard in the past.

"But my dear, nothing is new. The hateful words of today are the same as they were centuries ago. And so, for us, can we expect anything less?" Yosef wanted Bashira to understand the cost he had to consider, but that he was willing to explore how to make this event possible.

"Yeshua told us, 'If the world hates you, you know that it hated Me before it hated you. If they persecuted Me, they will also persecute you. Go and love your enemies, do good to those who hate you.' On our own, it's impossible to love like this, but through Yeshua all things are possible."

"For greater is He that is in us than he that is in the world." Bashira said, as she looked up into the kind face of her beloved uncle's friend.

"And Jesus has overcome the world," Yosef said, placing his hand on her shoulder. "Tell your uncle that an old friend can still hear the voice of our Elder Brother. Let me pray about the timing of your request and talk with the elders. I'll get back to you. No matter what, you've been a blessing today that I won't forget."

One of the tour groups approached. Yosef and Bashira hugged as she turned toward the door.

"You are welcome to stay."

"I can't. I'm supposed to be at the well. You know, a young maiden waiting for her possible husband."

Bashira stepped out of the door as the group began to enter. She had to make her way down the stony path, walking against the flow of the crowd. Yosef stepped outside to watch her go. Some of the tourists bumped into Bashira. She smiled to them politely as she passed.

Yosef said to himself, "And there goes one of the living stones."

He then turned to the tourists saying, "Welcome, my friends! Welcome, today, to our humble place of worship."

Chapter 29

YOSEF'S DILEMMA

*L*ater in the afternoon, Bashira returned home. During dinner, sitting at the table, she began to share with her aunt and uncle her excitement about seeing Rabbi Yosef. Rashad smiled as he listened, but Dalia looked concerned, showing restraint as Bashira recounted their conversation.

"*Amo*, you wouldn't believe it. We were both dressed as though we were back in the time of Jesus, he's reading the Scriptures from the scrolls. We talked about how the body of Christ has become so divided. I explained my desire to hold a joint ceremony where all could see that Jesus can forgive, restore, and reconcile us to Himself and to each other. He heard my heart. It was a truly amazing experience." Bashira's face was radiant as she looked over at Dalia.

"So, what did he say?" Dalia asked. "Is he going to participate or not?"

Bashira stopped smiling for a moment. "Well, first, he asked me to forgive him."

Dalia put down her utensils. Rashad raised his eyebrows and leaned in closer to Bashira. "Say again," said Rashad.

"*Amo*, he asked me to forgive him. He talked about how he had allowed old prejudices and animosity to separate him and his congregation from us. I was shocked. It's as if the Lord was in the room helping us ask each other for forgiveness. He told me how much he wished you could have been there with us and said to tell you that 'an old friend can still hear the voice of our Elder Brother.'"

A slight glistening of tears formed in Rashad's eyes as he listened to his beloved niece.

"I asked him if he would be willing to take part in a ceremony where you and he would baptize me with both of our congregations present."

Dalia interrupted with angst in her voice. "So what did he say?"

Bashira gathered her thoughts. "It took a few minutes for him to respond. He said that this wouldn't be easy for his family or his congregation, especially now, but he's going to talk to his elders. You know, as he talked, I could see in his face that this request touched his heart, and in the end, whatever the cost, I believe this is going to happen."

No one spoke for a moment.

Then, Dalia reached over and put her hand on Bashira's. "Amazing! You press on, *habibti*. The Lord is in this, and we're going to see it through."

Bashira grabbed both Rashad and Dalia's hands. "Thank you so much for standing with me. I love you both so much. Here I've said all this, but how did your time go with Mike?"

"It was a bit mixed. Reporting on the bombing has taken a toll on him. In some ways, it's hardened him a bit toward the gospel."

Bashira and Dalia both looked at Rashad with concern.

"It's understandable," he continued. "I told him I don't know how he and Jack do their jobs. I can't imagine getting up that close, seeing the horror firsthand as they do, and then having to bury their emotions in order to objectively report the news. I guess I never really thought through what it takes to be a journalist." Rashad tilted his head, recounting his conversation with Mike earlier in the day and wondered, *Was it enough? Could I have said more?*

Rashad then straightened himself to say, "We've sown the seed of the Lord's love into Mike. Now we need to pray that it will grow into saving grace. I certainly hope so. Only time will tell."

Bashira's face reflected her concern for Mike. "I'll be praying," she said.

Dalia added, "Let's all keep praying for Mike and Jack and for Yosef and his elders to find the heart of the Lord."

Bashira gave her aunt's hand a reassuring squeeze.

◇◇◇◇◇◇◇◇◇◇◇◇◇◇

On the short drive home from Nazareth Village, Yosef knew that he would need to set aside some time to spend with the Lord before he met with the elders. Right now, he needed wisdom for how to share what had happened today with his wife and his father, who lived with them in their small home. He could not ignore the profound impact his time with Bashira had had on him. Arriving home, he sat in his car for a while, staring out the window and thinking.

Yosef knew the Lord had allowed this special time for him to see the reflection of his own bigotry in Bashira's face. He wasn't proud of what he saw. It had become clear to him that his pride had allowed prejudice to break the unity within the body of believers. He knew the Lord was calling him to help restore that unity.

He recognized the difficulty this news would bring to the leadership of the congregation. But now he needed to speak with his father. That was another matter altogether.

Yosef's parents had emigrated from Germany to Israel during the Zionist migration following World War II. The entire family had accepted Yeshua as their Savior and Messiah years later while attending a "Jews for Jesus" meeting on the shore of the Sea of Galilee.

In that moment, realizing that Yeshua was the Messiah they had been waiting for, their lives were changed forever. Although his mother and father adhered to many of the old traditions, the family rejoiced in discovering the hope they had found in Yeshua. After Yosef's mother died, only ten months ago, his father needed the care he and his wife could provide. Yosef took a deep breath, opened the car door, and entered his home.

On the walls of Yosef's small home hung various photos of family members dating back to the early days in Europe, before their arrival in Israel. A narrow hallway led into his small living room where more family photographs hung on the walls.

A small table in the corner of the room held a framed picture of a happy couple in Germany attending a celebration. Another small table in the adjacent corner displayed a scrapbook filled with news clippings, opened to a page showing photos of women prisoners in the death camp at Auschwitz reaching out to crying children on the other side of a barbed-wire fence. One of the women had a circle around her face. It was Yosef's grandmother.

Yosef greeted his father, sitting on the couch between the two tables, and immediately excused himself to his study, an even smaller room set aside as a space for him to think, write, and pray. Once inside, he paused to look at a photo of him and Rashad and Bashira that he kept on the shelf behind his desk. The photo had been taken at an earlier time when they had been together in the forest at one of their meetings.

He released a sigh, wondering how he could have let their friendship split apart. *How it must grieve Adonai for us to separate ourselves from one another like this,* he thought.

As he stared at the picture, with their smiles beaming back at him, Yosef couldn't help but smile in return, knowing that Bashira, who he had known since she was a small child, was now a champion for the faith. *She is the one teaching her elders,* he thought. He turned and set the photo on the center of his desk, sat down in his small worn office chair, and prayed for the wisdom of the Lord to fall on him during the conversation with his father that he knew he would have after dinner that evening.

∞∞∞∞∞∞∞∞∞∞∞

Voices came from the kitchen, growing louder as the conversation took on more heat. Yosef's father stood. Yosef still sat at the table, looking at his open Bible, his hands resting on the worn pages. His father, red-faced and fuming, stood over him holding a small pair of old baby shoes. Yosef's wife listened to his ranting as she washed the dishes, glancing back at the men each time Yosef's father's voice rose with anger.

"You can't do this, regardless of how close you are to this Arab girl and her family. She can certainly find her own pastor for this ceremony, no matter what you call it."

"*Abba*, it's not just a ceremony. It's an opportunity for us to proclaim publicly that we are in unity as one body of believers in Yeshua. Bashira simply wants this to be a setting in which we declare our love for each other. We've allowed this conflict to split us apart. It's time to restore the blessings of our fellowship together in Yeshua.

"You call this a blessing, Yosef. But is it? My fear is that it will only bring more suspicion and false accusation against us. How many times do we need to hear our neighbors accuse us of being missionaries and outsiders or renouncing our Jewish heritage by embracing Yeshua? What blessing is there in possibly fueling this resentment even further by this public display. It makes no sense!"

"*Abba*, you know what saddens me the most is how we've become subject to our own bigotry. What we detest in the way we've been treated by others has become the way we treat our Arab brothers and sisters. We've allowed suspicion and accusations to separate and divide His Body. You've seen it. We all have. It can't be denied. We're the ones that need to ask for forgiveness."

"You speak of forgiveness, Yosef. How much have we endured and forgiven already?" His father clutched the old, worn baby shoes to his chest.

"Yes, *Abba,* but should the pain of the past rob us of a blessing in the present? Yeshua said it's by the love we have for one another that men will know we are His disciples."

Yosef rose from his chair. His father continued to stare at him in bewilderment and anger. Yosef looked his father in the eyes. His father stared, unflinching, back at him; his gaze seemed to demand that Yosef change his mind.

"*Abba*, Yeshua gave us His forgiveness and love even when we were His enemies. Shall we not obey His Word and love one another?"

His father's countenance broke. The words—forgiveness and love—seemed to have pierced his heart. Tears welled up in his eyes and began to trickle down his cheeks. He had come face to face with a truth that he could neither deny nor escape.

Yosef reached out to squeeze his father's shoulders with affection. They looked at each other for a silent moment.

"Yosef, I don't know if this is a good thing or not. I do know that if you believe it is of Yeshua it is what you will do."

His father turned and began to shuffle out of the kitchen and down the hall toward the living room. Yosef watched him go as his wife came up beside him. She grabbed his arm. Together they moved forward to stand at the doorway of the kitchen. There she laid her head on his shoulder and whispered gently into his ear.

"Do you think he will ever be reconciled to this?" she said.

"I don't know. It's something only Adonai can do in his heart."

As their eyes followed Yosef's father, he paused and lifted his hand to touch an old photo on the wall, showing a young couple with a baby. A yellow star of David was pinned to their clothes. The image showed them waiting for the transport trains to take them to the camps in Germany where death's fatal embrace awaited so many members of the family. He kissed the baby shoes that he held in his hands and slowly, reverently, continued toward his room. Yosef and his wife remained staring down the hall after him.

"Well, soon," Yosef said, breaking the silence, "I have to face another set of men. They may not be as understanding as my father. Pray for me."

Yosef's wife gave him a loving, supportive look. "God will be with you, my beloved." Yosef looked at his wife with gratefulness in his heart. God had given him a special woman with whom to share his life. He admired her strength and love for Yeshua. She, too, longed to do what was right before Him.

As she turned to put the dinner plates away, Yosef walked quietly down the hall past his father's bedroom and said a prayer for him. He then walked into his study. Once again, he saw the photo on his desk of Rashad and Bashira. He paused, then spoke softly to himself quoting Psalm 133, "Behold, how good and how pleasant it is for brethren to dwell together in unity!"

He turned out the light and climbed the stairs to their bedroom, continuing with the psalm, "It is like the dew of Hermon, descending upon the mountains of Zion; for there the Lord commanded the blessing—life forevermore."

Yosef stopped, looked back down the stairs, and thought, *The blessing of the Lord awaits us as we come together in Him.*

He hoped sleep would come quickly, bringing a sweet release from the day, for the morning, and his next conversation, would come soon enough.

Chapter 30

THE ELDERS

The monthly elders' meeting had been scheduled before Bashira had made her request. Yosef had spent the intervening weeks seeking wisdom from the Lord. Now the time had come; they all gathered inside the assembly hall. The dim light in the room hardly seemed enough to read by but it did reveal the intensity on their faces. Some of the elders sat on plain wooden chairs. Those not sitting paced about, waving their arms when it was their turn to speak. The atmosphere was tense.

Yosef sat on a stool in the middle of the room holding an open Bible. The men talked over one another and around him as if he was no longer there. In the shadows of the corner of the room stood a silent uniformed man whose face remained hidden.

One of the elders directed the conversation back toward the center of the room. "But Yosef, why now, and she's from Bethlehem! What if she doesn't have the proper papers? We could then be in trouble with the authorities."

"And what shall we say to God?" replied Yosef. "Heavenly Father, I'm sorry we couldn't gather together in the name of Yeshua because our neighbor didn't have the right papers." He looked around the room, his gaze falling on each man, studying them, praying for wisdom and the way forward.

"Okay, Yosef," said another, "what if the issue is not whether we should meet but instead about the timing? Look at the mess the country is in right now."

Yosef looked at the elder who had just spoken and said, with kindness in his voice, "My friend, when is it the right time for broken hearts to be healed?"

And then, addressing the entire group, he said, "Brothers, the Bible is clear. It tells us to endeavor to keep the unity of the Spirit in the bond of peace. We are to do this in gentleness, with long-suffering, bearing with one another in love. There are no conditions for gathering together except that we love each other."

One of the elders who had been pacing turned toward Yosef to speak sharply to him. "Then why us? Let her own people have the ceremony—if you want to call it that!"

Yosef, still sitting, looked down at his lap. His hands rested on the pages of his Bible. He looked up to answer firmly, "Her own people?" Yosef said again, with a look of incredulity, "Her own people? Brothers, is this not really the heart of the problem?"

He paused to gain their undivided attention. "Is not this the issue at hand: her people versus our people? Listen to what you are saying."

Yosef shook his head from side to side, rubbing his forehead with both hands, and then looked down at his Bible. The men fell silent.

Yosef let the men reflect as he looked around the room before he spoke again. "Is it not from every tongue and tribe around the globe that Yeshua makes us one in Him? He tells us that the world will know that we are His disciples. How? By our love for one another!" Yosef paused again, while many of the men in the room looked back and forth at each other. Some stared at the floor, others turned their eyes toward him; each man listened in his own way.

Yosef gave a deep sigh and spoke solemnly. "After being with Bashira and witnessing her humility and courage, I found myself ashamed of how I've withdrawn my hand of fellowship from our Arab brothers and sisters. What greater victory can the devil have, my friends, than to divide us as he has and keep us apart. We're the ones that need to ask for forgiveness for treating our Arab brothers and sisters as foreigners who don't belong to the body of Yeshua."

Yosef paused to turn his gaze on each of the men in the room. When he saw that he still had their full attention, he drove home his point. From his Bible he read, "Blessed are the peacemakers for they will be called the sons of God. . . . Blessed are you when men hate you, when they exclude you, revile you, and cast out your name as evil, for the Son of Man's sake. Rejoice and be glad for your reward in heaven is great."

Yosef placed his finger on the page, continuing to recite from memory as he looked up and into the faces of each man present. "Bless those who curse you, pray for those who spitefully use you. To him who strikes you on the one cheek, offer the other. Love your enemies, be merciful, just as your Father in Heaven is merciful." He let these words sink into the thoughts of the elders before speaking again.

"We of all people know how the world can treat a person with scorn and indignation. Many of you in this room have felt the loss of family and friends in receiving Yeshua as the long-awaited Messiah and Savior of the world. The same is true for Bashira and her family. Yet she reached out to us in love, seeking only fellowship and the recognition that in Yeshua there is no longer a wall of separation between us. What is being asked of us is that we love our neighbor and thus fulfill the law of love given to us by Yeshua."

Everyone now stared at the floor in silence, thinking through their own response to Yosef's admonition. Then the man in uniform stepped out from the shadows. The soldier slowly walked into the light.

Calev began to speak. "Brothers, compared with you I'm a relatively new believer in Yeshua and don't pretend to have the insight into God's Word and His purpose that you do. Who I do know is this young woman."

The men all turned toward Calev.

He continued. "We were on patrol, setting up a barricade in the heart of Bethlehem. It was an intense night. The people were angry over the enforced curfew and were trying to push their way through our perimeter. We held them back and arrested quite a few of them in the process. It was sheer chaos.

"My squad became exhausted. In the middle of it all, this young woman approached our barricade. She kept telling my men that she was a nurse and that she had to get through to the hospital, but she lacked the credentials she needed. My soldiers tried turning her away, but she kept persisting.

"When my team had had enough, they pulled her through the barrier to arrest her. The shouting, pushing, and shoving on all sides made things pretty rough on everyone. Bashira got caught in the middle of the altercation and experienced rough treatment from my troops.

"What caught my attention was hearing her exclaim that a TV news crew had visited her hospital that week. I realized that I knew this newsman. He and his cameraman had been embedded in my platoon, and he told me of his plans to visit a children's hospital. I intervened at this point, had her tell me her story to verify her claim, and released her with a pass.

"I'll never forget what happened next. It was obvious that she was still shaken by the whole ordeal, but from her bag she took a few small sacks of fruit and some candy that she was taking to the children at the hospital and asked me to give these gifts to my men. I was dumbfounded.

"She said, 'Maybe in this small way your soldiers might see the love of Jesus.' To say such a thing in that moment sounded insane."

The elders all shook their heads as though each one recognized how incredible it sounded. A few of the elders took quick glances at each other. Calev had not finished his testimony.

"What kept nagging me, pounding in my head, was the thought, 'What drove this young woman to share her meager belongings with those who had just threatened to arrest her?'"

Calev's eyes now roamed the room. "I had forgotten about this exchange until my brother was killed in the bombing at the Hebrew University, and Yosef came to comfort our family."

Calev turned to look at Yosef. "You said, 'Calev, it is impossible for a man to heal a broken heart. Only God can comfort us in our sorrow and pain.' And then you added, 'He's the only One Who can remove the anger and hatred from our souls that thirsts for vengeance.' I'll never forget shouting, 'How, Rabbi?! Tell me how God can do this?!' You said, 'Through the death and resurrection of His only Son, Yeshua.'"

Calev turned back to the elders. "I can still hear myself screaming, 'Rabbi, you're telling me the price for healing my heart required more death and suffering? How can this be?'"

Calev walked over to where Yosef sat and put his hand on his shoulder. The rest of the group focused on Calev. Yosef kept his eyes on his Bible as Calev looked around the room again. Turning to Yosef, he said, "And then you told me, 'It is because of love, Calev. For God so loved the world that He gave His only Son to save us from the horror of our sin—our anger against Him and our hatred toward one another.'

"It was in that moment that I realized I was God's enemy, hating Him and everyone who had anything to do with the death of my brother. Yet here was God, reaching out in His lovingkindness to set me free from everything that sought to drive me further away from Him. In that hour with you, Rabbi, I remembered that night at the barricade. I saw then what forgiveness looked like in the face of Bashira. She exchanged her pain for His love, and then she extended His love to me, even though I was her enemy.

"Rabbi, during your visit to our home, a miracle occurred in my life. I received the love of God in Yeshua for me that day and my broken heart was healed. In His forgiveness, I was able to forgive others, even my enemies."

Turning now to the elders, Calev continued. "And what have you taught me from Scripture, brothers? Is it not that we are all baptized into one body in Yeshua? It doesn't matter if we are Jews or Arabs. We now have the same Father in heaven. This makes us brothers and sisters in Yeshua. Will we deny our sister this opportunity to share her love with us?"

The question hung in the air as each one in the room had to face this challenge. Yosef stood up and put his arm around Calev. With Calev by his side, he turned to the rest saying, "Yeshua told us, 'Greater love has no one than this: to lay down his life for his friends. You are My friends if you do what I command. This is My command: Love one another.'

"It's clear my brothers, that we must act if we hope to walk in the liberty of love that He gave us. Come brothers, let's gather around and pray."

The men looked at each other as one by one they stepped forward, forming a circle, placing their arms around each other.

Yosef said, "Love drove Bashira to ask for our forgiveness and request that we join her in this rededication ceremony. Let's first rededicate ourselves to Him and then ask the Lord to bless our decision to not only obey Him but to celebrate the love and unity we have in Him."

The elders bowed their heads as one group and prayed together.

Chapter 31

LIVING HOPE

The day set aside for the celebration was glorious. The sunbathed Jordan River shone in translucent emerald-green against a bright blue sky. There was not a cloud to be seen. The banks of the Jordan, full of lush reeds and palms, had welcomed visitors seeking to be baptized along its shores for thousands of years. The ceremony would take place at the Yardenit Baptismal Site, a popular pilgrimage location near the city of Tiberias at the headwaters of the Jordan River. Everyone who had been invited to join Bashira today agreed that this was the perfect place; so many people from around the globe, with different backgrounds and cultures, came here to worship the risen Lord together. Today Yardenit would become hallowed ground for Bashira and the two congregations who gathered to celebrate the unity they had rediscovered in Christ.

Those who had come to participate with Bashira in her stance of hope began to arrive in the parking area. Rabbi Yosef and the members of his congregation waited at the front gate to welcome the guests as they arrived.

Rashad parked his van. He walked to the entrance with his arm around Bashira and with Dalia at his side. When they approached the gate, Yosef reached out to give Rashad a big hug.

"Welcome, my friend, it's good to see you."

"Thank you, Yosi. What a day to celebrate the goodness of the Lord."

"And it is all because of this young lady," said Yosef, smiling at Bashira who blushed in response.

Rashad squeezed her close to his side.

"Come, my friends." Together they walked through the gate. The large property stretched out along the west bank of the river. This site contained all the facilities necessary to host a celebration.

"Here, *yakirati*," Yosef's wife said, "there is a changing room over there. Let me show you. Come, Dalia," she beckoned. Dalia held Bashira's arm as they hurried her off to change.

Rashad and Yosef looked at each other. They both began to speak at the same time. "No, my friend, please go first," said Rashad.

"What I was going to say is how happy I am that we are doing this today, even though it saddens me for how long it's taken us to get together again."

"I feel the same way," said Rashad. He grabbed Yosef by his shoulders. "But, my brother, today we get to celebrate."

They both embraced, saying, "Praise the Lord." Many families from each of their congregations walked by, heading to the riverbank.

"We better get down to the river, or the ceremony will go on without us," Yosef said with a hearty smile.

Rashad chuckled. "You first, my friend."

As the family members gathered by the river, buses full of tourists oblivious to the event unfolding before them arrived in the parking lot.

∞∞∞∞∞∞∞∞∞∞∞

Bashira exited the dressing room with the women. A deep sense of peace enveloped her, bringing a reassurance in her spirit that she was doing the right thing. She gazed toward the riverbank, grateful for what the Lord had done by bringing so many people together.

She saw Yosef and Rashad standing beside each other, waiting at the top of the ramp that led down to the river, each holding their Bibles in their right hand. Everyone waited at the river's edge for Bashira to join them. She walked over to meet Rashad and Yosef.

Upon seeing her, Yosef spoke up, "Come, everyone. Let's make some room for Bashira." The people moved aside to let her through.

As they passed, all those assembled began to regroup. Calev, the elders, some members of the Messianic congregation along with the leaders and friends from Rashad's local church in Nazareth all edged their way forward. The group crowded in as close as possible to see Rashad and Yosef usher Bashira toward the water.

They turned around at the bottom of the ramp. Bashira looked back toward the crowd of tourists that was now attentive to their activity.

Rashad spoke. "Come in closer, everyone." The crowd pressed in, and as they did, Rashad opened his Bible.

When the people stopped shuffling, he addressed them. "What a glorious day we have here with one another on the banks of this ancient river. I wonder if this day might be similar to the one when our Lord and Savior faced John the Baptist on the bank of this same river. You will recall that on that day John declared, 'Behold, the Lamb of God, Who takes away the sins of the world.'

"Well, we are here today to honor Jesus, Yeshua, the Lamb of God, Whom John spoke of so long ago, perhaps at this very site, as being the one Who, in His great love gave Himself willingly unto death upon the cross to purchase our forgiveness before our Holy God.

"We assemble here to celebrate His great victory; that through Him and by His saving grace we are born again to a *living hope*. It is this living hope that Bashira, along with all of us, declare is our inheritance as born-again believers in Jesus of Nazareth, the Messiah, Yeshua Hamashiach, the Son of the true and only living God. Together we stand here at the river's edge to declare that there is only one true peace between God and mankind—the peace found in Jesus, Who by His death and resurrection has made us one in Him, His Church universal."

Rashad then stepped back a little to give Yosef the opportunity to come forward and speak.

Yosef looked over the crowd and with a strong voice began, "When you look around today, you see Jews and Arabs gathered together today on this riverbank. Some would say this is a miracle, and certainly it is. The Bible tells us that if you belong to Yeshua, then you are Abraham's seed and you become an heir to His promises. But what does it mean to belong to Yeshua? What causes a courageous young woman to come here today and proclaim to the world that our only hope in this life, and in the one to come, is in Messiah Yeshua? Where does this hope come from? It comes from recognizing Who Yeshua is. He is God's perfect Son, our long awaited Messiah, the One by Whom and for Whom everything in heaven and earth was made. Yet the Bible tells us that He did not hold onto His equality with God as something to be grasped, but willingly gave His life for us that we might be saved.

"And I would be remiss today if I didn't address what it means to be saved and born again. An influential rabbi, Nicodemus, asked this question of Jesus centuries ago, as recorded in the Gospel of John." Rabbi Yosef paused to open his Bible. "Jesus said to him, 'I tell you the truth, unless you are born again, you cannot see the Kingdom of God. For God sent His Son into the world not to judge the world, but to save the world through Him; for whoever believes in Him shall be saved. There is no other way unto the Father except through Him, for whoever believes in Him will in no way be cast out, but rather they will be received, and God will grant them life eternal.'

"Some of you may say, 'But, Rabbi, we're already saved.' Yes, I know, but the question to us today is: How many of us have tarnished this miracle of salvation by holding onto our own bigotries? Have our prejudices, fueled by the seemingly endless conflict in this land where we live, built walls of separation between us?

"We have failed to obey one of Yeshua's greatest commands. Instead of loving one another as He has first loved us, we've withheld our fellowship and have contributed to the breaking down of the unity in His Body of believers. This is why we are here today: to ask forgiveness for our role in partnering with this divisiveness.

"And so today, in the forgiveness we are asking from and giving to one another, we acknowledge that for us who have received Yeshua as our Savior 'there is only one body and one Spirit, one Lord, one faith, one baptism, one God and Father of all, Who is above all, and through all, and in all.' This is what Bashira reminds us of today: that His love is ours to share with each other so that the world might see Yeshua Hamashiach living in us as Lord and King of kings."

Yosef paused and turned toward Rashad welcoming him to continue. Rashad began to speak.

"My friends, the unity we are experiencing today as the Body of believers is through grace alone, by faith alone, in Christ alone. It is a gift of God so that no one can boast. If there is any boasting today, it is in Jesus, Who willingly went to the cross and died for us but is risen and now sits at the right hand of God the Father interceding for us. It's this same Jesus Who will one day return to establish His kingdom with a new heaven and a new earth where sin, death, or sorrow will be no more. Until then, He tells us to love one another as He has loved us.

"How important is this love? The Apostle Paul makes it crystal clear in his first letter to the church in Corinth." Rashad opened his Bible and began to read.

> "Though I speak with the tongues of men and of angels, but have not love, I have become a sounding brass or a clanging cymbal. And though I have the gift of prophecy, and understand all mysteries and all knowledge, and though I have all faith, so that I could remove mountains, but have not love, I am nothing. And though I bestow all my goods to feed the poor, and though I give my body to be burned, but have not love, it profits me nothing.
>
> "Love suffers long and is kind; love does not envy; love does not parade itself, is not puffed up; does not behave rudely, does not seek its own, is not provoked, thinks no evil; does not rejoice in iniquity, but rejoices in the truth; bears all things, believes all

things, hopes all things, endures all things. Love *never* fails. . . . Amen."

The moment had come. Rashad turned to Bashira. "Are you ready, *habibti*?"

Bashira looked up at Rashad with beaming eyes and said, "Yes, *Amo*."

Rashad and Yosef handed their Bibles to Dalia, who stood by on the ramp. They both stepped into the cool water. They beckoned Bashira to come to them. She entered the water to stand between them. Rashad and Yosef placed their arms behind her shoulders.

Rashad spoke to Bashira. "This immersion represents your rededication to Christ and His unfailing love. Your rising up from the water declares the unity we have in the love of Christ. Today you proclaim the wonder of God's great mercy and love in Christ Jesus. To God be the glory."

Rashad grasped Bashira's nose, covering her mouth with his hand. They lowered her backwards into and under the water. As she came up, the crowd began to cheer and clap, praising God. Bashira hugged the two men who had been so dear to her for so long. Dalia came forward with a towel for Bashira and handed the Bibles back to Rashad and Yosef as they all stepped out of the water. The crowd continued clapping and cheering as Bashira made her way up the ramp with Dalia's arms holding her tight.

Yosef, smiling at Rashad, turned to look at the crowd and said, "Well, my friend, our Elder Brother sure brought Ishmael and Isaac together today!"

Chapter 32

REUNITED

ashad and Yosef walked up the ramp together in the afterglow of an experience they both knew that only the Lord could have orchestrated. At the top, Yosef's father came walking toward him through the crowd. As his father drew closer, Yosef grabbed Rashad's arm. "Rashad, let me introduce you to someone special. *Abba*, here is my good friend Rashad."

Yosef's father extended his hand. "It's a pleasure to meet you. My son has spoken fondly of you and your family."

"Thank you. And what a special day for us all to be together."

Yosef then gave his father a warm hug. "You were right in following your heart, my son," his father said.

Rashad gave them space and began to look around for Bashira. He saw her making her way through the crowd. Beyond her, he saw Mike standing with Bashira's mother and father. Mike waved to get Bashira's attention. Rashad had asked Mike to help his family get the permits they needed to leave the West Bank. The family had been able to spend the previous days in Nazareth with Bashira. Rashad said a short prayer in his heart for Mike, thanking the Lord for His blessing to make a way for his family to be together today.

<hr>

Bashira saw her family in the crowd. She lit up with a beaming smile, skipped going to the changing room, and ran over to meet them. Her mother embraced her. She gave her father a hug and kiss. She turned to her grandparents and said, with delight in her voice, "*Sido. Teta.* I'm so glad you are here!" Her grandmother grabbed her hand and squeezed it, starting to cry. Her grandfather gave her a kiss. "Well, if it weren't for this young man," he touched Mike's shoulder while looking at Bashira with a smile, "we wouldn't be."

Bashira turned to Mike, "Thank you, Mike. I'm so glad you could be here to share this day with us." It was impossible for Bashira to hide how happy she was to see Mike. His presence made the day even more complete.

"I wouldn't have missed it for anything. It's not often a reporter gets to see you *and* a gathering like this," he said. "It couldn't be a better day," he added with a lighthearted smile.

Bashira blushed slightly and looked down and over to her parents. She didn't want them to be alarmed in any way by Mike's comment, even though her heart leapt within her at the sound of his voice. She looked to her uncle to bail her out of what felt like an awkward moment. She didn't want to draw attention to herself or let the others recognize her feelings for Mike.

Rashad picked up on her look of concern. Just then, he saw Yosef and his family walking by.

"Yosi," he called out to them. "Let me now introduce you to my family."

He welcomed Yosef, his wife, and Yosef's father into their circle. "Yosef," Rashad said, "this is my father, Abu Rashad, and my mother, Em Rashad, along with my brother, Samir and his wife, Miriam.

"Welcome, everyone," Yosef said.

"Thank you," Rashad's family replied, almost in unison.

"And what a special day it is for everyone," said Abu Rashad.

Yosef's father added, "A miracle, I would say."

Bashira felt the same way. She was thankful for the moment the introductions had given her to gather her thoughts now that Mike was here.

◊◊◊◊◊◊◊◊◊◊◊◊◊

Mike stood by. He was thrilled to see this family reunited after the tragedy they had endured, but he now felt unsteady and vulnerable, sensing that he couldn't enter into this celebration of faith.

Rashad reached out and grabbed his arm, pulling him closer. He then reached out to Yosef, tapping him on the shoulder. Yosef turned. "Yosi, let me introduce a friend of ours. This is Mike Olson. He helped get the rest of the family here today."

Mike extended his hand to Yosef. "It's my pleasure to meet you."

They shook hands. Yosef said, "I've heard a lot about you and have seen your reporting."

"Well, don't believe everything you hear, and certainly not everything you see on TV," Mike said with a wink.

"When it comes to reporting in the Middle East, you do a pretty good job. What do you think of this gathering?"

"I'd say it's remarkable, but I guess that's what you come to expect when Bashira is involved."

"Yes," said Rashad, "and what a great day for all of us. It's so good to see you and Jack. I wasn't sure you could make it, so I didn't say anything to Bashira about you coming. We are all glad that you both are here.

"We'll have to hurry, though. Everyone is waiting for lunch. Bashira, now's a good time to get out of that wet robe. Mike, you and Jack will join us for lunch, right?"

Jack came up behind Mike, biting into a falafel ball. "You betcha; can't wait." Mike looked at him with surprise and then with a scowl. Jack threw up his hands, looking at Mike with a smirk on his face. "What? It was offered to me. They're awesome."

Bashira tightened the towel around her shoulders. "I'll be right back," she said to everyone. She gave Mike one last look with a smile and turned to walk away toward the dressing rooms. Mike followed her with his gaze. Beyond her, he saw a familiar face. Calev was talking with friends in the crowd.

"Excuse me, everyone, there's somebody I have to see." Mike worked his way over to Calev from behind. He put his hands on Calev's shoulder. Calev turned and stepped back startled. He certainly did not expect to see Mike at this gathering. They then shook hands vigorously.

"What are you doing here, Calev?"

"I could ask you the same thing. But I realize if it involves a certain young Arab woman and any newsworthy story, you would be here. Or should I say, forget the news, and now it's all about the girl?"

They both laughed. "Seriously, I would have never dreamed of seeing you here either." Mike said. "By the way, that hard-hearted colonel of yours is the one who helped get Bashira's family here today."

"Really? What is it you say in the states, 'The Lord works in mysterious ways?'"

"Yeah, if he could speak through a donkey, I guess he can use a colonel."

"I'm impressed you know the Scriptures so well," Calev said.

"Not really. It's that goofy cameraman of mine. He said something like that about me once."

"It's so good to see you, Mike."

"Likewise, but you still didn't answer my question. Why are you here? Don't tell me you're one of these believers?" Mike asked the question with jest in his voice.

Calev paused for a minute and stared at Mike intently. "Yes, I am."

Mike's jaw dropped. "You're kidding me."

"No, really. Born again, like Yosef shared."

"'Wow!" said Mike. He felt his world shrink. *Calev is a believer too? Is all this real?* he wondered. Then, both he and Calev saw Bashira exiting from the dressing room looking beautiful in her simple white dress.

"Pretty amazing, huh?" said Calev.

Mike stared at Bashira, mumbling under his breath, "Yes, amazing."

"I didn't just mean the young lady," Calev said with a grin.

Mike shook himself away from the vision of Bashira. "Yeah. I meant today was amazing."

"Sure," said Calev, teasing Mike with a grin. Mike grimaced but was soon distracted with the sound of laughter. He turned to see Jack grabbing a handful of falafel balls. He and Calev both chuckled at the voracious antics of his colleague.

"That guy," said Mike. "We better head over to lunch before Jack eats it all." He and Calev walked together toward the tables where lunch had been laid out.

Everyone sat around tables set with generous servings of pita, hummus, salads, and fruit. Children played on the grass beyond the lunch tables. Rashad, Yosef, their wives, Bashira's parents and grandparents all sat at one table. Mixed groups of Jews and Arabs sat at the other tables, eating and talking, smiling and laughing, together.

Most of the seating was filled by the time Mike made it over to the eating area. He saw that Bashira was still standing, too, engaged in conversation with one of the older ladies in the group. He went over to her. Bashira turned toward him. Mike realized he had interrupted their conversation with his presence. "Sorry to interrupt," he said awkwardly, "but I wondered Bashira, do you have a place to sit? If you don't, I thought I might join you, if that's okay?" The older woman smiled, gave Bashira's arm a tender squeeze, and stepped aside.

Bashira looked deeply into Mike's eyes and then looked about to see several people clearing their places, leaving a table empty. "Why don't we sit over there."

"Sounds good to me." They got some food on their way to the table.

Their conversation was upbeat and lighthearted. Bashira thanked Mike again for coming and asked how he was doing after reporting on the bombing, now several weeks past. Mike shared that he had been able to put it all behind him and move on. He didn't want to bring any negative emotions into his time with her.

Sitting this close to Bashira, Mike felt his heart pounding in his chest. Just being in her presence was intoxicating. Even though they were surrounded by her friends and family, the slight separation they had achieved by sitting at a table alone was all Mike needed to feel that he had her for himself at last. He had patiently waited a long time for this moment.

Chapter 33

A LIVING STONE

"Mike," said Bashira, "I have something to tell you." Over the weeks before the day of the celebration, Bashira's conviction had grown, and her family agreed, that she needed to help her uncle by going to Iraq to assist the advanced preparations for the medical supply delivery. The need there was becoming a crisis; much had to be done to get ready to receive the supplies on the ground in Iraq.

She had spent a lot of time discussing her conviction about going with her uncle and family. It had become clear to all that she should go. The decision had been both a practical one, based on necessity for the care of the people they knew and loved in Iraq, and a response to the call Christ had put on her heart to share the hope and life He had given her, especially with other Christians suffering persecution and loss.

After many hours of prayer, the decision had been confirmed by everyone she respected. They had chosen today to be the day of her departure. Her family knew how hard it would be for them all to be together again. They took the time they were with her that week to pray and help with some of the arrangements. Mike was instrumental in them all being together, but he had no idea of the urgency this day contained. Bashira's family had planned for her to leave that night.

She broke the news to Mike. The atmosphere between them changed dramatically. For all the joy of the ceremony and the vision of her beauty before him, a cloud of despair descended over Mike's countenance. The angst on Mike's face was palpable. He couldn't believe what he was hearing. "Bashira, I don't get it. How can you be leaving? So much is going on in my life right now. There's more I want to tell you—more I want to share."

"I know, and I'd like to tell you more, but I'm afraid you just won't understand."

"I'm trying to understand. Why do you think I came here today? I came to see you. I love your family, but it's you I care about. More than care, I want to see you more. And now you are leaving? I mean, look what happened today, people are together, things are changing. Why can't I see you anymore?"

Bashira stared at the table for a moment. "A long time ago, someone once said, 'Follow Me.' That's what I'm doing."

With exasperation in his voice, Mike said, "Great. You talk in riddles. Is there another guy? Are you going to be with him?" Mike sighed in frustration.

"It's not like what you think," said Bashira. Tears welled up in her eyes, causing them to glisten and shine. "Mike, a blind man can see that I care for you, but the Lord says in His Word, 'Follow Me.' He tells us to share the good news that His salvation reaches to the ends of the earth. It's Him I'm following. He wants those who are suffering to know how much He loves them—including our friends in Iraq."

"Iraq!" he exclaimed. "Do you realize how dangerous it is in Iraq right now? You've seen the TV coverage. They're on the edge of war!"

"I know, Mike, but I've been there before, and the people we help there with medical aid are our friends. They love the Lord, and it's not about me, my life, or anything else it's—"

"It's about being crazy, Bashira. Do your father and uncle know?"

"My family and I and the leadership of the church have prayed and discussed it for weeks. That's partly why they are all here, to say good-bye. I'm leaving tonight."

Mike stared at the table, still shocked by what he heard. Bashira slowly reached out to gently touch his hand with her soft fingertips.

"I realize that this is the last thing you expected to hear today. I didn't know if or when I might see you again. And I wish there was more time to let you know how I feel and why I'm going."

Mike glanced up at her but then looked back down at the table. He found himself at a loss for words—lost in time without direction. Bashira's gentle eyes told him all he needed to know. Her decision was made. All he could think about now was if he would ever see her again.

⋄⋄⋄⋄⋄⋄⋄⋄⋄⋄⋄⋄⋄

Rashad and Yosef got up to clear their table. Rashad looked over at Mike and Bashira talking intently to each other. Yosef placed his hand on Rashad's shoulder.

"Poor guy, it looks like she's told him." Rashad had shared Bashira's plans to go to Iraq while he and Yosef had worked out the details of her baptism.

"If that young man ever gets saved, we might be having more than a baptism," Rashad replied.

"Well, clearly the Lord is not finished with those two yet. I bet there will be another story to be told."

Calev stood behind them and said, "I think we need to go over and help the guy. He's not looking too good."

The three men started working their way over to Mike and Bashira.

⋄⋄⋄⋄⋄⋄⋄⋄⋄⋄⋄⋄⋄

"Mike, look at me," said Bashira. "I'm so grateful you came and made it possible for my family to be here. We can't thank you enough. I'll be praying for you every day."

Mike gazed into her eyes. "If I knew how to pray, I'd ask God for you to stay. All I know is that if I loved Him as much as I love you, I'd probably be racing ahead of you."

Bashira's tears overflowed and began to trickle down her cheeks. Mike continued to stare into her captivating eyes. He then took a napkin from the table and reached up to gently dab her tears.

Rashad, Yosef, and Calev came up alongside them.

"Now, we can't have tears," said Rashad. "This is a day of celebration." His voice startled the two who were deeply engaged in the moment with each other. Mike turned toward Rashad with a quizzical look. *What now?* he wondered. *No more surprises, please.*

"*Habibti*, I hate to interrupt, but you have to be leaving or you'll miss your flight. There's a lot still to be done," said Rashad.

Bashira got up from the table. Mike started to get up more slowly. She hugged her uncle and gave him a kiss on the cheek. She hugged Yosef, smiled at Calev, and looked back to Rashad.

"Thank you all. You made this day so wonderful. I will never forget it. I will be praying for you," she said.

"We're the ones who will not forget, and we'll be praying for you," Yosef said. "Return soon and tell us all the good things God has done."

"Your father will be along soon to take you to the airport," said Rashad.

Bashira looked at Mike, now on his feet, standing beside Calev, and said softly, "I'll look for you on TV and pray for you every day." She smiled and reached out to touch his sleeve. They all began to walk back to the entrance.

More buses full of tourists arrived in the parking area. She heard a horn honk and saw her father waving to her from the car. Walking towards him, she turned back briefly to say, "I love you all. God bless you!"

The men stood in silence. Rashad placed his hand on Mike's shoulder. They all watched her walk through the crowd of tourists getting off the buses. An American tourist rushed past Bashira. As he did, another person, loaded with cameras, bumped into her, pushing her aside. He didn't turn or stop to say a word. Bashira looked at him with a smile and continued walking.

Yosef interrupted the silence. "There they go chasing after the *dead stones* as a *living stone* passes them by."

Acknowledgments

It is nearly impossible to acknowledge all those who have stood by and encouraged me in the undertaking that was the writing of this story.

First and foremost, I want to thank my lovely bride, Janie, who for all these years believed in the effort to try to write the living testimony of those in the land of Israel who shared their lives with me. Her support and encouragement helped me to press on through flawed writing skills, lost laptops, and frayed hopes that longed to see this project completed.

Then, I'd like to thank all the others who said, "This story must be told." My closest friends, Michael and Sue Buzbee at Open Hearts in Nicaragua loved to hear this story told to the guests who came on the mission field to share their lives in the love of Christ. The lawyer and movie producer, Todd Burns, patiently listened to the story in its infancy and gave of his time to encourage the effort each step of the way.

The story itself is not my own. It is the story of close evangelical Arab friends of mine living in the land of Israel whose lives are the testimony of God's love. This fellowship of deep friendships developed through traveling for over a quarter of a century with those who reside in the land as a living testimony of the saving grace of Jesus Christ. This is Najed and Gail Azzam's story—told by the characters created in this book who proclaim the good news of the gospel of Jesus Christ.

Other faithful friendships developed over time with those serving with Friends of Nazareth, a NEMA Corporation. Donna Chisam, Retired Executive Director, willingly read each draft and provided insight into the nuances of truth that needed to be shared more clearly.

A story like this written by a novice writer cannot be completed without the endless work and patience of a loving editor. David Bedell at Destiny Writers filled this role. What began as a simple undertaking became an arduous labor of love and prayer that strained all the skills honed by one whom God raised up for this task. For his help, I am grateful.

There are so many others who have been there in the moment with the timely inspiration to press on. Several authors offered their insight to the endless rewriting to improve what is recorded here. Kristen Ingebretson worked unwaveringly through the initial ideas to create an inspirational cover image that captures the heart and message of the story.

And to so many other family members and friends, I give you my thanks. Your encouragement provided me with hope that this final product would meet, even possibly exceed, your expectations. It is with heartfelt gratitude to you that I dedicate this novel to the "glory of our God and great Savior Jesus Christ" (Titus 2:11-13).

Many blessings to you all,
Robert M. Booth

ROBERT M. BOOTH is a retired businessman who spent over a quarter of a century working with a global cellular technology company headquartered in Israel. His experience in international business development allowed him to travel the globe with an Israeli Arab Executive Vice President and Jewish Director of Engineering. These three men developed a lifelong friendship. Together, they shared the experience of living in the complex environment of Israel.

Rob's time spent with his colleagues and their families allowed him special insight into their lives to discover the challenges they face. This experience also provided Rob the opportunity to spend time with evangelical Arab Christian leaders, Messianic Christians, and those believers in Christ from America and all over the world who have chosen to live in the land to share the gospel. The stories they told became the backdrop for the writing of *Tearful Triumph*, sharing the good news of the gospel from the perspective of disciples of Christ living in the Holy Land.

Rob lives in California with his wife, Janie. He is blessed with three adult children and nine grandchildren, all of whom he adores.

Living Hope Publishing

Pray for the peace of Jerusalem and for peace in Israel to be established through the Prince of Peace, Jesus Christ.

Visit our website at:

www.livinghopepublishing.org